"If you think a book about aging can't be a fun and engrossing read—think again. Alan Castel's *Better with Age* blends cutting-edge research with personal accounts from well-known Americans to create a roadmap for the later years. This engaging and inspirational book should be read by everyone who wants to know how to ensure a happy and healthy old age."

—Karl Pillemer, Professor of Human Development, Cornell University and author of *30 Lessons for Living: Tried and True Advice from the Wisest Americans*

"Reading *Better with Age*, you will regret not having read it at an earlier age. Professor Castel combines the wisdom of remarkable people he interviewed, with the latest research findings, to provide a masterful guide to become better with age."

—Moshe F. Rubinstein, Professor of Engineering and Business at UCLA, author of *Extraordinary Outcomes*, age 87

"This evocative, compelling, insightful, thought provoking, readable, comprehensively researched book is a stunning celebration of not just aging but of all of life. As presented: age is no better or worse than youth, the 80's or 90's no better or worse than the 20's or 30's. Age is one of the phases of life, but like all phases, it must be mindfully lived differently. This symphony of life has been composed from a massive quantity of disciplined studies and powerfully expressive scenarios from real lives such that the reader can design custom tailored optimum phases for themselves. If only enough people would engage this thinking, the trajectory of the human species would be elevated into a new realm."

—Story Musgrave, loving daddy to seven children, ages 57 to 11, grand-daddy to many, student of life, professor, pilot, trauma surgeon, astronaut on six flights

Better with Age

Better with Age

The Psychology of Successful Aging

ALAN D. CASTEL, PhD

OXFORD
UNIVERSITY PRESS

OXFORD
UNIVERSITY PRESS

Oxford University Press is a department of the University of Oxford. It furthers
the University's objective of excellence in research, scholarship, and education
by publishing worldwide. Oxford is a registered trade mark of Oxford University
Press in the UK and certain other countries.

Published in the United States of America by Oxford University Press
198 Madison Avenue, New York, NY 10016, United States of America.

Library of Congress Cataloging-in-Publication Data
Names: Castel, Alan D., author.
Title: Better with age: the psychology of successful aging / Alan D. Castel.
Description: New York, NY: Oxford University Press, [2019] |
Includes bibliographical references and index.
Identifiers: LCCN 2017052747 | ISBN 978-0-19-027998-1 (alk. paper)
Subjects: LCSH: Adulthood—Psychological aspects. | Aging—Psychological
aspects. | Aging—Social aspects.
Classification: LCC BF724.5.C37 2018 | DDC 155.67—dc23
LC record available at https://lccn.loc.gov/2017052747

Printed by Sheridan Books, Inc., United States of America

Contents

Prologue: How I Got Interested in Successful Aging at a Young Age

I learned to love old age early in life. I had one grandparent who celebrated with large birthday parties, and another who lied constantly about her age. My grandfather was very uninhibited and told me many funny and risqué jokes that I still remember to this day. My grandparents taught me my family history, sent chocolate in the mail, and showed me how to clean a penny in Coca-Cola. My early exposure to old age was filled with a cast of colorful characters.

As a child who grew up in Canada, I was able to escape many harsh winters by visiting my grandparents in sunny South Florida. Children were a cherished minority in the "snowbird" retirement community where we stayed each winter. My retired older relatives would take walks every day, visit orange groves, and rejoice in the warm, humid weather. Older adults taught me to play golf, chess, and shuffleboard. They also taught me when to yell at the TV while watching football. We would meet my older relatives at hotels and museums, often going out for early dinners and having ice cream. In my young eyes, old age looked pretty fun, literally like fun in the sun.

I used to have a great memory. In high school, I memorized all of the chemical elements in the periodic table. The names of those elements were mostly nonsense to me, so I just made up a catchy jingle to remember them. Was I good at chemistry, or simply good at memorizing? In college, I quickly forgot most of the chemistry I had memorized and learned that I had little interest in a deeper understanding of chemistry. Luckily, I took a class in psychology my first year of college, and discovered an interest in how we learn and why we forget. I learned about the scientific study of memory and aging and the "booming" field of gerontology. My early interest in older adults and aging was rekindled.

Our memories are our very identities, and my research at UCLA seeks to understand how we remember what is important to us, especially as we get older. As we age, we might actually get better at knowing what is important to remember—something that college students often find challenging. The ability to remember what is important is essential in a world overflowing with enticing but useless information. Memory and aging go hand in hand, as memory decline is one of the first things that concern most people as they age. But changes in memory really happen over a lifetime. In my 40s, I sometimes struggle to remember names and where I put my wallet or sunglasses. But I am also struck by how many older adults vividly recall remote memories and what is most important to them, even if some names are forgotten on occasion.

People often think about old age in a negative light, in terms of aches and pains. But when does old age actually begin? A few years before I turned 40, I hurt my back. I had a herniated disk, the result of an ill-advised zip-line adventure. I felt shooting pain in my lower back and nerve sensations in my toes for months. I had to hobble around, sometimes hunched over. People told me I was "just getting old." It probably didn't help that my hair was also thinning. My young daughters would say, "Daddy, why are you walking like Grandpa?" I would struggle with carrying my children, installing car seats, and lifting anything heavy. I wasn't exercising as much as I used to, and I was complaining more about my various aches. I lost my prescription sunglasses enough times that I now have my name and phone number engraved on them. Sadly, some of my once-close friends died unexpectedly. Was this an early taste of what to expect in older age? Why didn't getting older look like what I saw in sunny South Florida as a child?

Some people say you are only as old are you feel. I felt old when I started college, which in fact was a place where I often acted like a child. Later in life, my back injury led to people telling me I was getting old. I feel even older now that I have a mortgage. We learn as we grow older. I have learned from the people I've interviewed about successful aging, as well as from the students and older adults who do our research studies at UCLA. I see many impressive role models of aging, as well as those who struggle in older age. Having studied aging for several decades, I know we are never too young, or too old, to learn about the effects of aging.

If you haven't yet reached old age, then you are training to become an older adult. Our expectations about aging shape what we do in older age, and our expectations are influenced by observing how others age. Aging isn't all downhill unless most of life is an uphill battle. Then navigating the downhill portions can be a challenging yet enjoyable journey. Frank Sinatra sings "The Best Is Yet To Come," and the Robert Browning poem says "the best is yet to be." The book title, *Better with Age*, may make one think of a fine wine that ages well with time, but like wine making, successful aging can be an active and involved process that requires development over time. This book shows how we can get better with age, and enjoy the benefits of old age.

Introduction: The Benefits of Aging and the Psychology of Successful Aging

Some say age is just a number, but it is an important number. Our age determines when we can vote and buy beer, and there are social age expectations about when we should marry, have children, and retire. However, most people feel younger than their actual age. While we celebrate birthdays, we also fear the aging process and spend time and money trying to conceal the signs of aging. The psychology of aging tries to make sense of not only how we age, but also our beliefs about aging and how expectations influence the way we age.

There are many measurable changes as we age. For example, we aren't as fast as we used to be, and we tend to forget what's-her-name's name more often. We also adapt as we age so that we don't need to be as fast, and we learn to compensate for memory challenges. As a cognitive psychologist, I have done hundreds of experiments to study the aging processes. My research team has measured reaction times, quantified memory accuracy and strategies, and uncovered pitfalls and unexpected strengths of thousands of older adults. I have also conducted structured interviews with many older adults, listening to their life stories. While research studies are very informative, this book is also about these real-life stories. I discuss what makes people happier and how people improve with age, as well as what frustrates and challenges older adults.

Thinking about people whom we respect and admire, and how well they have aged, can provide us with inspiring role models. This book presents many examples, with insights from Maya Angelou, Warren Buffett, Phyllis Diller, Bob Newhart, Frank Gehry, Dave Brubeck, David Letterman, Bill Clinton, Jack LaLanne, Jared Diamond, Kareem Abdul-Jabbar, John Glenn, Sully Sullenberger, Vin Scully, Dr. Ruth Westheimer, and John Wooden, many of whom I was able to interview. I thank the exceptional individuals who agreed to share their thoughts and insights on successful aging during personal interviews with me—a true highlight of doing research on successful aging is interacting with these amazingly interesting people. This list could be much longer, for when I tell people about these interviews on successful aging, they quickly suggest someone else that I should interview, meaning that we all know many impressive older adults.

Humans may be a unique species in that we celebrate and fear the aging process. In some ways, old age can sneak up on us, as most people think of "being old" as more distant than our current age. While we may not have control over the gift of good genes, how we think and behave can have a substantial impact on how we age. The habits, routines, and behaviors we have established well before we reach older age can persist but are also highly modifiable. Diet, exercise, beliefs, social interactions, curiosity, positivity, and a sense of purpose in life can greatly influence how we experience old age. People who have a positive attitude about older age are often good at successful aging. Our stereotypes and expectations about aging can influence how well we age. In fact, reading this book can lead to a more positive attitude about aging.

I recently got a birthday card saying, "What is the difference between you and a senior citizen?" I opened the card for the thought-provoking answer: "A lot less than there used to be." This book is not just for older adults, as successful aging does not start at some particular age, when you get gray hair, when you are balding, or when you retire. Whether you are young or old, middle-aged, or not thinking at all about your age, you have already started this journey. Today is a great time to be getting older, and if you are healthy, then tomorrow may be even better. While people have some negative attitudes about aging, it is *not* all downhill. Recent research on the psychology of aging has led to many surprising discoveries about the benefits of old age. This book is an exposé of the benefits of aging and the many paradoxes that surround aging. Successful aging can start at any age, and there is a lot you can do now to enjoy the benefits of old age.

Better with Age

What Is Successful Aging?

I will never be an old man. To me, old age is always 15 years older than I am.

—Francis Bacon, English philosopher, scientist, and author

MANY POPULAR BOOKS ABOUT AGING FOCUS ON HOW to prevent or avoid aging. Terms like *enhancing longevity* are used instead of *aging*, as people think the word *aging* implies decline. The phrase "successful aging" has grown in popularity over the past few decades. At some point in life, people become concerned about aging and want to know what to expect, what to avoid, and ways to adapt. New research has shown that important paradoxes exist regarding how we think about old age and how we actually age. A paradox exists when we have expectations about old age, but these expectations are almost the opposite of what *actually* happens in old age. This book outlines some of these paradoxes and describes when, how, and why we can get better with age.

At a basic level, aging involves our continuing survival—a race against time. We often associate negative outcomes with getting older. If you start complaining about a bad back and aching joints or struggle to remember names of people you have met, "you're getting old" is often used as an explanation. But this type of "old age" can really begin at any age. I will sometimes complain about my bad back to my 70-year-old colleague, who has no back issues. Getting older isn't the leading cause of back injuries, joint pain, or memory problems. If you are happy, active, and enjoy spending time with friends and family, people never say "it's because you are getting old."

Adults often do not get excited about aging or even talking about their age. Simply asking someone's age is often a faux pas in our youth-obsessed society. Bring the topic up at a party, and most people will avoid it or want to know how to prevent or slow the process. But if you visit a children's playground (as I frequently do with my young children), parents often quickly volunteer their children's very specific ages. For example, "My son is two and three-quarters" is often met with a response like "My, he is big (or fast or strong) for his age." We rarely discuss age as openly when we see middle-aged adults. However, we are often impressed with a healthy, active 90-year-old, which suggests we search for good examples of aging.

Happy Birthday! Again Already?

> How old would you be if you didn't know how old you were?
> —Satchel Paige, baseball player

Paige began his Major League Baseball career at age 42 and retired at age 59, becoming the oldest player both to begin his playing career (at age 42) and to play (age 59) in the major leagues.

A casual look at the birthday card section at a drug store reveals both the humor and remorse associated with old age. Some examples of the birthday card messages include "Happy Birthday, You Old Fart" and "The good thing about growing old with your friends is they have forgotten all of your secrets." Most of these cards focus on the negative aspects of aging, often mocking how little control we have over aging.[1] Perhaps the best messages in some of these birthday cards include the wisdom to know how to enjoy old age. Fitting with the title of this book, one card said, "Like a great wine we get better as we get older! Or rather, as we get older we feel better with wine." The birthday card you choose for someone, and how to interpret their messages, says a lot about how we think about aging.

While birthdays remind us of aging, they also may motivate us to do something important in life. They are the landmarks on the map of life. People run marathons because of upcoming birthdays, go on long anticipated trips, or have large parties with friends. Some research[2] suggests that when people approach a new decade in life (a so-called "landmark birthday," like turning 40, 50, 60, etc.) they search for meaning. People may buy a new car, join a gym, get married, date online, or even read books about aging!

Jack LaLanne, the legendary fitness guru who led a nation to learn new ways to exercise, celebrated his various birthdays in unique and impressive ways: At age 45, he did 1,000 jumping Jacks (which some say were named after him) and 1,000 pull-ups in 1 hour and 22 minutes. At age 60, he swam from Alcatraz to Fisherman's Wharf in the San Francisco Bay, not only wearing handcuffs but also towing a 1,000-pound boat. On his 70th birthday, he swam 1.5 miles while towing 70 boats filled with 70 people—and again while wearing hand-cuffs and shackles on his arms and legs! His wife of over 50 years, Elaine LaLanne, said, "You can't be around him without being enthusiastic. He wanted to show people that just because you're older doesn't mean that you have to give up, or stop exercising. You don't have to become a couch potato. He wanted to prove that anything in life is possible, and *you* can make it happen."[3]

What Do We Call Older Adults: Elderly? Boomers? Them? Just Call Us by Our Names!

What is "old age"? In a large-scale survey of nearly 3,000 people over the age of 65,[4] respondents said that the "average person" enters old age at age 68. However, that number is deceiving, as those same people said that for *themselves*, old age starts at age 85. This elusive age for defining old age may be elusive because most "older people" don't report actually feeling that old.

Another issue is how to address older adults: names such as boomers, seniors, elderly, old folks, golden age (not to mention graybeards, geezers, or codgers) may all carry negative connotations. Using the wrong words to describe a demographic can alienate an audience or individual. In one poll[5] of persons over 60, more than half responded that they are not comfortable with the term *senior*, but many more were comfortable with the term *baby boomer*. In today's environment, boomers are caring for aging parents and usually don't view themselves as seniors yet. The poll also found that when considering "old age homes," people hated the term *nursing home* but liked *retirement community*. One younger person who worked in a retirement community, when asked what seniors like to be called, said, "Their names!"[6] Throughout this book, I use mostly the term *older adults*, but I also realize various other descriptors can be used, besides simply being older than younger or middle-aged adults.

What Is Successful Aging? Hard to Define, But We Know It When We See It

The term *successful aging* was made popular in 1987, when the scientists John Wallis Rowe and Robert Kahn published an influential book entitled *Successful Aging.*[7] Rowe and Kahn were interested in the multidimensional aspects of aging. They stated that successful aging involved three main factors: (1) being free of disability or disease, (2) having high cognitive and physical abilities, and (3) interacting with others in meaningful ways. Importantly, Rowe and Kahn acknowledged that successful aging involved both intrinsic genetic factors and extrinsic lifestyle factors. Extrinsic factors such as diet, exercise, personal habits, and psychosocial aspects of aging are often underestimated if one takes the simplistic view that aging is guided by genetics.

Today, an exact definition of successful aging is an open debate. It is even unclear whether aging is a process or an outcome. Researchers have offered over 80 unique and different operational definitions of successful aging,[8] with some estimating that only 1% of people achieve successful aging, while others estimate that close to 90% of people can achieve it. Despite these discrepancies, most people can easily identify someone who exemplifies successful aging, without subjecting that person to medical testing or any psychological evaluation. Thus, successful aging is often something we simply "know it when we see it."

Many people consider Warren Buffett to be very successful professionally. After all, he is a billionaire philanthropist, and he is now 86. Is he then a model of successful aging? What are the secrets to successful aging for Warren Buffett? He is an avid Coca-Cola drinker (he reportedly drinks five cans a day), noting, "I'm about one-quarter

Coca-Cola" and that he had seen no evidence that switching to "water and broccoli" would make it easier for him to make it to age 100. Of course, Buffett's eating habits may not be the path to successful aging, but he has identified one key to his success. Buffett credits his own success to reading voraciously; he typically spends 80% of his day reading. He says that reading is something many people can do at almost any point in their lives, and especially later in life, but that people rarely do enough of it.[9] Buffett has no plans to retire and he loves his work—he's clearly successful professionally and apparently very happy. However, simply making money and living well in old age is only one way to conceptualize successful aging.

What about Jeanne Louis Calment, from France, who was born in 1875 and has the longest confirmed human lifespan on record, living to the age of 122 years? She said her longevity could be attributed to a diet rich in olive oil, but also to drinking port wine and eating large amounts of chocolate (not to mention smoking a few cigarettes a day since she was 20). She also stated that being calm allowed her to age well ("that's why they call me Calment," she said). She outlived both her daughter and her grandson by several decades. Calment reportedly remained mentally sharp until she died in 1997, at age 122, saying, "I'm interested in everything but passionate about nothing."[10]

In Western culture we tend to "medicalize" aging, looking for the hidden secrets of health and longevity, ideally in a pill or bottle. Health is viewed as a biological state, and "good or bad" aging as the outcome of our medical or physiological state. However, people can alter this state and have the most control over the behavioral aspects of aging—how we eat, exercise, think, and interact with others—behaviors that have a strong impact on our biological health. Successful aging can start in childhood, as people develop habits and work ethics and learn to exercise and eat well. We often focus on the physical health of people as they age, and we assume that psychological well-being follows this trend. While physical and mental health are related, there is more to life than simply being in good physical shape. Older people often say that successful aging involves being productive, being mentally fit, and, most importantly, being able to lead a meaningful life.

Pulitzer prize–winning author Jared Diamond says successful aging for him is enjoying life, being productive, and continuing to do the things he is good at doing. He told me that age 70 was one of the best times in his life. His said his father was a physician who continued to see patients until he was 93. Today, Diamond finds ways to balance his writing with his family activities. He is currently working on his seventh book, at age 80, while also finding more time to travel with his family. Diamond says his closest professional colleague and mentor was the biologist Ernst Mayr, who published his twenty-second book on his hundredth birthday—certainly a role model for Professor Diamond. Successful aging involves focusing on what is important to you, and being able to do what you want to do in old age.

While successful aging may be one way to describe how well we age, the concept of "meaningful aging" may be another important way to consider how to age well. Meaningful aging does not involve "winners or losers" in terms of longevity and health, but rather the need to focus on what is most meaningful to a person, especially in older age. Sometimes this involves not doing more to stay active but, perhaps, doing less, giving up some control over our lives, being more mindful of others, and being aware of the need to forgive and forget. Meaningful aging encourages us all to find meaning and peace in our lives, and the effects that these practices have on how we age can, in fact, lead to a form of successful aging. Other terms, such as *healthy aging*, *productive aging*, or *joyful aging*, convey the many themes that are associated with a more encompassing phrase of successful aging.

Too Young to Die: The Case of Unsuccessful Aging

This book places a large emphasis on successful or meaningful aging and the benefits of growing old. While I focus on successful aging and have interacted with and interviewed many who fit that bill, one could say they are aging well because of the success they have had in life. For example, U.S. presidents live longer than the average adult male, despite the stress associated with the presidency. This is likely because of a number of factors, including diet, education, social support, and the financial means allowing them to live well.[11] On the other hand, what is *un*successful aging? Unsuccessful aging may involve not reaching old age in the first place. The English rock band The Who's famous song "My Generation" had the lyric "I hope I die before I get old." Interestingly, when The Who's singer Pete

Townshend was asked about it, he said that when he wrote the lyrics (on his twentieth birthday), to him "old" meant "very rich."[12]

One unfortunate culprit contributing to unsuccessful aging is addictions to alcohol, drugs, and prescription medications. Today, drugs such as opiates are one of the leading causes of accidental deaths in middle age. Some individuals have incredible talent, and overcome amazing odds and circumstances to become superstars and legends, only to succumb to the dark side of their own success. Such individuals include Michael Jackson, Kurt Cobain, Jim Morrison, Prince, Philip Seymour Hoffman, Whitney Houston, and Amy Winehouse, to name a few, and sadly, the list grows daily. Today, access to addictive painkillers leads to many drug overdoses for those at any age. Interestingly, younger adults may think of Michael Jackson, Prince, or Whitney Houston as success stories, yet may not have a similar level of admiration for people such as a war veteran or Holocaust survivor.

It seems that in some cases extreme success does not lead to successful aging, and sometimes it can lead to quite the opposite. What habits and obstacles were overcome for older adults to age well, and how can we appreciate the benefits of old age ourselves? One way is to better understand the paradoxes of aging early in life and conform our lifestyle respectively for successful aging. Simply put, surviving one's youth and middle age to reach old age is the first step to successful aging. Some who have experienced success early in life can fail the challenge to reach even middle age. But the concept of "middle age" brings up an important question: How do we define and measure these age ranges?

Chronological Age, Biological Age, and Subjective Age: How Old Do You Feel?

How old are you? Chances are you are referencing a date from your birth certificate—this is your objective chronological age. You aren't necessarily checking in with your body for a more biological signal, such as "I have the lungs of a 50-year-old," or "a recent bone scan shows I have bones like that of a 70-year-old." Brain training technology will attempt to tell you your "brain age," by giving you feedback about your score on a brain game, and to show you that you can modify this age. Yet the best marker for your age, and your longevity and overall health, is how old you feel—something known as your *subjective age.* Research has shown that subjective age (how old you feel), not your actual age, is in fact a better predictor of your overall health, memory abilities, physical strength, and longevity.[13] Thus, instead of asking "How old are you?" (which is impolite in most social settings anyway), a better question may, in fact, be "How old do you feel?" People often report feeling anywhere from 5 to 15 years younger than their chronological age. In general, once we hit 40, we report feeling 20% younger, such that a 40-year-old feels 32, a 60-year-old feels 48, and an 80-year-old feels 60.[14] Paradoxically, we feel younger as we age.[15]

In a culture obsessed with youth and anti-aging, the idea of "feeling younger" can be misleading. When people report that their subjective age is younger than their actual objective chronological age, they aren't denying or hiding their age, but merely reporting that they feel healthier than they expected to feel at that particular age. Dr. Laura Carstensen, founding director of the Stanford Center on Longevity, has shown that when older people are asked how old they would like to be, people typically say they wish to be about 10 years younger—80-year-olds want to be 70, and 60-year-olds wish to be 50—mostly because they feel they were healthier then. None of the older adults yearned to be 20 or 30 again, which is telling, since those cherished years may be considered very challenging relative to older age, and not necessarily times we want to relive.[16]

Unlike our chronological age, which is only modifiable by the actual passage of time into the future (we can't get any younger), our subjective age, and how old we feel, is modifiable. If we are around others who are younger, we might feel younger. For example, the actor Dick Van Dyke, at age 86, married Arlene Silver, age 40, and we can think of many other examples of large age differences in couples who marry or remarry. The older person married to the younger person may have a younger subjective age; he or she feels younger and acts younger and, according to Van Dyke, might even sing and dance more. Van Dyke, now in his 90s, said, "I have a beautiful, young wife who sings and dances, so there's a lot of duetting going on at my house."[17]

Dr. Ellen Langer, a social psychologist at Harvard, suggests that cues about our age (such as balding or having children later in life) can influence our subjective age and associated outcomes.[18] For example, women who bear children later in life are then often surrounded by younger age-related cues (younger mothers), and these relatively older mothers have a longer life expectancy than that of women who bear children earlier in life. Large differences in spousal age can result in "age-incongruent cues" (women with older men might see more aging up close and feel older). These younger spouses tend to live shorter lives, whereas older spouses live longer lives, although it is very difficult to determine any causal factors. The point is that being reminded about aging can change how old we feel, and feeling older or younger can certainly make a difference.

Interestingly, people may actually want to look younger, not just for vanity but to appreciate the associated health benefits and societal expectations associated with a younger subjective age—feeling younger may make us act younger. A surprising finding from Langer's research is that women who think they look younger after having their hair colored or cut actually show a decrease in blood pressure, and they also appear younger to others. For men, baldness certainly is a reminder about advancing to old age. Men who go bald prematurely see an older self in the mirror and may, in fact, "age faster," as there is some evidence that prematurely bald men have an excess risk of getting prostate cancer and coronary heart disease compared to men who do not prematurely bald. Thus, the search for more hair in men (either toupee or via regrowth, a booming industry) could actually have some health-related benefits if people firmly believe that they feel younger when they look younger.[19] This may be one reason we are often surprised to see an older-looking face in the mirror.

What does it mean to be older adults today, compared to being an older adult 20 or 30 years ago? Today, older people think old age starts around 85, and that is much different than 20 years ago. When we think of an older adult, we often think of our parents or grandparents, or other family or friends who fit that description—but does that mean that is what we will be like in older age? Based on a large-scale study conducted in Berlin,[20] relying on data collected in 2014 from people age 75 and comparing them to data from a similar study conducted in 1990, researchers were able to closely examine the differences between the two sets of data. More impressively, the researchers were able to identify and compare "statistical twins"—one person of the same sex from each of the two studies who were similar to each other in terms of age, health, and education. On average, today's 75-year-olds are cognitively much fitter than those from 20 years ago, performing much like 55-year-olds from the earlier study and reporting higher levels of well-being and a more positive mood. The researchers suggest that a possible explanation is that there have been improvements in physical fitness and higher levels of independence in older adults today compared to 25 years ago. This fits with the notion that we just might be getting smarter, stronger, and even faster, an argument that has been made on the basis of faster marathon and triathlon finish times over the last 50 years, and the older ages of those who complete these endurance races.

When and How to Study Successful Aging: It Happens So Fast and So Slowly

We are all constantly observing aging, in ourselves and in our families. In many ways, we are all students of aging as we follow our children, parents, and grandparents through the course of life, observing changes in them and in ourselves, and wondering what we will be like when we are older.[21] I certainly notice how my memory has changed over the years (and my more frequent memory blunders), possibly because my career is focused on memory and aging. However, I am continually in awe of older adults who are sharp, witty, and wise and are role models in some way. That is how this book got its momentum—from interacting with older adults who age in many different ways, and asking what we can learn about successful aging from people of all ages. But how can we do scientific research on aging?

Constraints and Caveats When Doing Research on Aging

When studying aging in humans, it is hard to do experiments in the pure sense of the term, for a variety of reasons. Barring a time machine, we are limited by time and waiting to observe any outcomes that might result from introducing that variable. For example, if one introduces some variable or intervention (such as eating more blueberries or getting more exercise) to see if it has an effect on aging (such as better memory or a longer lifespan), one needs to wait in order to observe any long-term effects. Also, it is hard to determine if any health benefits are due to the variable or to some other sequence of events or changes in behavior that occur during the aging process.

As a result, we often rely on observing associations or correlations, assuming that time or aging plays a key role. In order to attempt to isolate aging in more detail and determine what really causes age-related changes or age differences, one can either patiently follow a group of people for years (referred to as a "longitudinal study") or, more simply, compare two different age groups at some set point in time (referred to as a "cross-sectional study").

Watching our children grow up or our parents grow old is our personal longitudinal study of aging. Comparing ourselves to our children is more cross-sectional and illustrates both how times have changed and how people may change. While individuals and case studies can provide useful insights, it is hard to draw firm conclusions based on one person; ideally a large group or sample of hundreds or thousands of people is best in order to make generalizations. Often anecdotes may support larger research studies[22] or provide the necessary stepping stones for additional research that may or may not support anecdotal evidence. In addition, nonhuman animal studies can give greater control over the aging process, and a shorter lifespan to study. For example, the lifespan of a fruit fly is several weeks or months,[23] so experiments that manipulate genes can attempt to extend this short lifespan and make important discoveries without waiting years, decades, or a human lifetime to observe any results regarding enhancing longevity.[24] Finally, we scientists tend to study questions we find interesting and important about aging, so in a sense we choose what to study about our own aging process, which leads to potential biases right from the start of any experiment. Thus, research can be driven by our own interests and motivation. I am reminded of a joke about what motivates us to want to study the brain: "I used to think the brain was the most interesting thing to study, and then I thought, wait, who is telling me that?"

College Students and the "Worried Well" Older Adults Who Like Research

Studying aging requires a lot of time, quite literally. In experimental psychology, there are various methods of studying how people age, without waiting years and years to watch them age. In fact, most studies of "aging" are really looking at "age-related" differences between groups of people. These cross-sectional studies compare younger adults to older adults at one given point in time. They are, by and large, the most convenient and cost-effective, and they often take place on university campuses. As a matter of convenience, they usually involve college students for the younger group, who participate for course credits or sometimes are paid for their time. The older adults are often the "worried well," healthy older people concerned about their memory, worried it doesn't work, and wanting to do something about it. These older adults are recruited from the community, living independently, and getting paid for their time, though often they may do it for free or sometimes donate the money. Their motivation might be to keep sharp, stay in touch with the latest research, and learn more about their own memory.

One thing to note is that these cross-sectional studies involve the comparison of different cohorts of people. An older adult today was likely a teenager in the 1950s and maybe went to college in the 1960s. These older adults are then compared to college students of today—a much different time than when older adults were young. Even a college degree "in that day and age" differs from a college degree today, as many more people are now attending college. So, in addition to age differences, there are cohort differences, and these can play a role in how people perceive the world. This is important to keep in mind when comparing younger adults today to older adults, who grew up in a different world.

Don't Forget to Come Back: Longitudinal Studies of Aging

The more involved form of studying aging is through longitudinal designs—emphasis on *long*—as it involves following groups of people as they age. This takes time (often decades) and resources (usually grant money). Participants in these studies may drop out over the years as people move, don't respond, lose interest, or die. As a result, sometimes it is the healthiest and more interested and dedicated participants who keep on coming back for their dose of research participation. Worldwide, the most famous of these longitudinal studies have been conducted in Berlin, Baltimore, Victoria, Seattle, and Sweden; another famous study is the Harvard Study of Adult Development.

Interestingly, in some of the longitudinal studies, very small declines, or sometimes even no deficits at all, are found on some tests of memory, reasoning, and vocabulary for people well into their 90s.[25]

One challenge of longitudinal studies is that if you bring people back each year to test their memory on the *same* test of memory, they will show "practice effects," as they have taken these tests several times. However, the same type of effect could be said about college students who are constantly taking memory tests in their classes. In one longitudinal study in Sweden, researchers compared different age groups with those groups that came back regularly and found that when controlling for these practice effects, there were still only small decrements in memory, starting around age 60, and fewer deficits on tests of verbal memory and vocabulary. They also found that education levels influenced cohort effects in the cross-sectional studies.[26] Given these issues, a complete picture of how things change with age relies on various measures that all come with their own challenges, for practical and interpretative reasons.

One of the more unique longitudinal studies was an eight-decade study, starting with young school children born around the year 1910. The study was conducted by a Stanford psychologist named Lewis Terman, who was famous for his studies of intelligence. He selected 1,500 high-functioning and gifted boys and girls, arranging for various types of tests early in life to better understand what made people leaders later in life. Decades later, it was found that the children's performance on these early-life tests was related to various impressive achievements later in life, although it remains unclear if these early blooming children were any better at such achievements than those who weren't identified as gifted early in life. There were also some surprising findings, such as while early reading ability in these children was associated with later academic success, it was less associated with lifelong educational attainment and was hardly related to measures of midlife adjustment. In addition, the children who entered school at an early age actually completed fewer years of education in life, had worse midlife adjustment, and had an increased mortality risk.[27] Although many of the selected children ended up living long, healthy lives, it was unclear whether they lived any longer than others who were not identified as gifted early in life. These selected children, sometimes referred to as "Terman's Termites," are almost all dead now, but their legacy lives on in terms of treasure troves of data and stories about their lives as long-serving test subjects. Further research is needed to successfully track how our current information age, with a technology-driven cohort, will age over the next few decades and how our constant access to information will shape knowledge, wisdom, well-being, and aging.

In terms of how our own memory has changed over the years, without doing any formal experiments, we often rely simply on our own self-reporting: How is your memory these days? Relative to what? When you were 20, or relative to college students today? We need to carefully compare ourselves to an appropriate time or group in order to draw valid conclusions. Often our own subjective assessment of our health or memory and of how we age can be very accurate.[28] In addition, our companions and close family members who know us well can provide some insights regarding the possible onset or presence of dementia.[29] Thus, over the course of our lives, we know ourselves pretty well, and we notice the changes that come with age.

With Age Comes Selectivity? Theories of Selective Goals in Old Age

While there are various theories of what happens to us psychologically as we age, most center on decline or how things get worse: we get slower, fall down, don't sleep well, and have trouble remembering things. However, notable exceptions to this are lifespan development theories that don't focus on declines with age but rather what things change in different ways as we get older, some for the better and some for the worse. Two prominent qualitative theories of aging are known as *selective optimization with compensation* and *socioemotional selectivity theory*, and both make important and accurate predictions that, as we age, we selectively and strategically focus on different activities, different information, and different goals, and we are not simply falling apart, relative to our younger selves or counterparts.

As we get older, we have a better understanding of what activities we like, how to better allocate our time, and the physical limitations that might accompany older age. Older adults may be considered connoisseurs in how to spend time and how to choose activities while still trying new things. Goals change with age, and we may be more selective about what to focus on when we are older, often focusing on emotionally meaningful goals, such as spending time with family and friends and doing things that might have an impact on the next generation.

Selective Optimization and Compensation

One dominant theory about aging is that we become more selective about what we pursue and how we pursue it. Proposed by Professor Paul Baltes and colleagues, this highly influential theory is known as *selective optimization with compensation.*[30] According to this theory, we select what activities or goals we wish to achieve, optimize the time and abilities we have to achieve these goals, and compensate for any declines or deficiencies that might result from aging. For example, an older person with fading eyesight who loves music and singing could selectively spend more time and attention on singing, listening to music, and perhaps even joining a new choir. At the same time, this person might reduce time spent reading or playing cards and on other activities that rely heavily on vision.

The great pianist Arthur Rubinstein, who performed well into his late 80s and lived to 95, was a good example of selective optimization with compensation. In older age, he practiced fewer pieces, focusing on the ones he loved most, and performed in public. He also described how he stopped performing extremely complicated pieces in older age. But when he did perform fast and complex music, he said he learned to slow down his speed of playing prior to fast movements, thereby producing a contrast that enhanced the *impression* of speed.[31] I witnessed a similar approach when I saw legendary guitarist Chuck Berry perform at the jazz bar Blueberry Hill in St. Louis. Berry employed similar strategies in his 80s, varying tempo, substituting words, and, in general, improvising as he saw fit, as a true, aging artist.

While habits are often hard to break, it can be adaptive to reassess what activities are modifiable in older age. If one played basketball or jogged for years and now experiences knee or joint deterioration and pain, taking up swimming, walking, and birdwatching would be consistent with selective optimization and compensation. Substituting activities that are more age-friendly is adaptive, such as replacing racquetball with golf, or even taking up these sports earlier in life, knowing they are ones that can be enjoyed well into old age. Astronaut and Senator John Glenn used to jog regularly, but in his 90s, he walked most days instead, getting exercise in a different manner. The Pulitzer prize–winning author Jared Diamond, who used to do challenging 20-mile hikes, now enjoys a regular 3-mile bird-watching walk every morning near his house. Overall, this model suggests that older people should take an active approach in their aging process, by selecting what activities to pursue, based on current resources and abilities, and setting reasonable and meaningful goals.

Emotional Goals in Older Age: Socioemotional Selectivity Theory

A related theory explains how our goals shift with age, such that a college student or young employee often is focused on accumulating information or knowledge, whereas an older adult often is more focused on emotionally meaningful goals. Those goals may involve family or broader professional pursuits, such as mentoring, directing, or finding ways to make bigger changes in the world and contribute to the next generation. This idea, known as *socioemotional selectivity theory*, is a highly influential notion proposed by Professor Laura Carstensen and colleagues at Stanford University, and is outlined in her popular book, *A Long Bright Future*.[32] This theory suggests that older adults are aware of the finite limits of life and, as a result, will focus more on positive information, emotional goals, and spending time with loved ones, compared to younger adults, who may focus more on negative information for survival, accumulating knowledge, and making new friends and connections, sometimes at the expense of spending time with family.

Remembering What Really Matters in Life: Value-Directed Remembering

My own research program expands these two dominant theories, suggesting that despite or possibly because of encountering more memory challenges with age, older adults are actually very good at selecting what is important. This selectivity is partly because older adults have better "metacognition"—an awareness about the challenges of remembering a lot of information. As a result, as we age, we are more selective about what is important to us and what we will remember. We might focus on positive emotions or important names, and on what interests us or what we are curious about. We remember foods that our children or grandchildren are allergic to, sale prices of grocery items we frequently buy, or names of birds if we are avid birdwatchers. Quite simply, as we get older, we may get better at knowing how to be selective and knowing what we want, what to remember, how to use our time, and what makes us happy.

Grumpy Old Man? Our Stereotypes about Old Age May Be Biased

Societal stereotypes or our own cultural expectations profoundly affect our aging. When you think about an older adult, what comes to mind? People associate both positive and negative traits with older people as a group, although there tend to be more negative trait associations than positive ones.[33] One way to assess this is to ask people to come up with the first 10 words they think of when imagining a "typical" older adult. You can try this for yourself—what are the words that come to mind?

Usually words like *gray hair, grandparent, slow, Florida, frail, dementia, grumpy, cane, frugal, wrinkles, forgetful, wisdom, mumble, medications,* and *retired* come to mind. In many ways, the media can be partly to blame because of the emphasis on the negative aspects of aging in television commercials and in the media. In fact, one study showed that the more TV one watches, the more negative attitudes one has about aging.[34] While some stereotypes certainly are often valid, such as having wrinkles and being a grandparent, older adults often defy many negative stereotypes. Older adults may hold very different opinions from those of younger adults about what old age means. Thus, while younger adults may have certain attitudes and opinions about what old age is all about, many of these may be inaccurate, based on limited interactions with older adults, or both. This is an important paradox, as one's attitude is very important in terms of how we age.

Research shows that the attitudes one holds about aging are related to how well one actually ages—even when these attitudes are assessed years before one enters old age.[35] Negative attitudes about aging have been found to be associated with not only developing dementia at an earlier age but also with the degree to which dementia-related brain pathology exists in older age.[36] These attitudes may be most important in younger middle age, as one study found that young, healthy people under 50 who held negative attitudes toward older adults were more likely to experience a cardiovascular disorder later in life compared to their peers who had a more positive view of the elderly.[37] Our attitudes about the aging of others can have a strong influence on our own health.

Research has shown that how people feel inside, and their expectations of their capabilities in older age, can have a greater impact on health, happiness, and even longevity than the date on their birth certificate. Our physical environment can also make us act young or old. In her book *Counterclockwise*,[38] Dr. Ellen Langer, a Harvard University social psychologist, describes a study she conducted in 1979 in which men in their 70s and 80s went to a week-long retreat to a converted motel that was quite literally retrofitted so that the décor, music, and even the newspapers in the lobby were staged to feel like it was 1959, a year when these older adults were middle-aged. Langer divided her subjects into two groups. One group was told to reminisce about the year 1959, a year when they were 20 years younger, and the other group was told to act like they were 20 years younger, but they were not given instructions to actually reminisce about that earlier time in their lives. Upon entering the study, both groups of men had been highly reliant on relatives to help do things for them. However, at the end of the week, both groups were observed to be functioning more independently, actively completing various activities (some were playing catch with a football), and, amazingly, had significant improvements in hearing, memory, strength, and scores on some intelligence tests. The group told to behave like they were 20 years younger also showed better dexterity and flexibility and even looked younger, according to outside observers who judged photos of the participants taken before and after the retreat.

While this creative and labor-intensive study has not been repeated or conducted in other settings, you might experience similar effects of feeling younger when you attend a high school reunion, visit where you went to college (complete with additional alcohol consumption), or spend time with old friends reminiscing about the past and reliving your younger years. Older adults may even feel younger in their home if it is decorated from an era they associate with being younger. For this reason, many older adults do not want to move from their home, because moving to a retirement community might lead to reminders about aging and make them feel old. I find that coaching my daughters' basketball team (a group of talented, energetic 7- and 8-year-olds) makes me feel, if not act, younger than my age. Several of the children said that since they often see me wearing my UCLA T-shirt, they assumed I was a college student, suggesting that they see me as much younger than my actual age.

Do we attribute decline to being a natural part of aging? This ranges from a bad back to forgetting where you parked your car or the name of someone you just met. When a young adult forgets a name or forgets where they parked their car, it is often attributed to being busy or distracted (thanks, smartphones, for a great excuse for our absentmindedness), but when a middle-aged or older adult forgets something, we chalk it up to aging, or even worry about dementia, as a possible reason. Thus, our attributions can invoke and support negative attitudes about aging. People forget things, but how we interpret this can have profound implications.

All in Your Head? Nuns without Dementia Who Have Brains with Dementia

This book addresses the very powerful impact of the psychology of aging. While biological variables can certainly play key roles, it is also important to highlight how our behavior can modify biology and your brain. Biological aging and psychological function share an intimate relationship, but one that can also be perplexing. One of the most common biological markers of Alzheimer's disease is the appearance of plaques and tangles in the brain—something that can only be definitively diagnosed after death, at autopsy. A very unique longitudinal study of aging[39] was conducted with nuns, the Sisters of Notre Dame—an ideal group to easily track and study for decades because of their dedicated commitment to the church; they are unlikely to drop out of the study or move away. The nuns completed a variety of cognitive tests over many years, and when they eventually died, their brains were examined for the telltale biological signs of Alzheimer's disease.[40] What was most surprising and striking was that many of these nuns did have the plaques and tangles present in their brains, but they did not show any psychological signs of Alzheimer's disease while they were living; they did well on the memory tests, led active lives, and behaved in ways that gave no indication of dementia. Also, the level of mental activity that the nuns engaged in earlier in life was related to the amount of brain pathology found at autopsy: more engagement in stimulating activity early in life reduced the likelihood of the presence of plaques and tangles in the brain.[41] In addition, these nuns may have had brain benefits from hours of mindfulness, meditation, and prayer, which may involve harnessing the power of patience. Practices such as tai chi and yoga may serve a similar purpose. Thus, simply having biological markers, such as the plaques and tangles in the brain that are related to dementia, does not necessarily mean you will behave like you have dementia. Research suggests that higher education and continued mental activity throughout life can be protective factors.

New research supports the complex ways our brains change with age, and some studies show *qualitative* differences in the patterns of brain activity in older adults, relative to younger adults, when doing a challenging memory task—not simply *reduced* activity or less blood flow. The brain of an older adult is different from that of a younger adult because different regions, and not just fewer parts of the brain, are activated for any given specific tasks.[42] Thus, qualitative differences, and not just declines and atrophy, are important to consider, and exciting work suggests that as we age, we may build up some form of cognitive reserve to combat memory challenges,[43] as well as different types of neural scaffoldings[44] that can buffer against age-related cognitive decline.

Another understated factor is social connections, often with friends or family, sometimes through religious affiliations and activities. One's social network, and especially the quality of social connections, and not simply the number of Facebook friends, can also be protective, especially for people who already have high levels of brain pathology.[45] Parties, singing, and dancing may be very important for older adults, especially those with dementia. Moderate amounts of physical exercise, such as walking, and diet can play an important role and can modify the brain and body in important ways, reducing the likelihood of developing dementia. Research shows volumetric changes in the brain after the introduction of walking several times a week, leading to improvements in memory.[46] Thus, the brain can provide some markers of pathology, but our behaviors need not always map on to what the hardware in our head might show. This suggests that there are important ways in which psychology can influence how our brains physically change with age and can help us to age successfully.

Role Models and Interviews about Successful Aging

Do you have a role model who is successfully aging—a parent, grandparent, relative, teacher, coach, car mechanic, plumber, or a good friend—who exhibits many positive aspects of aging? Someone you might hope to emulate one day? When I started this book, I certainly had many people in mind. When I told people about the interviews I was conducting, people often had many suggestions for role models of successful aging. Insights are very informative, opening new doors for research, sometimes confirming the current science, but also sometimes casting it in doubt or revealing important gaps in our knowledge of what it takes to be successful in older age. In addition, when we reflect on what happens as we go through life, we may make important observations; in fact, these thoughts about aging and mortality can often lead to a clearer perspective on what is most meaningful in life.

Role models can change attitudes and beliefs. Changing attitudes about aging, possibly by seeing or having role models of aging, can have an impact on our impression of older adults and what we hope to accomplish in older age. This book attempts to illustrate many impressive things that older adults are doing and the new avenues that older adults may take on, ranging from a part-time jobs with Uber or Home Depot to teaching tennis or Pilates. Defying many stereotypes of old age, astronaut John Glenn traveled to outer space at the age of 77 for scientific research, in order to better understand how space travel can influence the physiological functioning of an older adult. It will be interesting to see how attitudes change about older adults in the future, especially given the demographics of healthy older adults living longer. With more healthy older adults living longer lives and acting as role models, a younger generation may update their stereotypes and expectations of their own old age and of what one can accomplish in old age.

Summary

This book is meant to illustrate some benefits of old age, highlighting both the foundational and latest research, using role models of aging to illustrate how things are not all downhill or negative, and arriving at insights that can help the current generation of soon-to-be older adults. Combining anecdotes, insights, and research studies, this is not simply a book about the sage advice from our elders, although this advice is an important source of information.[47] Talking to older people can be illuminating. Socrates said, "I enjoy talking with very old people. They have gone before us on a road by which we, too, may have to travel, and I think we do well to learn from them what it is like." Socrates wasn't alone in his enjoyment of being around older people; physicians (geriatricians) who specialize in aging and work closely with older adults are one of the happiest groups of physicians, despite often being paid the least.[48] In this book, I highlight some intriguing aspects of aging that still might not be well understood and that for a long time have been viewed in a negative light. This bias may have led to inaccurate perceptions of what really happens as we age.

Happiness: A Funny Thing Happens as We Get Older

Wrinkles should merely indicate where smiles have been.
——Mark Twain

It takes no more time to see the good side of life than to see the bad.
——Jimmy Buffett, musician

G RUMPY OLD MAN, CURMUDGEON, CODGER—THERE ARE so many negative stereotypes associated with old age, it is sometimes hard to avoid them. At some level, the media may be to blame. One study showed that the more television you watch, the more these stereotypes become ingrained[1] (think of Archie Bunker, Grampa Simpson, Golden Girls, and Grace and Frankie, depending on your era and TV interests). In the media, youth is usually associated with joyfulness, carefree living, and being full of adventure and life experiences. What is rarely emphasized, and what we don't focus on when we think of our "good old days," is how our youth may have also been full of conflict, turmoil, and many emotional highs and lows. Relatively speaking, older age might allow for emotional stability, a greater sense of control, and, in some cases, more freedom.

Do you think people are happier when they are younger or older? For younger adults, it may be a difficult question to answer, as young people will likely base this assessment on stereotypes or case studies of aging, rather than on their personal experience of older adults in their lives. The media certainly provides plenty of stereotypes to persuade us that old age is not a happy time. This focus on the negative aspects of aging then leads to the perception that older people must not be happy—quite the contrary to what people actually experience. Dr. Becca Levy found that people who hold a negative belief about aging earlier in life actually have poorer memory in old age and are more likely to suffer from age-related hearing loss.[2] In addition, if you have lower expectations about aging, you are less likely to exercise in old age—and exercise in older age is associated with health, happiness, and longevity.[3] Thus, there are benefits to learning about the bright side of aging, and how you might actually be happier than you think in older age.

Old age is not for sissies, many have said (such as Bette Davis and Art Linkletter, and echoed by many others). The truth is, as we enter older age, there are clear physical signs and symptoms: our muscles may weaken; our bones may become more brittle; we get wrinkles; our hearing and vision can deteriorate; it seems harder to remember names of people we recently met; we can't run or walk as fast as we used to; and we start to notice more aches and pains in parts of our bodies that we may never have even noticed before. So, despite all of these changes, why might we get happier in old age?

Happiness and Life Satisfaction: The Dual Benefits of Old Age?

Happiness can be defined as both the feeling of pleasure and the feeling of overall contentment. When discussing happiness, it is important to make a distinction between the current emotional state of happiness (as experienced currently or in the recent past, such as sometime earlier today or yesterday) and a more retrospective feeling of contentment with life. On a day-to-day basis, we seek pleasure and want to avoid pain. This form of happiness, a person's experience of pleasure, is also known as the hedonic state of well-being. *Life satisfaction* refers to one's contentment with one's overall life, but is a fundamentally different form of emotional assessment. Life satisfaction involves reflecting on our accomplishments and goals, and if we have achieved what we want in life.

Is life satisfaction only obtainable in old age? Ambition may fuel us early in life to strive for goals, making a lack of current life satisfaction very motivating, if at times frustrating. It was, after all, a young Mick Jagger and Keith Richards who wrote the 1965 song, "(I Can't Get No) Satisfaction." They might not have these same feelings now, after impressive 50-year musical careers—the senior citizen Rolling Stones are still rocking and rolling, with both Jagger and Richards in their 70s (how's that for life satisfaction?).

How do researchers measure happiness on a day-to-day basis? In one large study,[4] researchers gave people of different ages beepers (remember those?). For 1 week, at five randomly selected times each day, the researchers paged these participants, who then completed questionnaires asking them to rate how much they felt different emotions, including anger, sadness, amusement, boredom, and joy. The researchers then followed up with these people 5 and 10 years later, to see how this changed with age. As the participants aged, their moods, as assessed by the ratio of positive to negative emotions, steadily improved. Professor Laura Carstensen, an author of this study and the book, *A Long Bright Future*, said, "contrary to the popular view that youth is the best time of life, the peak of emotional life may not occur until well into the seventh decade."[5] Thus, our day-to-day happiness may change substantially as we get older, but often in ways we might not predict when we are younger.

Ask the World: Larger-Scale Studies of Happiness and Emotional Well-Being

This conclusion from the beeper study has been supported by a number of larger-scale studies, including one from 2010 that polled over 300,000 people in the United States about their day-to-day emotional experiences.[6] The survey also examined "global well-being" by asking each person to rank his or her overall life satisfaction on a 10-point scale, an assessment many people may make on their own from time to time, such as on birthdays or when reminded about their age and accomplishments in life. Happiness appears to peak in young adulthood, hit a low point during the late 40s and 50s, and then increase again into later life and old age.[7] This is something known as the U-shaped curve, and perhaps it no coincidence that this curve looks like a subtle smile across the range of ages.

The researchers also asked several questions about more immediate emotional states. They asked people: "Did you experience the following feelings during a large part of the day yesterday: enjoyment, happiness, stress, worry, anger, sadness?" They found that stress declines from age 22 onward, reaching its lowest point at 85; worry stays fairly steady until age 50, then sharply drops off; anger decreases steadily from age 18 on; and sadness rises to a peak at age 50, declines at 75, then rises slightly again at 85. Enjoyment and happiness have similar curves: they both decrease gradually until we hit 50, rise steadily for the next 25 years, and then decline very slightly at the end, but they never again reach the low point of our early 50s.

To sum up the study results, during the period of ages 50 to 70, positive emotions were found to increase while negative emotions decreased, and, overall, older adults had a higher positive-relative-to-negative emotional experience compared to those who were younger. Thus, for those people who have yet to reach the pinnacle of age 50 and may sometimes feel gloomy, you can actually have something good to look forward to: you are only going to get older and, ideally, also happier.

Despite all the data to the contrary, whether you're old or young, chances are you think of young people as being happier. In one study, researchers asked groups of 30-year-olds and 70-year-olds which age group (30 or 70) they thought would be happier. Both groups choose the hypothetical 30-year-olds, but when they rated their own happiness levels, the 70-year-olds scored higher than the 30-year-olds.[8] These false beliefs about happiness could be damaging to both age groups. If younger people inaccurately anticipate older age as being a miserable time in life, these younger people may make risky decisions, such as not taking care of themselves, because they think old age is an inevitably unhappy time.

Focusing on the Positives in Old Age: Socioemotional Selectivity Theory

Why are people happier in old age, if our society often portrays old age in a negative light? One reason is that we simply choose to be happy, and focus on positive events and people. While there are terrible tragedies in our lives, and some people feel the world might not get better, as we get older we might focus on the positives in life, leading to greater happiness. This is the main tenet of a highly influential socioemotional selectivity theory, proposed by Professor Laura Carstensen and her colleagues at Stanford University. Carstensen has suggested that, in early adulthood, we are focused on gathering information and achieving future-oriented goals—think of a college student who is trying to learn and consume information, find a job, find a spouse, and establish a rewarding if not high-income career to support a family. However, when we are older, we focus more on being present in the moment and on realizing more emotionally relevant goals. As a result, older adults tend to focus on, and later remember, positive emotional information.

This has been examined in a number of studies, in which older adults will focus on smiling faces, look away from sad or angry faces, and later remember the smiling people.[9] Remembering mostly positive information may be an important mechanism that can lead to greater positive moods, happiness, and emotional well-being. This positivity also appears to be a goal or mental choice. When older adults are distracted or their attention is divided, they will act more like younger adults and focus on the negative. In addition, parts of the brain involved in processing emotional information (the amygdala) appear to be relatively intact and active in older age. Thus, older adults are using mental resources to direct their attention to what is positive, and attempt to minimize looking at the negative. As a result, healthy older people are actually happier and more satisfied with their lives than younger people. They experience more positive emotions and fewer negative ones, and their emotional experience is more stable and less sensitive to the vagaries of life, the ups and downs, and the daily negativity and stressors that might be present.

Socioemotional selectivity theory suggests that as we enter older age, our priorities shift. We begin to recognize that our years are limited, and we fundamentally change our perspective about life. The shorter time horizon motivates us to become more present-oriented and to invest our (relatively limited) time and effort into the things in life that really matter. This isn't just true for older adults. It has also been found in persons with terminal illness and in people of all ages after a major negative life event (such as the terrorist attacks of

9/11). When we are made aware of how fragile life is and that we all have a finite period on this earth, our most meaningful relationships become much more of a priority than meeting new people or taking risks or adventures. We then invest more of our energy in these more meaningful relationships and dissociate with those that are not very supportive, and we avoid conflict.

Fewer But Better Friends in Old Age Reduces Loneliness and Leads to Happiness

One reason older adults might be happier has to do with the quality, not just the number, of relationships they have with others. While older adults tend to have smaller social circles than those of younger adults (who might have many Facebook friends), this decrease in total number of friends might result in nurturing more important friendships.[10] As a result, some studies suggest that friendships tend to improve with age, and this may extend to having a better marital relationship and to avoiding relationships that are full of conflict. Professor Karen Fingerman studies how older adults cultivate relationships and how this differs from younger adults. She said, "Older adults typically report better marriages, more supportive friendships, less conflict with children and siblings, and closer ties with members of their social networks than younger adults."[11] Her research suggests that, overall, older adults have more close ties than younger people, and they have fewer problematic and conflicting relationships that cause stress.[12]

A related study,[13] led by Laura Carstensen and colleagues, followed people for a 10-year period, and asked them to classify their friends and relatives into three possible categories: an inner circle, consisting of people they felt very close to; a middle circle, people who were important but they felt a little less close; and an outer circle, people they know but with whom they don't feel a strong connection. Every few years, the researchers also asked the participants to rate the intensity of positive and negative emotions they felt for these people. While the researchers found that socials circles tended to enlarge until about age 50, at that point people started to reduce interactions with those they felt less close to and to spend more time with closer friends and family. In addition, people rated these closer relationships as those that were more emotionally satisfying—likely contributing to greater life satisfaction and overall happiness. Based on this research, Carstensen said, "Their loved ones seem to mean more than ever, and that is protective against loneliness."[14] She suggests that while this doesn't mean loneliness isn't a problem for some older people, on average, older adults are, in fact, less lonely than young people.

As we get older, we might focus on the positives in life, leading to greater happiness. Consistent with Carstensen's socioemotional selectivity theory, one thing younger adults do a lot is think about the future: future jobs, future spouses, future houses and cities to live in, the future names of children (and if, how, and when to have them). This future-oriented approach may not lead to day-to-day happiness, as one is ambitiously pursuing the future while not considering the present. Older adults, by contrast, have accomplished many of these pursuits, and as a result have greater life satisfaction. Thus, the types of experiences that make younger and older adults happy are different. Some research[15] has shown that young people tend to seek out and highly value *extraordinary* experiences—such as adventure travel (yes, I did feel the need to hike the Inca trail in my 20s), falling in love, or thrill-seeking events, which can help them to build a greater sense of personal identity. Older adults may prioritize more ordinary experiences (e.g., going to an interesting restaurant) and everyday emotional pleasures, such as seeing good friends and spending time with family, and derive their identity from these types of experiences.

According to socioemotional selectivity theory, the second half of life is thought to promote happiness in several important ways. Knowing that our time is limited, combined with the increased maturity and social skills that come with every decade, motivates us to maximize our well-being and to control our emotions more successfully (a form of emotional wisdom discussed in Chapter 3). For example, we might do our best to make ourselves feel better when we are feeling down, anxious, or angry and avoid spending time with people or in situations that have made us unhappy in the past. Maintaining feelings of contentment, serenity, gladness, or closeness may also come more easily as we get older, because more mature people have been found to show a positivity bias in attention and memory. In other words, the older we are, the more likely we are to focus on and remember the positive features (and overlook the negative ones) of our neighborhoods, our relationships, our life histories, and even random bits of information. This positivity bias may be a result of deliberate emotion-regulation strategies (e.g., the older we are, the more consciously we try to turn a blind eye to criticism), or a result of the brain structures associated with the processing of negative emotions experiencing atrophy with age. However, the credit for our happiness in later life lies not only with us but also with everyone who interacts with us. As a result, older adults may surround themselves with people who make them feel positive, are upbeat and jovial, and enjoy reminiscing about the good old days.

Data assessing happiness across the lifespan suggest that high levels of happiness can be maintained well into older old age (e.g., after age 85), although it is important to interpret these findings carefully. While these older-old adults may report greater happiness and life satisfaction relative to younger adults, it is important to qualify these observations in terms of healthy older adults who are relatively free of disease or illness and who are living in their preferred community, which is often at home or a retirement community that allows them to be active and socially connected. Many older adults over the age of 90 will still report high levels of life satisfaction, and an overall sense of happiness, but might also qualify this by stating they are sad to have lost a spouse, see their friends pass away, and have less independence.

The potential onset of dementia, loss of friends, lack of family support, and a sense of loneliness can all contribute to lower levels of happiness, although this may be tempered by having a high sense of life satisfaction. Some research certainly supports that notion, as well as the idea that part of the reason for a lower level of happiness is the possible onset of dementia or other illnesses, limited amounts of social support, loss of independence, and feelings of loneliness.[16] Loneliness often goes unnoticed by others and has been characterized as a "silent killer." It is estimated that 40% of adults over the age of 65 will experience loneliness.[17] But loneliness is not specific to old age; those starting college, enlisting in the military, or divorcing from a partner often experience loneliness.

The Dwarfs of Happiness: Sadness, Regret, and Anger in Older Age

When describing emotions in old age, we tend to focus almost exclusively on happiness and don't consider how other related emotions might change with age. Even historically, to paraphrase Thomas Jefferson, we are a nation obsessed with "the pursuit of happiness."[18] It is important to consider how sadness, anger, and regret are experienced in old age in many forms, and how they are dealt with in ways that can have an impact on levels of happiness.

Sadness

Older adults will report that they feel sad to see their own group of friends and family pass away. Losing a loved one (especially a spouse) elicits long-lasting sadness. Widows will often say they miss their spouse "every day." John Wooden, the long-time UCLA basketball coach and 10-time national championship winner, lost his wife Nell more than 25 years before he passed away. Wooden would write a letter to his wife each month, and would not sleep on her side of the bed, even though she had been gone for many years. In addition to losing loved ones, the loss of social status, physical abilities, housing, or professional roles can bring about sadness. Since all of these forms of loss can lead to sadness, are most older adults sad because of these sometimes inevitable events of life? While some studies show increased sadness in old age, other studies show no change.[19] Often when sadness peaks, it is at times in life when one's parents pass away or when friends and spouses die, but the death of friends and family is a universal experience as we age. However, when considering emotional reactions to interpersonal conflicts (such as siblings fighting), younger and older adults report similar levels of sadness.[20] But older adults do express greater levels of sadness after watching movies related to death or dementia, something younger adults might not feel is in their imminent future.[21] While sadness might be more accessible for older adults, simply because more unfortunate events and deaths befall them, the interpretation of this sadness can influence one's overall mood and the balance of day-to-day happiness and sadness.

Regret

One interesting, if perhaps overly personal, question to ask an older adult is: "Is there anything you regret in life?" This can be a very sensitive question, as regret often involves conflicting emotions, sadness, or remorse over past events. As older adults have had more life experiences than younger adults, they have more possible actions that they could re-gret. But do older people regret more than younger people? Surprisingly, older adults are, in fact, less likely to express regret, despite having had more opportunity to experience it. For example, in one study,[22] people ages 40–85 were asked to complete the following sentence:

"When looking back on my life, I regret . . ."

At first, you might think, *well—where do I start?* Interestingly, the likelihood of reporting nothing to regret was more common in older adults than in the middle-aged adults. Another study[23] involving an even broader age range (19–89) found that not only did older adults report fewer regrets relative to the younger adults, but the associated emotional intensity and duration of regrets were less in older adults. So, perhaps time does heal all wounds.

In a more experimental context, regret can be simulated in laboratory-based tasks, such as gambling on a particular outcome and losing. For example, imagine losing money when gambling at the roulette table. In this type of situation, healthy older adults tend to focus less on the regretful decision to bet in the task and more on the potential for possible (unrealized) gains.[24] In addition, older adults are more likely to remember people who owe them money than people they owe money to, in a simulated game in which players want to maximize total income.[25] Interestingly, de-pressed older adults will show similar amounts of regret to that of non-depressed younger adults. This suggests that healthy younger adults are actively attempting to avoid regret, which might induce greater happiness. One study[26] found that acceptance of what can't be changed is a significant predictor of satisfaction in later life. One way older adults may alleviate regret is noticing that one often has little control over regretful situations, and that one can emerge from them as healthy and relatively happy individuals despite the nega-tive outcomes of those events. This provides evidence that cognitive strategies are used to defend against regret.

Anger

While we look to gain greater happiness and reduce sadness, there are risks, as our emotional response can sometimes be dangerous.

The expression and experience of anger and anxiety can actually be quite hazardous to one's health, as these emotions can trigger heart attacks.[27] Are older adults better at controlling their anger? Self-report measures of anger suggest that anger increases during young adulthood but then decreases into old age.[28] Older adults may display a calmer demeanor, "mellow" in old age, and use strategies such as removing oneself from situations that can invoke anger, or they may avoid emotional outbursts that may be more common in younger adults.[29] One byproduct of reduced levels of anger in old age may be greater patience, both in terms of interpersonal affairs, such as avoiding conflict and heated arguments, and not rushing through things, as when reading to children or interacting with grandchildren.

Anger over certain events may fade as we age, as may the level of anger associated with outcomes that we don't have control over. Becoming aware of what we have control over and what is beyond our control can lead us to feel happier and gain more context about ourselves and our outcomes in life. Many of the famous older adults I interviewed made one thing clear: they had life satisfaction and confidence in themselves, mixed with some anxiety associated with their pursuits, but they were still actively pursuing both new and established goals. In some cases this included performing live music, doing stand-up comedy, building new buildings that would be critically acclaimed, and learning new languages. Each of these goals involved levels of anxiety, frustration, and pleasure in the end result. Thus, having a balance of emotions, coupled with an awareness of what one has control over, can help us as we age.

Why Look for the Fountain of Youth if Old Age Is Happy?

With so many people concerned about the negative aspects of aging and seeking anti-aging treatments or elixirs, perhaps there is something to learn from happy older adults. Can we make younger adults think like older adults and appreciate life? Some research[30] addresses this by looking at how younger adults behave when faced with terminal illness or grim events in history (e.g., the attacks on 9/11/2001). These younger adults behave like older adults, by wanting to spend more time with family, perhaps appreciating the finite aspects of life, but this doesn't last—after 6 months, younger adults are back to being concerned about their own issues.

However, people still seek to avoid the signs of old age, especially given the negative stereotypes associated with aging. Professor Ellen Langer has demonstrated that doing things to make us look younger (e.g., dying one's hair) makes us feel younger; in contrast, men who are balding see themselves as aging faster.[31] Comedienne Phyllis Diller, as much as she joked about aging later in life, was upfront about having numerous facelifts in order to appear younger and, possibly, to act younger (although it is unclear for her what acting younger might have entailed). Thus, despite the apparent happiness associated with old age, and the fact that older adults report being happy for the most part, some older people want to look and feel young, perhaps not appreciating happiness in old age or accepting that they might look the part.

A Smile Goes a Long Way: It Can Even Add 5 to 10 Years to Your Life!

One of my favorite sets of studies on how happiness can influence longevity involves smiles from baseball cards and nuns' diaries. These studies are unique in that they rely on archives and old dairy entries that were reanalyzed years later to see if they might relate to longevity.

Can a smile indicate not only how happy you are, but how long you will live? One creative study examined whether one's expression of a smile when being photographed indicates happiness, and if those who smile more intensely have greater longevity. Researchers used a retrospective study design, in which they examined baseball card photos from the Major League Baseball Registry database from players who started their careers before 1950.[32] They separated the players' photos into three groups: (1) those with no smiles, (2) those with partial smiles, and (3) those with full, genuine smiles. They then determined when the players had died, and found that those players with no smiles lived to an average age of about 72 years, those with partial smiles lived 75 years, and those with full smiles lived almost 80 years. The intensity of the players' smiles predicted the span of their lives—and big smiles were associated with 7 more years of life.

As another way to examine how happiness might be related to longevity, researchers studied another unique population: a group of long-living Catholic nuns. The researchers analyzed the nuns' early personal diary entries, made in the 1930s and 1940s when the nuns were in their 20s, to determine the nuns' overall level of happiness during their earlier years.[33] At age 80, the most cheerful nuns (as rated on the basis of their diary entries from over 50 years ago) had a survival rate of 75%, while only 40% of the least cheerful group had survived. In fact, the happiest nuns lived 10 years longer than the least happy nuns. Subsequently, a recent review[34] suggested that happiness increases how long we live by 4 to 10 years. As an added bonus, based on the reviewed research on happiness and aging, those additional years are likely to be happy ones.

Older Adults Show Happiness in Different Ways Than Young People Do

One reason people (both young and old) think older adults are less happy than young adults might lie in how people show their happiness. We think of happiness in terms of smiling, laughing, and maybe being playful or silly. Children also show this type of behavior. Some research suggests that babies laugh up to 300 times a day, whereas adults laugh 20 times a day.[35] Older adults might show happiness in terms of stability and emotion regulation, which might not result in these overt signs of happiness all the time. However, many older adults enjoy hearing and sharing a good joke, and often their jokes and the ensuing laughter occur in social settings.[36]

In addition to the sheer enjoyment we might get from a good joke, there are many physiological benefits of laughing as well. Norman Cousins, the famous journalist, author, and UCLA professor, was told he had little chance of surviving heart disease and reactive arthritis, initially diagnosed as ankylosing spondylitis. As his condition worsened, he checked into a hotel and treated himself with a regimen of large doses of vitamin C, Marx Brothers films, and episodes of *Candid Camera*. This treatment resulted in a lot of laughs that he said calmed his pain for hours; within weeks, his disease mysteriously faded into remission.[37]

However, what Cousins did isn't necessarily the best way to get a good dose of laughter. Being around other people makes people laugh a lot. Laughing has a strong social component, to the point that people are more likely to laugh when they are in the company of others. Professor Robert Provine, who studies laughter and is author of the book *Laughter: A Scientific Investigation*, theorized that laughter can be thought of as a social lubricant, such that we use it to bond with others. This notion is supported by the observation that people laugh 30 times more often in the presence of others than they do when they're alone in a room. Interestingly, it also explains why nitrous oxide (a.k.a. laughing gas) won't make you burst out laughing if inhaled while you are alone, but will when others are in the room. The mere presence of people makes you laugh, not just the joke or the laughing gas, and this may be why being around others can be important in older age. And you don't need to go to a comedy club to experience laughter. *Laughter yoga* is a group-setting yoga class that combines yoga with some initially forced laughter, until it becomes a sincere and uncontrollable laughter. Laughter yoga can be a great way to enjoy the contagiousness and health benefits of laughter in a social setting.

Laughing Well into Old Age . . .

He who laughs, lasts.

—Mary Pettibone Poole

George Burns and Bob Hope both lived to be 100 years old, and Phyllis Diller passed away at the age of 95, reportedly with a smile on her face. Bob Newhart (in his 80s) is still active and enjoying life. What do they all have in common? They laugh, and they make people laugh, a lot. Is one key to successful aging having a good sense of humor? Some would say YES. When asked whether she missed performing her comedy routine on stage, Phyllis Diller answered, "I don't miss the travel. I miss the laughter. I do miss the actual hour. I don't want to sound like I'm on dope, but that hour is a high; it's as good as you can feel. A wonderful, wonderful happiness, and great power."[38]

Burns joked, "If you live to the age of a hundred you have it made because very few people die past the age of a hundred." When asked in his late 90s if his doctor knew he still smoked, Burns said, "No . . . he's dead."

It isn't that you should smile in order to age well, it's why you smile. Bob Newhart quoted Nathanial West, the author of *Day of the Locust*, who said that the universe is against us, so the only intelligent response is laughter. Newhart added, "If you want to get through this place you better learn how to laugh, otherwise it is over!" When asked about how to age successfully, Newhart said, "Laugh, or make people laugh. I give commencement addresses, and I end on that note: keep your sense of humor because you are going to need it!"

Not All Rosy: Negative Events Recounted by Grandparents and Holocaust Survivors

Despite all the focus on positivity and happiness, older adults may need to discuss the past in a negative light, especially when it can help a future generation better understand life. For example, grandparents and parents might inform children of all the dangers of talking to strangers and crossing the street on their own, and provide detailed accounts of what has happened to children under graver circumstances, including their own stories of the past.

A grandmother might feel the need to read the warning label on a package of glue to a young grandchild, stating as printed on the warning label that the glue could cause blindness if placed in the eye. This is something my daughter reported to me when I came home after her grandmother had been babysitting. Reading and remembering warning labels on medication can be critical, as can recalling past episodes of illness and their resulting antecedents and ways others may have gotten sick. As an extreme example, survivors of the Holocaust might never be able to forget their experiences, and some will recount and document them; my grandmother dedicated her life to this cause.[39] Many survivors may also try to limit the horrors they recount, in order to lead a normal life. Joshua Kaufman, a family friend and 90-year-old survivor of the concentration death camp Dachau, would rarely talk to his four daughters when they were younger about what happened to him during that time. However, now that his daughters are adults, he shares his memories with them and with others. Older people may try to focus on the positives in life, sometimes in order to overcome past tragedies, and older adults are an important link to the past.

Bright and Early: Happiness and Stability in Younger Morning Larks and Older Adults

> How does a happy person start the day? The answer seems to be: "Early."

It is clear that some people are morning types, while others are night owls. As we age, our circadian rhythms change, and people often shift from being night owls when they were younger to morning larks in older age. While I used to work well into the wee morning hours as a graduate student (and I enjoyed the solitude of the night), as I grew older and had children who wake up early, I became a full-fledged morning type. Just a simple survey of who is eating break-fast at the local restaurant or coffee shop at 7 a.m. will tell you who is a morning person (the many older adults who are up and at 'em early in the day) and who isn't (the crabby younger waitress who was up late last night). There is research[40] suggesting that being an early riser is associated with greater emotional stability and levels of happiness. This was found in both morning-type younger adults (the few that exist) and older adults (who tend to more naturally be morning types). In addition, this research suggests that, in general, morning types tend to be higher in positive affect relative to night owls. Thus, behaving like an older adult can have its advantages. In terms of memory, older adults also perform better on memory tests during their optimal time of day, usually in the morning, while most college students avoid early mornings (as evidenced by the lower attendance when I teach an 8 a.m. class at UCLA).

Summary: Why Do Funny Things Happen in Old Age?

The pursuit of happiness might be a major motivational factor as we age, and a large amount of research shows that when people are happy, they experience health benefits. There are certainly good reasons to focus on negative information, especially when we are young, to avoid danger, learn from mistakes, and survive. While there are a variety of physical challenges that can accompany older age, healthy older adults report high levels of happiness and life satisfaction. Some refer to this as the "life satisfaction paradox": despite various declines in physical or sensory abilities, older adults display high levels of happiness and life satisfaction by focusing on positive information and mood. There may be adaptive reasons for this paradox, as research has shown that levels of happiness predict success in many domains[41] and can also play a role in helping people develop resilience to challenging circumstances.[42] Thus, the pursuit of happiness in old age can have benefits, in terms of both physical and mental health.

Memory:
Our Memory Becomes
More Selective with Age

[I]t is a triumph of life that old people lose their memories of in-essential things, though memory does not often fail with regards to things that are of real interest to us. Cicero illustrated this with the stroke of a pen: "No old man forgets where he has hidden his treasure."

—Gabriel Garcia Márquez, writer and winner of 1982
Nobel Prize in Literature

A S WE GET OLDER, AND EVEN AFTER THE AGE OF 20, OUR memory starts to change in many different ways, some for the good. But there are also clear and concerning declines in various types of memory.[1] These may include the ability to remember names, the combination of the gym locker you haven't used in a while, and why you just walked into a room. Faces may feel familiar, but you can't recall how you know the person, let alone their name. One notion is that *episodic memory*—the ability to recall specific instances from the past—declines with age, but *semantic memory*—knowing things like the capital of France—might actually get better with age. Our vocabulary continues to increase as we get older, a reason why many older adults may enjoy, and excel, at crossword puzzles. However, given the sheer amount of words stored in semantic memory, older people experience some word-retrieval problems, or more tip-of-the-tongue experiences—when you know a word to say but just can't recall it right now. One benefit of semantic knowledge is that older adults are good at proofreading sentinces, partly due to ectensive reading experience and accumulated vocabulary (if you are reading closely, perhaps you noticed the two spelling errors in this sentence?).[2] In general, while changes in memory can be worrying for people at any age, often they are the natural byproduct of having a lot of information in the brain (or on one's mind, if one is multitasking)—much like a messy attic chock full of old valuables but also plenty of useless things that haven't been touched in years.

A vast amount of research has documented the memory deficits that accompany aging. Most people aren't surprised that memory declines with age, so this is sometimes referred to as the less exciting or "dull hypothesis" of aging.[3] However, recent work shows that memory is not simply impaired in old age—there are many things older adults remember quite well.[4] What can't be explained by pure deficit models of cognitive aging is that, as we age, we can almost effortlessly remember many things: our childhood address or home phone number from 40 years ago, the lyrics to "Yesterday," by the Beatles (and memories associated with that song), and how to ride a bike or play the piano, especially if those skills were learned earlier in life.

Most of us have beliefs and negative expectations about memory declines due to aging. "Stereotype threat" can make you perform "stereotypically"—consistent with what you think is expected of you—and often make you underperform. Stereotype threat has been examined in various memory studies in the lab to determine if it causes older adults to underperform on tests of memory.[5] Labeling something a memory test, or asking people to come to a memory study, can invoke anxiety. Research has shown that simply relabeling it as a "wisdom test" (and then administering the same memory test) actually leads to better performance by older adults.[6] Thus, simply taking a memory test can be anxiety-provoking and make you feel older.

Some research has also shown that doing a short memory test in a doctor's office can underestimate an older adult's memory ability, because of the stress associated with a potential dementia diagnosis[7]—just saying the word *Alzheimer's* can make people very nervous about their memory. Interestingly, it is often the "young" older adults (those in their 60s and 70s) who are most susceptible to this threat.[8] These relatively healthy younger-old adults may be considered the "worried well"—people concerned about their memory, worried it doesn't work, and wanting to do something about it. Older adults in their 80s and 90s are not as surprised about memory changes in old age, as they have had sufficient experience with memory challenges. Some of these older adults would even say, "Tell me something I don't know," in response to any declines in memory in older age.

What might be even more interesting is that as we age and experience these memory "challenges" (I prefer not to call them failures), we get better at knowing about how and when our memory works. *Metamemory* is the term used to describe the self-awareness of how one's memory works and when it does not work well. It may be enhanced in old age, as older adults have more life experience working with their memory. Older adults are adept at using strategies that allow for greater selectivity about what to remember. For example, an older adult may be better at summarizing and communicating the main points from a recent movie they saw, perhaps by recalling the gist of the movie, whereas a younger adult may give many more details, but not necessarily capture the main message of the movie. For older adults, these adaptive strategies may be compensatory in nature and allow for both the recruitment and development of brain areas that can improve memory.

The other day, my daughter was watching a movie at home. Having missed the first 15 minutes, I asked her what I had missed. She proceeded to give me a very detailed report, including plot lines, character traits, and even the music that accompanied various parts of the movie. This took about 10 minutes. When I ask my wife the same type of question, her response is usually, "Oh, nothing," or perhaps a very brief, 10-second summary of the movie ("This is the bad guy," etc.). My wife is aware that I will likely catch up by watching the next 10 minutes, that no key information has been missed that needs to be relayed to me at the cost of missing more of the movie. With age, we are better at taking a listener's perspective, whether that of another adult or of a child.[9] What this illustrates is that, with experience, we might get better at summarizing and at knowing what someone needs to know.

Based on a functional approach to memory use, what is actually important for us to remember? At a very basic evolutionary level, we need to remember the last time we ate (though our stomach gives us good reminders) and where to find food. We need to know our predators and what foods make us sick. Knowing what allergies our children or grandchildren have is critical. We need to know how to navigate our environment so we don't get lost. In our modern era, we need to remember to take our medications at certain times and feed the dog. It is helpful to remember anniversaries and the likes and dislikes of loved ones, and we also use memory to enjoy reminiscing about the past. However, by far the most common complaint about memory is that names are hard to remember, and we feel very embarrassed if we have forgotten someone's name, whether it is someone we just met or someone we know quite well but haven't seen in a while.

I'll Never Forget What's His Name: The Cost of Knowing Too Many People

Whenever I talk to a large audience of older adults about memory and aging, often a worried or concerned person will pull me aside and tell me that they have a very specific memory deficit: they are great at remembering many things, hold down a very demanding job, but simply cannot remember names. This isn't just a problem for older adults. I assure them that this is due to some simple memory principles: names are somewhat arbitrary. For many people, a face might look familiar, but we can't remember the name of the person, or perhaps where we met them. One day I played basketball at UCLA with some friends and someone who looked very familiar, but I couldn't quite place him. He reminded me of my brother in some ways, and he was fairly funny. After 2 hours of playing with him, my friends, who knew exactly who he was, told me: he was the comedian and actor Adam Sandler. Of course, this can often happen in Los Angeles, where we see familiar faces from movies or commercials and we feel like we know them, even though we don't know them personally.

This "name amnesia" is a common experience at parties: you've *just* heard the person's name and talked to the person for 5 minutes, and then you are embarrassed when you have to introduce them to your spouse. We just quickly forget names. A long time ago, the baker in town was "Mr. Baker," and the barber was "Mr. Barber," but times have changed. In addition, names usually aren't nearly as interesting as other information (e.g., the person's profession or where the person is from), although often a name is related to one's background. One study showed that the word *barber* is more poorly remembered when used as a name (Mr. Barber is a lawyer) than when used as the occupation (e.g., Mr. Jones is a barber)—and this is especially true for older adults.[10] Thus, it isn't just the name itself but the fact that we don't connect a name like we would if it was an occupation. However, sometimes having a meaningful name can also lead to confusion. Our children's doctor when they were born was named Dr. Crane, a name I constantly confused, often calling him Dr. Stork.

When you meet people, you usually move past introductions into more interesting conversation, so you often don't even pay attention to the name, or even notice if the person actually said their name. In addition, as we get older, we have met more people with the same name (e.g., Alan, Allan, and Allen), which interferes with learning the name of yet another person with the same name (Alan). However, we can use prior knowledge to create an image to help remember a name. For example, my last name, Castel, rhymes with Pastel, and my grandfather was a famous painter who used pastels. Also, the name looks like Castle, but is spelled Castel. The cost of doing these brain tricks is that people then often call me Alan Pastel or Alan Castle.

Forgetting proper names doesn't just happen when you are "older"—when you are 65 or have gray hair. It can frequently happen to people in their 20s, 30s, and 40s, given distraction or lack of attention, but it doesn't mean we all have a specific deficit in name learning. The use of simple mnemonics and principles of cognitive psychology (testing, imagery, cues, and connections) can be used to effectively remember names at any age. Although sometimes it is simply easier to ask people to repeat their name if you are having trouble remembering it. This usually works well for me. My joke, after telling people I recently met that I study memory and aging, is to then ask them, "What's your name again?" They usually then say it with a laugh.

Recently, I forgot the name of a person whom I had met many times. I saw him at a local ice cream shop, and just couldn't recall his name—which was most embarrassing and frustrating. I dealt with it the way many of us do (and I think the way he did as well during our brief chat)—I pretended I knew his name but just never used it when talking to him. I knew exactly who he was, where I knew him from, and many other details: he is the father of a child at my daughter's school. I knew he has a clothing business, and I even remembered his dog's name. I told my wife, Jami, that I forgot his name and was having trouble remembering it, despite recalling all of these other details about him. She looked at me with shock, and astonished said, "Really, you can't remember his name?!" My wife had to remind me, much to my own surprise, that his name was Jamie. Thus, I knew the name well, but didn't associate it with this person.

As I study memory and aging, people tell me all the time, "I can't remember names." The reason we do not remember names is that we don't do much to remember them, as we hear them and rapidly forget them. As I age, I am very aware of the memory mistakes and challenges that I encounter, and my children are even more aware. Like many parents, I often get their names briefly confused, as these names are stored closely together in my brain. My children know I study memory, and I often ask them questions about their own memory. Recently, before I was to give a talk to a group about memory, my daughter advised me, "Daddy, I don't think you should talk about how great your memory is, because you often forget which toothbrush is mine, and yesterday you brushed my teeth with Eden's [her sister's] toothbrush. Maybe it's because sometimes you call me 'Eden' and not 'Claire'—so you should take a class on memory, too."

Memory for the Mundane or the Essentials? The Price of Bananas, and the Weather

A lot of memory research focuses on what might be considered mundane—word lists, face–name pairs, studying and being tested on pictures that might resemble someone's photographs from their last vacation—and it is unclear why this might be important to remember. How about things that are of real concern or interest? Imagine you just read the weather forecast. Could you now recall which day it is forecasted to rain? If you just went to the store and bought soup, bananas, and milk, you might later recall the prices of these items (especially if the bananas were on sale this week for 29 cents a pound).[11] These are the sorts of things older adults do well, and perhaps memory becomes more geared to what is essential as we get older. My grandparents would literally brag about where they found oranges or coffee on sale, and would recall the current and past prices of these items, even if they had to drive across town (and didn't factor in spending more money on gas) to get the best prices.

Older adults also remember emotional information very well, as this likely carries greater importance and might activate the parts of the brain (the amygdala) that work well in old age and support memory for emotions.[12] In addition, decades of experience can influence what we remember, such that accountants remember financial information, and retired air traffic controller fare extremely well when remembering simulated air traffic control information. If you like baseball or basketball, you will be able to remember the score of the game you last watched or read about. When I spoke with 97-year-old John Wooden about his memory for sporting events, he could recall the Los Angeles Dodgers' score from the other night, as well as the score from the 1975 NCAA championship game.[13] A long-time real estate agent might recall the price of the first few homes they sold 30 years ago, as well as the current price of local real estate. These observations show that one can remember what is both remote and recent, as long as it was important at some point in one's life.

Information Overload: Selectivity to the Rescue (Especially in Old Age)

We are often overwhelmed with information. Today, we can easily access endless amounts of information on the Internet. This can lead to information overload and can then limit what we will later remember. One key to avoiding information overload and to rejuvenating our memory capacity is to be selective about what we attempt to remember. Thus, the most important part of regulating memory is deciding what to remember. Selectively focusing on what is important is critical and may actually be a skill that is enhanced in old age, as a necessary byproduct of not being able to remember everything.

Often, I feel like I remember too much insignificant information and need to direct more attention to what is important. This ability to focus on what is important may be something older adults do quite well. The ability to monitor our memory ability is a form of metamemory. While there is a lot of research showing that memory tends to decline with age, metamemory appears to remain intact.[14] Thus, with age, older adults learn what they will remember and what might be quickly forgotten. The trick is to remember what is important, and perhaps it is then okay to forget the rest. I realize I have gotten good at forgetting, but also *knowing* what I will forget. As a result, I regularly use my cell phone camera to take pictures of things I know I will lose or forget[15] (such as handwritten shopping lists, receipts, things I see at museums) and would rather offload to my camera so that I can later reference them, if and when that is later needed.

Imagine you are packing for a trip—you want to make sure to include all the important items, as forgetting them would be very costly and have great consequences (e.g., forgetting your passport or wallet would not make for a fun start to a vacation). To examine this in the lab (it would have been more fun to follow people on their vacations, and see what they actually forgot!), we presented 20 possible items a person might pack on a trip (e.g., passport, medications, sunscreen, toothbrush, phone charger, deodorant, swimsuit, sandals).[16] When we later asked people to recall the items, the older adults recalled more of the items they felt were important, despite remembering fewer items. This illustrates that despite memory not being strong in terms of the sheer amount of information that is recalled, older adults were able to selectively remember the necessary information. Much like the real world, there are consequences if you forget something important (e.g., a spouse's birthday), and older adults are usually pretty good at remembering the consequential information. We have since done many studies showing that older adults will remember important medication side effects from a long list, dangerous allergens of a grandchild, and the words paired with the most reward (relative to words paired with less reward). Imagine you are given a list of words to remember, but some of the words are more important (and paired with higher point-values or rewards) than other words that are less important (and are associated with lower point-values or rewards). When the goal is to maximize your overall memory reward, you remember the words paired with the highest values, and that is especially the case for older adults. Older adults remember fewer words overall, but they remember just as many of the highest-value words as younger adults—so there are no deficits in memory for the highest-value information for older adults.

Interestingly, functional magnetic resonance imaging (fMRI) of people's brains when they do this task with higher- and lower-value words to remember shows that both younger and older adults recruit similar areas associated with semantic processing. This means both groups are able to focus on the high-value words and use imagery to remember them. The age differences emerge for the lower-value words: older adults' brains don't show as much activation for these words.[17] Thus, the key to being selective is not just to focus on what is important but to down-regulate what is less important. Trying to remember every detail can be problematic, even if we think that is what memory is for—to remember as much as we can. In fact, the regions of the brain that direct our attention (the frontal lobes) might have evolved to allow us to focus on what is important, since we cannot, and perhaps should not, remember everything.

The Crowded Library of Memory in Old Age and the Benefits of Forgetting

One theory of why memory is impaired in older adults is that, as we age, we have too much stored in memory, and this leads to interference. Much like an overstocked library, it is great to have this information, but it then takes longer to find things, and other things can get in the way when we try to recall something specific. Older adults often have a better vocabulary than younger adults, but this can also lead to more tip-of-the-tongue experiences, when you momentarily can't recall a word you know well.[18] Interestingly, you can try to simulate crowding by creating a model of a younger adult using a computer. This "younger" adult simulation on a computer involves stuffing its hard drive with lots of new vocabulary. This younger but highly knowledgeable computer then behaves much like an older adult, taking longer to recall things, sometimes having trouble with similar information interfering. The same thing happens with people who are bilingual—it takes them longer to access words, and they report more tip-of-the-tongue experiences—but bilingualism is also related to many cognitive benefits. One perspective, in a report entitled "The Myth of Cognitive Decline in Old Age,"[19] suggests that memory doesn't actually decline with age. We simply have more stored in our memory, so it is harder to find things quickly in this massive warehouse of information in our brain. So, it is not that our memory just gets worse with age, it's that there is much more to contemplate in the search, which takes longer!

Proactive interference is when information learned earlier in life interferes with new learning, and this can be a problem as we age. If you need to recall where you parked your car today, past locations in the same parking lot can get in the way of recalling where your car is now (hence the wayward person walking around trying to find their car by sound, using their key alarm). Most of the time, we are pretty good at ignoring irrelevant information. For example, you stop noticing the humming of the refrigerator in your kitchen or the sound of traffic. We might stop noticing things because they aren't relevant to the task at hand, or because we don't want to burden our memory with something unimportant. At UCLA, much like most office buildings, we have fire extinguishers posted in high-traffic areas in our building so that they are highly visible. But do we notice them, or can we later recall where they are? In one study,[20] we found that despite seeing the fire extinguishers every day, people stopped noticing them and forgot where they are. This was especially true for older people, even after having been in the office building and having seen these fire extinguishers for over 30 years. This is a good example of how, as we age, we stop noticing things that may not be directly relevant to us.

A Prospective Memory Paradox: Older Adults Can Remember in the Future

Sometimes the most important things to remember involve doing something in the future. This is known as *prospective memory* and can take the form of remembering to take medications at a future time, or returning a library book at some future date. While prospective memory may be worse in older age, there are some important exceptions. Researchers have found what is known as the "prospective memory paradox": despite older adults doing poorly on laboratory-based tasks of prospective memory, older adults fare well in the real world. A lot of lab-based research shows that older adults experience prospective memory impairments on tasks such as "when you see the word *president* on the next page, please raise your hand." You get so focused on reading, you forget what to do when you see the word *president*—but does that mirror the forget-fulness of not taking your medication tomorrow at noon (or was it 10 a.m.?).

Older adults often have good strategies in place to remember to do things in the future (e.g., put the wallet by the front door and medications by the reading glasses). Why might older adults perform poorly on lab-based prospective memory tasks but much better on those that happen in the real world? To bridge this gap, one study[21] asked people who came to the lab to mail back postcards each week, to determine how many younger and older adults would remember to do this prospective memory task. To the researchers' surprise, it was the older adults who diligently mailed in the postcards each week. There are times when prospective memory is needed to remember to take medications or attend upcoming appointments, although often older adults will remember the old fashioned way: write it down in a calendar that can be consulted each day. When I called retired basketball coach John Wooden, at age 97, to schedule an interview, he wrote it in his handwritten and very full calendar, and even called me the day before to confirm I was still coming—he was reminding me!

Multitasking Ruins Memory Making, Burns Breakfast, and Can Kill Infants

Staying on task can be difficult, and when we have opportunities to multitask, it is hard not to give in to the possibility of getting lots of things done at the same time. What are the memory consequences of always being busy with several other tasks? Is it hard to multitask in old age? In one study,[22] people were asked to start cooking break-fast on a simulated computer-based oven display, with the main task being to start cooking eggs and to turn the eggs off in 2 minutes. During these 2 minutes, other tasks had to be completed, such as preparing toast, making coffee, and setting the table. Older adults had a lot of trouble doing all of these tasks simultaneously and often would forget to turn the eggs off after the 2 minutes and would burn the toast. Thus, multitasking can ruin the ability to focus on what is important, and also lead you to burn your breakfast in the study just described or, worse yet, cause you to forget to turn off the stove before you leave the house.

In the most extreme cases, prospective memory failures can cause people to forget an infant in the backseat of their car, something referred to as "forgotten baby syndrome."[23] It happens more often than one might think, about three to four times a month in the United States alone. This can happen to anyone: new or experienced parents, parents of any age or profession or level of education, including a rocket scientist, professor, doctor, Army-trained professional, office manager, and teacher. The truth is, we can get consumed by other things, our own routines and habits, trains of thought, cell phone conversations, thinking about an important meeting scheduled for later in the day—any of which can make us completely lose track of what is important in the here and now.

Getting the Basics and Remembering the Gist

In general, how we see things influences what we remember. We use context to interpret what we see, and that then guides what we remember. There are many benefits to using our prior knowledge and context to interpret incoming information. Computers can remember details quite well and maintain the literal sense of letters and words. However, unlike computers, human experts are better at remembering the gist, or the general theme. For example, older doctors may remember the diagnosis of a recent patient, but might forget the exact symptoms or even misremember certain symptoms that are consistent with the diagnosis.[24] This could represent a dark side of expertise, but it also shows that an expert is more likely to process details to make useful conclusions. It is often these conclusions that are most meaningful and later remembered.

One thing that may get better with age is summarizing, getting to the bottom line, and remembering the gist of something. Try now to remember the following words for a memory test:

BED, REST, AWAKE, TIRED, DREAM, WAKE, SNOOZE, BLANKET, DOZE, SLUMBER, SNORE, NAP, PEACE, YAWN, DROWSY

Without looking back, can you recall them? Either say them out loud, or better, write them down on a piece of paper. How many did you get?

Now try another type of test for the words, a recognition test: Was DROWSY on this list? How about BED? How about WINDOW? How about SLEEP?

You might remember a few of them or recall that they were all related to sleep. Was the word *sleep* on the list? You might believe that you saw it, but it was *not* on the original list of words. People of all ages falsely recall seeing *sleep* in the list when in fact it wasn't—it was all in their head.[25] Is this a worrisome false memory? Should you be concerned that your memory is failing you? No, it is just a by-product of how we remember. When we try to remember things, our brain makes associations, creates images, and interprets semantics, and this leads to a good memory, but also memory for things that didn't quite happen that way.

It may actually be a benefit of not having a perfect memory if you can't recall exactly everything about this book or the movie you saw last week; you will likely still give a good summary, without remembering all the details. Sometimes this involves overemphasizing the important parts, while also some recall of things that didn't quite happen but are related to the topic. Often older adults will remember the gist, which also involves remembering *sleep* being on that list, even when that exact word was not presented but was the main theme of the list.[26] While some interpret this as false memory, it is also one way that the brain helps us, as it allows us to remember main themes and not all of the specifics. One theory is that we have better schemas to incorporate new information and that the brain builds scaffoldings to organize new information with what we already know, leading to better interpretations but sometimes predictable inaccuracies in terms of recalling details.

Gone But Not Forgotten: Context as Memory Cues, Walking into Rooms and Reunions

Our surroundings can influence how and when we remember something. Hearing a song from long ago, or smelling perfume, freshly cut grass, or wood burning in a fireplace can bring back a flood of memories, sometimes ones we hadn't thought of in years or in decades. Research has shown that people are better at remembering things if the context matches the place where they originally learned it—for example, scuba divers are better at remembering things underwater that they saw underwater. Likewise, if you were in a positive mood when you learned something, you are better at remembering it if you are in the same positive mood later.

Imagine going back to your high school or college reunion. When you walk into the building again, there are many triggers for things you hadn't thought about in decades. The same can be true for visiting your childhood home or the town where you grew up. Seeing grandchildren can revive memories of your own children, especially if there is a family resemblance or similar character traits. All of these examples show that memories don't just get forgotten, they are simply temporarily inaccessible without the right cues.

Have you ever walked into a room and forgotten why you went into that room? This is a common occurrence, especially for older adults. We know that we were looking for something or that we needed to walk into the room to get something, but we are here now, and it is forgotten. Some research suggests that walking through doorways or crossing physical boundaries can actually trigger forgetting.[27] When you move from one place to the next, the entry/exit doorway will lead to a new environment that does not provide the necessary cues to remember what you were doing in the other room. As you enter the new room, your brain must keep in mind or recreate what you were thinking when you were in the other room—but our minds are often wandering as we go to another room, or we start to thinking about something else. The best way to remember what you need is to actually walk back into the first room where you originally had the thought of why you needed to walk to the other room. The context of that original room can trigger your original intention. In addition, as you will see in the following chapters, walking is one of the best ways to keep memory sharp. My mother-in-law recently said she experiences this doorways-cause-forgetting effect often. Now that she knows that walking can help memory, she feels it is actually a good thing as she spends more time walking around her house, going back and forth from room to room, trying to remember why she went to the other room. With enough time and walking, it eventually comes back. Betty White said[28] something similar: "I have a two-story house and a very bad memory, I'm up and down those stairs all the time."

Anxiety about Memory: Forget about It

> Don't get upset when you forget something . . . just wait and it will come back!
>
> —Dr. Ruth Westheimer, sex therapist

One common observation among older adults is that their memory isn't what it used to be, or that they have trouble keeping things in short-term memory. This is actually normal for people in older age (meaning it is common and not a source of disease). Many older adults become accustomed to it and deal with memory challenges in simple ways, such as just allowing more time to remember something or writing down things that are important to remember. It is among the young-old "worried well" who are most consumed by anxiety-provoking memory concerns, whereas older-old adults (over the age of 80, who have been dealing with these issues for decades) will not be as concerned; they know it is simply something that comes with age. There are clearly many types of memory that are not impaired in old age, as well as ways to remember important things. One benefit of older age is that we might forget what isn't important and focus instead on what is important.

This book does not deal with issues regarding Alzheimer's disease or dementia— just the mention of them can invoke high levels of anxiety in some people. Diagnosis of early stages of dementia is quite challenging for doctors. It may be wise to consult a neurologist if you or a loved one is concerned about memory or attention problems or about changes in personality and everyday functioning. One joke is that it is normal to occasionally forget where you parked your car in a parking lot, but it is not normal to forget that you own a car. Don't sweat the small stuff: find your car and then remember how to get home—these are the important things to remember.

Memory for Jokes and Poetry in Old Age: The Benefits of Retrieval Practice and Relaxing

We remember lyrics to songs often without much effort, due to the repetition and frequency with which we hear them. Children can recite songs, starting from "Twinkle Twinkle Little Star" to Taylor Swift's latest hit, with great ease. One of the best ways to make sure you remember something isn't just to study or look at it. The best way is to test yourself and to try to retrieve the information first.[29] Sing the song from memory, or try to recall the person's name after you just met them. Do you remember my name? By going through the act of recalling it, as opposed to me just telling you again, you strengthen the pathway to this memory.

Bob Newhart uses a similar method to remember his jokes; he says a lot of comedians can't remember jokes. Newhart says, "I am a writer-comedian, so if you give me a punch-line, I build backwards, and can reconstruct it." By recalling a poem or jokes, you can further reinforce these pathways and be better at recalling them when needed. Testing your memory strengthens those memories, especially in old age.[30] However, you might find yourself telling the same jokes to people who have already heard them, partly because a particular person might trigger the recollection of a joke. I once started telling a joke to a friend, and halfway through, I got the sense that he had already heard the joke, and then I thought perhaps I had even told the person the same joke myself—not uncommon, but still embarrassing. Worse yet, my friend then informed me that he had told me the joke several weeks ago! Of course, this is easy to explain in terms of memory principles: his familiar face made me think of the joke; I forgot he had told it to me but had a feeling of some association between him and the joke that I then interpreted as, hmmm, he might find this joke funny.

You will forget things if you don't use them. For example, if you don't go to the gym for several weeks, you will forget your locker combination (I can attest to this). However, someone would not forget if they were regularly checking on their "treasure," or taking money out of a safe in their basement that contains large amounts of cash, or monitoring their bank account. Thus, the lesson is to use your memory like a bank, making regular transactions (both deposits and withdrawals) to ensure the balance is safe and has some frequent activity.

In our current digital age, we have easy access to information, and one result is that there is little emphasis placed on memorizing poetry. In the "olden days," people often memorized poetry, but today this seems to be a forgotten skill. Author Maya Angelou said to me, "If I don't recite it, when it goes away, it is as if I can do two lines, then I know the next two lines, but if I don't know the words I know the melody. I have access to some structure. If I stay still, and allow the melody to play itself out, then the words will come back."

Poetry can be also used as a form of relaxation, and as a test of memory. In his older age, basketball coach John Wooden recited poetry to fall asleep and to relax, and not just to test his memory. John Glenn told me he recited and tested himself with Robert W. Service poems. He frequently recited one he learned while in the Army, "The Shooting of Dan McGrew." He felt his memory was still fairly sharp. He and his wife joked that if they couldn't remember a name they were trying to remember, they would just wait 20 minutes and then it would come to one of them. There are also benefits to spouses using collaborative forms of memory to help recall what one may not be able to recall on his or her own—working as a team can bring brains together.[31]

The ability to remember poetry is a skill that can also be learned later in life. For example, at age 58, John Basinger began memorizing Milton's *Paradise Lost* as a form of mental activity to accompany his physical exercise at the gym.[32] Although he had memorized various short poems in earlier years, he had never attempted anything of this magnitude. He stated that he wanted to do something special to commemorate the then-upcoming millennium. He began by walking on a treadmill one day while trying to memorize the opening lines of the poem. Nine years and thousands of study hours later, he was able to recall from memory all 12 books of this 10,565-line poem over a 3-day period. While this represents an extreme feat, it shows that exceptional memorizers are made, not born, and that feats of memory can be demonstrated even in later adulthood with sufficient practice. A similar feat, with a much different goal, was accomplished by Douglas Hegdahl, then a 20-year-old prisoner of war in North Vietnam. As he would be one of the only prisoners granted early release, he desperately wanted to learn the names of other prisoners, in order to report this information to the United States. Hegdahl memorized names, capture dates, methods of capture, and personal information of about 256 other prisoners, to the tune of the nursery rhyme "Old MacDonald Had a Farm." Even today, in his older age, he can still recall all of these names.[33]

Reminiscing: The Role of Nostalgia and the Good Old Days

> I sometimes like to spend time in the past, with the things that have been important to me.
>
> —John Wooden[34]

Remember the good old days? One reason older adults might be happier is that they focus on and remember more positive information. Thinking about the past in a positive light is also the basis for reminiscing, something we tend to do when we are older. Nostalgia may make us relive past moments in glorious terms (e.g., "the fish was THIS big," or "I used to walk 5 miles uphill in snow"). These moments can be interpreted as defining images from a person's past of overcoming hardships or challenges. Research[35] also shows that nostalgia serves an existential function by bolstering a sense of meaning in life and social connectedness.

Nostalgia can take the form of remembering a childhood home, recalling listening to the radio broadcasts of the 1954 Cubs, and reliving the positive and sentimental moments of our past. Despite the now famous title of the book by Thomas Wolfe, *You Can't Go Home Again*, in our memory we can certainly go home again. The reminiscing process allows us to enjoy the events and experience of our past with even more positivity and revisit childhood memories like they were just yesterday. Research suggests that being nostalgic can add meaning to your life. Also, there is a certain amount of pleasure associated with recalling uplifting, emotional, and defining memories of the past. This might be a reason why older adults are happier.

Reminiscing about the past can involve discussing family history, and this can also connect younger family members to important historical events, leading to a richer understanding of who our parents and grandparents were before we knew them. As a result, some research suggests that the more children know about their family, the better connected they are to their family and the more secure they feel about their family identity, factors that are important for child development.[36] Thus, nostalgia can connect multiple generations in important ways.

Curiosity Guides Memory in Older Adults

> I have no special talents, I am only passionately curious.
>
> —Albert Einstein

Starting at an early age, we are curious. My son loves the adventures of the mischievous Curious George, and of learning about the world. He is curious, and I hope it stays with him his whole life. Our curiosity blossoms with age. But often we become curious about different things as we get older. What interests you might not interest me, and *Curious George* might not be the best bedtime reading for adults.

To test your own level of curiosity and memory, read the following trivia questions, decide how interested you are in learning the answers (on a scale of 1 to 10, with 1 being not interested at all, and 10 being extremely interested), and then try to come up with answers (the answers are in the notes section at the end of the chapter)[37]:

What mammal sleeps the shortest amount each day?
What was the first product to have a bar code?
What was the first nation to give women the right to vote?

These are fairly hard trivia questions, and some are more interesting than others. In a recent study,[38] younger and older adults tried to answer questions like those that you just read. Much like the questions you read, all of the questions were chosen such that almost none of the participants knew the correct answers. They then gave ratings of curiosity—how interested they were in learning the answer. They were then told the answers. A week later, these people were again presented with the questions and asked to recall the answers. It was the older adults who remembered the ones they were more curious about when tested a week later and forgot the less interesting ones. The younger adults didn't show this pattern. Thus, as we get older, we do tend to remember what piques our interest, and forget the rest.

There is a certain pleasure in recalling trivia, knowing about the world, and learning new information. Games like Trivial Pursuit might actually attract a crowd of all ages (adapted versions such as Pub Trivia are popular with younger adults). Older adults are often more knowledgeable about facts, history, and the types of question that show up on *Jeopardy*. The most popular games at senior centers and retirement communities often involve trivia. As we get older, we don't lose the ability to be curious, but we might be more selective about what we feel is important to learn and later remember.

Many people, both younger and older, will remark that they remember things when they find them interesting. That seems like a good strategy, especially in old age, if we have a lot of information stored in our brain and don't want to worry about other clutter. But sometimes trivia can be interesting, even if it has no useful value—it is just a curious interest.

The Roman philosopher Cicero described the elderly Cato Maior as an impressive example of mental sharpness, saying, "I've never heard of an old man who forgot where he buried his treasure; only keen interest is needed to stimulate the retention of mental strength in old age."[39] The need to remember information, or where our treasure is hidden, may be the necessary ingredient to having a level of curiosity that enhances our memory for what is important.

Summary: A Selective Memory Can Work Well in Old Age

As we get older, we become connoisseurs of what we need to remember. Memory is not like a video camera, and even if it were, it would become less so with age. While we might struggle with remembering certain details or names, the benefit is that we are more selective, we can focus on what is important, we filter out what is not relevant or of interest, and we are better at remembering and reporting on the gist of it. Sometimes remembering the overall conclusion or summary can be even more important than remembering minute details (as we can find those on Google or Wikipedia). It may be just as helpful to remember where to find information. More generally, remembering main themes or important lessons can be an efficient way to remember at any age. As we get older, our knowledge and awareness about our own memory (a form of metamemory) provides a deeper understanding of how to effectively use memory and what to do if and when it might fail us. Our beliefs about our memory can be very influential, as having negative beliefs about aging has shown to lead to later declines; thus, our beliefs can play an important role. There are reasons why memory declines with age, consistent with stereotypes of memory and aging. However, there are also a variety of ways in which memory works well in old age. In summary, older people don't forget where they have hidden their treasure (but where the hell are my glasses?).

Wisdom: The Benefits of Life Experiences and Creativity

The art of being wise is the art of knowing what to overlook.
—William James (1842–1910), psychologist, also known as the
"father" of American psychology

Knowledge speaks, but wisdom listens.
—Jimi Hendrix, rock guitarist and singer/songwriter

WHILE WE KNOW WRINKLES WHEN WE SEE THEM, wisdom has a more elusive definition. Are wrinkles really needed to have wisdom—or put another way, do we need to have many life experiences to have wisdom? Wisdom is more than knowledge, and wisdom is not Wikipedia. Wisdom can be thought of as the ability to think and act using prior knowledge, past experiences, common sense, and insight. One definition suggests that a wise person has expert knowledge about the practicalities and pragmatics of life.[1] Wisdom isn't just being very smart. Wisdom is considered to be a separate entity from intelligence or spirituality but involves the integration of various cognitive and emotional factors, things that may be more accessible and noticeable in older age.[2]

Wisdom is not just being very intelligent or knowledgeable. For example, Albert Einstein was once asked, "What is the speed of sound?" Einstein admitted that he did not know the precise answer, saying "[I do not] carry such information in my mind since it is readily available in books . . . . The value of a college education is not the learning of many facts but the training of the mind to think."[3] Thus, Einstein suggests there may be wisdom in knowing what needs to be personally remembered. Other information can be easily accessible, today often on the Internet.

While wisdom may seem elusive for people without experience, often wisdom allows people to see the obvious, or to use common sense without second-guessing themselves or the outcomes. Ask a child for a less complicated definition of wisdom: my 6-year-old daughter says, "Wisdom is being careful" (and her grandmother, when proofreading this text, agrees wholeheartedly with her). When I asked Maya Angelou, the writer and poet, how she would describe wisdom, she said, "I suppose it is the essence of the lessons one has learned, distilled by care and concern, honest evaluation, and then it is given to a listener using the best possible language. While everybody has some wisdom, an unwise person is unkind, cruel, brutish, not very smart, thick, doesn't use mother-wit, or common sense."[4]

Wisdom is also something that almost everyone will assume is a valued benefit of old age. The actor Brad Pitt commented, "Personally, I like aging. With age comes wisdom . . . . I'll take wisdom over youth any day." (Note that he didn't say I will take old age over youth, just the wisdom, please!)

While old age doesn't guarantee wisdom, experience may be a critical ingredient, something that often accumulates with age. However, wisdom also involves the creativity of not simply comparing a current situation to one that might have been experienced in the past. Making mistakes may enhance and inform wisdom, and older adults have made plenty of them. Thus, wisdom, expertise, and creativity may be intricately linked, and they may all be enhanced with age and considered a benefit of old age. In general, while we value wisdom, we don't always seek it out, or appreciate that older adults have knowledge and experiences that can provide insights that are critical in very practical ways. Older adults may enjoy passing on wisdom to appreciative ears and younger minds. Therefore, knowing when and how to access wisdom is important.

Who Has Wisdom and at What Age?

Where do we find wisdom—and what characteristics might lead to having wisdom? We often think of older adults as wise, and some research suggests that older adults, without formal psychology training, are, in fact, adept at analyzing interpersonal conflict, much like a trained clinical psychologist.[5] Another study[6] showed that regardless of education, IQ, or gender, older adults possess better reasoning skills about societal and interpersonal conflicts—a critical form of wisdom. People in this study read stories about conflicts between individuals and social groups, as well as letters from the "Dear Abby" advice column, and described problems between friends, siblings, and spouses. Participants were asked, "What do you think will happen after that?" and "Why do you think it will happen this way?" Their responses were audio recorded. After transcribing their responses and removing the age of the person from the record, the investigators then asked other participants who had received training to rate these responses on the basis of "wisdom." Wisdom was defined as the ability to see problems from multiple perspectives and show sensitivity to social relationships. The researchers then asked outside experts, including clergy and professional counselors, to rank a subset of the responses according to their own definitions of wisdom, a process that largely confirmed the accuracy of the students' ratings. The main finding was that the average age of those with scores in the top 20% was 65 years old, versus 46 years old for the remaining 80%. In addition, a follow-up study showed that distancing oneself from a situation or event can also trigger wise decisions. Thus, sometimes it is best not to consult someone who recently went through a similar problem, but rather someone who is more removed from the situation—possibly more removed because they are older.

Emotional Wisdom in Old Age

> He that can compose himself is wiser than he that composes books.
> —Benjamin Franklin

In the book *The Wisdom Paradox*, author Elkhonon Goldberg details the many ways the brain appears to deteriorate in older age, one being the simple (but not necessarily true) idea that as we age, brain cells die and mental operations become slower.[7] However, a lifetime of using intellect and observing others can then lead to empathy and the accurate awareness of others' emotions. Goldberg himself observes, "What I have lost with age in my capacity for hard mental work, I seem to have gained in my capacity for instantaneous, almost unfairly easy insight."

Experience is often necessary to have wisdom, make good decisions, and be a mentor for others. For example, CEOs of Fortune 500 companies are typically 50 to 70 years of age. These people score lower on laboratory computer-based tests of speed of processing, reasoning, and problem-solving relative to younger adults,[8] but they have a knack for guiding companies and making wise decisions. Yet wisdom involves more than making important financial decisions. Often the use of wisdom in problem-solving can involve emotional family issues. Think of the last time there was a large family gathering, such as at Thanksgiving, and how certain subtle family conflicts or even more major family squabbles were handled by family members of differing ages. Intellectual abilities may be different from more emotional wisdom or practical wit. As such, despite perhaps doing poorly on timed paper-and-pencil tests of reasoning and problem-solving, as might be measured on an SAT-type test, older adults may excel in terms of emotional regulation and practical problem-solving.

Consider this example of a somewhat complex emotional situation:

An older woman's daughter-in-law just gave birth to the older woman's fifth grandchild. However, the woman's daughter-in-law and son were quite insulting in instructing the older woman (the grandmother) on how to hold the baby. In order not to escalate the conflict, the older woman gently gave the baby back to the mother and left the hospital room so as not to vent her emotions to them. She did not want to cause any conflict with her family at such a vulnerable time. Controlling her emotional reaction to the situation made it easier for her to calmly revisit the issue with her family later, undistracted by the emotional upheaval of the earlier moment. The older woman's control of her emotions was effective and wise given the situation and her goal to avoid a fight. However, in another context, if this same older woman were administered a cognitive assessment battery in a laboratory setting, she would likely show cognitive decline on a number of tasks that assess various forms of memory and attentional abilities.[9]

The situation described here could have escalated quickly and resulted in a regrettable family conflict. Older adults can often handle these situations quite effectively, using a form of emotional wisdom and life experience. Computer-based tests of memory and cognitive function do not capture emotional wisdom—namely, the ability to handle conflict effectively, which is something that gets better with age. This type of wisdom can sometimes involve keeping emotions in check and deciding when and what to express to others. In terms of emotional responses, when dealing with an upsetting interpersonal situation, older adults report being less likely to engage in impulsive and aggressive responses, such as shouting or name-calling. Older adults are better able to "pick their battles" wisely, choosing to first wait and see if things will improve without the need for a strong emotional response.[10] As we age, we may also be more aware of the suffering of others, and the need for acceptance, forgiveness, and compassion, as expressed in Kenny Rogers' song, "The Gambler" (1978):

> You've got to know when to hold 'em. Know when to fold 'em. Know when to walk away . . .

The use of emotional wisdom can also extend to judging the character and intentions of others and appreciating the best of qualities that people possess. Drawing on a lifetime of experience, older adults may overlook certain flaws or characteristics of someone in order to draw conclusions about how or why that person might behave in a certain manner. In one study,[11] when given a list of behaviors of a fictional person, older people overlooked distracting but relatively unimportant actions and focused on those that were more pertinent and diagnostic of the person as a whole. Older adults may try to focus on the positive aspects rather than the flaws of a person. Relative to younger adults, older adults were more likely in this study to accurately label a stranger as dishonest or intelligent, which suggests that older adults have social expertise when judging others.

Being able to recognize a trustworthy person can be important in older age. Older adults are usually pretty good at sizing up people. In one study, older adults accurately identified which faces they were earlier told were either trustworthy or untrustworthy, but only when the faces were of a similar age to them.[12] When asked to judge the trustworthiness of unfamiliar faces, older adults tended to judge the "stranger" faces as more trustworthy than younger adults did. This suggests that older people are using wisdom for social analyses of character but may also be prone to trust people in general. This trait can be an issue when encountering con artists who attempt to take advantage of older adults. Older adults are targeted more frequently than younger adults because of their greater assets, but they are not necessarily more likely to be victimized in these situations[13] (see also Chapter 9 for scam methods and ways to avoid scams and con artists in older age). Knowing whom to trust can be an acquired skill and something that is learned with age. However, older adults who are lonely may be more inclined to trust people who seem friendly but aren't familiar, even if simply giving them the benefit of the doubt.

Creative Cognition: How Can We Measure Creativity?

When we see unique art or architecture, we often are impressed by creativity. There are many ways in which people can be creative in various domains. Like many other things that are hard to define, we know creativity when we see it. We like to debate and discuss creative contributions, like an unusual piece of art or the latest building by renowned architect Frank Gehry, but actually measuring creativity can be quite challenging. Gehry is famous not only for his creative design but also for using novel materials, such as cardboard, to make furniture. One classic measure of creativity is known as the "alternative uses task."[14] The task is fairly easy to administer, and easy to try for yourself. In this task, people are asked to list as many possible uses for a common object, such as a nail, table, or toothbrush.

For example, imagine a simple red brick. Now try to come up with as many uses of a brick as possible. Stop reading—and think of these different uses for a brick: what do you come up with?

You likely first came up with the more common uses—for building, perhaps—but then your mind starts to wander. This is the creative process at work. Coming up with more creative examples can be a fun endeavor, but also one that requires you to let go of your inhibitions. At first it might seem difficult, or even unrealistic (a brick is a brick is a brick). After a little while, you might get the creative juices flowing, shut down your inhibiting frontal lobes (a part of your brain that often keeps you focused and on task), and then come up with many funny and strange uses of a brick, such as "a weapon," "something to put in a toilet tank to save water," or "something to flatten a chicken while cooking it."

There are several ways to measure or score your creativity on this task. One way is to simply count how many things you came up with that represent alternative uses—ones that aren't directly related to houses, building, or construction (the total creative output). However, being creative often involves more novel insights and originality. Another way to analyze the creative output from this task is to tally the number of uses other people likely didn't come up with, as those answers are very unique or original uses. Also, you can have another person look at your responses and then rate each of the responses in terms of some level of creativity. While we might cringe at being judged by others, being evaluated by our peers is often the truest test.

You might expect older adults to be more set in their ways: a brick is used for building, that's it. This is known as *functional fixedness*— we get stuck on the common use of something and fail to see it as useful in another way. But in fact, older adults come up with just as many creative alternate uses for bricks as younger adults,[15] which suggests no declines in this form of creativity in older age.

As we age, we often need to be creative—with finances, family, and even to simply entertain ourselves. Surviving often involves creativity; as some say, "necessity is the mother of invention." While we might think younger minds are more apt to be creative, there are many reasons to believe that old age is a time for great creative contributions and insights, partly because older people have more experiences to draw on, and creativity often involves seeing commonalities and making novel connections. Often older adults are more open to alternate perspectives. Life experience teaches us that people will often see things differently. Being able to notice different points of view allows greater perspective and an awareness that not everything is as simple it seems.

Creative Contributions Late in Life, Large and Small

We may think that creativity peaks in young adulthood (think Steve Jobs or John Lennon), but it is clear that creative contributions are made throughout one's life, and often in different forms. Older age may allow us the opportunity to be more creative after having established some credibility in a domain, as is the case with the world-renowned architect Frank Gehry. Early in his career, he designed conventional buildings and shopping malls, but now he has the freedom to design the creative buildings he would only dream about when he was younger.

While some forms of creativity often peak earlier in adulthood, in complex domains such as pure mathematics and theoretical physics, for areas that require the use of accumulated knowledge, creative peaks typically occur later.[16] In support of this view, there are ways to attempt to measure creative output across the adult lifespan. For example, an analysis[17] of ages at which some 300 famous artists, poets, and novelists produced their most valuable or useful contributions, as measured by auction prices and the number of times specific works appeared in textbooks, suggests two peaks in life. The first peak occurs more frequently among conceptual artists, who often do their best work in their 20s and 30s, and the second peak, after age 60, occurs among experimental artists, who may need a few more decades to reach their full potential (perhaps being more akin to a Frank Gehry type, whose more creative output blossomed later in his career).

Of course, Gehry is not alone. People such as Mark Twain, Alfred Hitchcock, Paul Cézanne, Frank Lloyd Wright, Robert Frost, Laura Ingalls Wilder, Giuseppe Verdi, and Virginia Woolf are thought to have done their greatest work in middle to older age, relying more on forms of wisdom that allow for creative output. In some cases, this involved dealing with the physical challenges of old age; Monet began his famous water lily paintings at age 73, and many of his works were painted when Monet suffered from cataracts.

"Big C" and "little c" Creativity: How a Little Creativity Goes a Long Way

Creativity researchers have often classified creativity as either "Big C" or "little c."[18] *Big C creativity* refers to extraordinary, often famous and well-recognized accomplishments of great artists, scientists, and inventors. *Little c creativity* often involves more diverse subjects and personal things that affect only a few people. This could include more everyday creative output, such as creative ways to write memos, ways to teach a subject or skill, or ways one expresses oneself. We won't all make major creative contributions later in life, as that is often not the goal of older adults. Rather, we choose hobbies or activities in which we can express creativity, such as painting, gardening, photography, cooking, baking, poetry, or writing books.

My two daughters love to bake, but when they improvise, the results are sometimes inedible. As they learn through their mistakes, though (such as learning that baking powder has to be measured carefully, and not used too creatively), their accidental creations are unique and often delicious. When my wife improvises, sometimes the best discoveries are made—as she has a better understanding of what ingredients can be substituted or work well together. Many scientific discoveries arise from small mistakes and are serendipitous. Those scientists had the necessary levels of knowledge, creativity, and curiosity. Little c creativity allows people to muster up their creative talents in domains that they enjoy, and often these people go without much professional recognition or media attention but are provided with important creative outlets at any age. Gardening can provide a creative outlet and connection to both nature and nurturing life. Engaging in these types of creative tasks can stimulate cognitive function and well-being, and also demonstrates new ways that older adults can connect with creativity at any age. For example, Grandma Moses took on painting late in life, becoming nationally recognized in her 80s.[19] Thus, creativity blossoms at many different ages and in many areas.

A Miracle Landing on the Hudson: Wisdom and Creativity Working Together

On January 15, 2009, a cold winter day in New York City, US Airways Flight 1549 departed La Guardia Airport, on route to Charlotte, North Carolina, with 155 people on board. This was one of hundreds of flights that took off that day at that airport under routine conditions. However, just seconds after takeoff, the pilot, then 58-year-old Chesley "Sully" Sullenberger, reported to air traffic control that the plane had hit a large flock of birds, and both engines were disabled. Sullenberger had to immediately ask air traffic control about the possibilities of either returning to LaGuardia or attempting to land at the smaller Teterboro Airport, in New Jersey. With time as an issue, and no engine power, Sullenberger had to make a quick decision: either try to land at the airport, but risk crashing into a heavily populated area, or land the plane on water in the Hudson River, something he had never done before. Gliding over the New York City skyline with no engine power and with the Hudson River in sight, Sullenberger decided that reaching an airport was not feasible. He determined that an emergency water landing in the Hudson River was the best option for everyone's survival. There was little time for discussion. The co-pilot, Jeff Skiles, a veteran pilot with 32 years of experience, recounted how he responded to Captain Sullenberger's command:[20]

> Sully said, "We're going in the Hudson," and I was happy with that . . . I said, "Great," and went back to doing what I was doing.

Somewhat miraculously, Sullenberger was able to land the engineless plane in the Hudson River, saving the lives of all 155 people on board. While this was an exceptional feat, other dramatic aircraft disasters had also been averted over the years, and often they had something in common: a highly experienced team of pilots was involved in flying the plane. While other professional pilots agreed that it was the training and experience of these pilots that enabled them to respond successfully to the extreme challenges their planes faced, these pilots were older adults who on many tests of dexterity or reaction times would have fared worse than their younger counterparts. In many cases, the pilots were near their 60th birthday, an age at which U.S. airline pilots, prior to 2007, were required to retire.

What is now referred to as the "Miracle on the Hudson" didn't simply involve an experienced pilot's and co-pilot's fast reaction times in responding to improbable events. Captain Sullenberger was calm, knowing that time was a factor, and he had to make several contingency plans—no airport was close enough without engine thrust, so the river was the best option—and despite his many years of experience, he had no experience landing a plane in water. He had to rely on his understanding of certain principles of aviation, and some creativity, that in combination would allow for a miraculous feat.

That decision to land on the Hudson was made two and a half minutes after their routine takeoff, and just one minute after the birds had destroyed the engines, leaving the plane without power. Sullenberger and his co-pilot Skiles had to quickly plan and prepare for a water landing during this brief period. Speaking with news anchor Katie Couric, after the event,[21] Sullenberger said, "One way of looking at this might be that for 42 years, I've been making small, regular deposits in this bank of experience, education and training. And on January 15 the balance was sufficient so that I could make a very large withdrawal." Asked what was going through his head, Sullenberger told Couric, "I knew immediately that this, unlike every other flight I'd had for 42 years, was probably not going to end with the airplane undamaged on the runway."

One theory is that Sully might have had time to go back to the airport, but would have had to make this decision immediately, without contemplating any other options. This would have involved following a more routine mental set: planes are meant to land at airports, not on rivers. However, this might also have meant a catastrophic crash into a highly populated city. This dramatic theory of what could have been (gliding back at an airport with no engine power or a fiery crash into a densely populated city) was illustrated in the 2016 movie *Sully*, by Clint Eastwood. Interestingly, people likely would not have second-guessed a plan to circle back to the airport had it been successful. After all, that might be what one would expect if following routine procedures. However, this was no ordinary set of circumstances since ALL engines were destroyed by the bird strike. Sully was able to balance making a complex decision that could involve possibly two horrible outcomes with a level of creativity that resulted in one amazing outcome—even with no experience landing in water. Pilot Sullenberger and co-pilot Skiles didn't even have enough time to go through the entire crash landing checklist. For example, the ditch button, which seals the plane's vents and outlets from taking on water, was never pressed. That, coupled with the fact that the impact caused a breach near the plane's tail, resulted in the plane rapidly taking on water. Thus, in this case, wisdom is not necessarily linked to knowing the exact protocol for a water landing and remembering these details under pressure, but rather implementing important procedures and then improvising "on the fly."

Slow Down: The Benefits of Slowing in Old Age and the Wisdom of Taking Your Time

Make haste slowly.

—Jack LaLanne

Be quick but don't hurry.

—John Wooden

It is no surprise to many that as we age, we get slower (on the order of milliseconds). Slower reaction time to press a brake pedal when a car abruptly stops in front of us is a result of our neuronal signal slowing down, providing evidence for a general slowing theory of aging.[22] But there are exceptions, and forms of compensation, that mitigate this "general slowing." For example, expert older typists employ better strategies of anticipating words they will type, which can offset any slowing. Older musicians know to deliberately slow down, in order to make faster parts of the music appear to be played faster relative to other parts of the music. Older drivers are less likely than younger adults to get into high-speed car accidents, partly because of their driving experience, sticking to familiar routes, and not driving frequently at night, or when distracted, tired, or intoxicated.

Older pilots can rely on prior experience and knowledge to put themselves in a position to avoid the need to react quickly to a new situation, thereby reacting calmly while also regulating other emotions, as in the case of Captain Sullenberger. In terms of the unique conditions that Sullenberger encountered on that cold day in 2009, a younger pilot might have reacted more quickly to circle back to the airport in order to land on land. But by doing so, this pilot could also have risked a possible crash into a heavily populated area. Pilots usually have many routines to follow, and various checklists, that help aid the complex operations involved in flying an airplane. While these pilots are adept at calculating fuel consumption and mileage times, remembering new information can be a challenge. Memory, and the proactive interference of having flown many flights, can become cluttered. Much like the burden placed on older adults' memory for remembering names, interference leads to rapid forgetting. I once met a middle-aged commercial airline pilot who said that despite all the complicated equipment he used and the complex calculations he needed to make for each flight, the hardest thing to remember was the assigned gate arrival information at the airport where they would be landing. As this would often change, he would actually write it on a post-it note in order to remember it.

There is something to be gained by being slow if slowing down can make you more present, more mindful, and more aware of other people's perspectives. A slow communicator can be a highly effective one, allowing for natural pauses, such that the audience follows the speaker's train of thought. When I first started giving presentations and teaching classes to large audiences of 300 students, I was a rapid communicator. With my mind racing a mile a minute, I tried to say everything I knew about a topic in order to be thorough, but I noticed that the crowd didn't always follow along. Now I have only one note to myself that I need as a reminder or prompt before beginning a presentation: "PAUSE." I will incorporate more time for questions, get more audience participation, and gauge the level at which my message has been understood by the audience (especially when I need to compete with Facebook in the large lecture classes). With pauses and the right tempo, a clear message emerges, often with fewer words. Being a slow speaker can also make you a good listener, something that might improve with age.

Slowing down can also make you more aware of the simple dangers of walking and falling. Falls can be one major source of hospitalizations and mortality in old age. Taking one's time walking down steps, avoiding a tripping hazard, or being aware of slippery surfaces can be critical at any age. In a *New York Times* op-ed article about how to reduce risks in life, Pulitzer Prize–winning author and geographer Jared Diamond noted that bathrooms can be one of the more dangerous places for older adults, from slipping in the shower.[23] If you aren't careful, your daily shower, or the walk to the bathroom at night, can be very dangerous, especially in older age.

One byproduct or benefit of old age is that there might not be as much of a rush as for a younger person, and one can better appreciate the benefits of being careful or the need to do so. As an example, my "old age" back injury was recently aggravated because I tripped on a root while hiking in the mountains. I was too focused on what was 40 feet ahead of me while walking at a good clip and didn't notice the terrain directly in front of me. Slowing down might reduce the likelihood of a bad fall.

Carl Honoré, who has written books about the benefits of slowing down (*In Praise of Slowness* and *The Slow Fix*), notes that he has gotten speeding tickets and thus also appreciates the challenge of following his own advice. He describes how, after a long day, rushing to make dinner and get the children ready for bed, he has often tried to skip lines or pages when reading to his children at night. Contrast the dad's need for a speedy story time with the story time of grandparents, who likely have more patience, partly because they spend less time with these children. Grandparents will read or provide detailed stories and answer questions thoroughly when telling bedtime stories. My mother-in-law, who has endless patience when reading to her grandchildren, often provides rich and detailed explanations for concepts they have yet to encounter (e.g., when reading *Annie*: what is an orphan, what is a widow, why do orphans have pet dogs and we don't?). This can lead to tangential lessons about life that can only be provided by patient and experienced storytellers, often grandparents or other older adults. As Saint Augustine wrote, "Patience is the companion of wisdom."

Grandparents as a Source of Wisdom (and Overqualified Babysitters)

> When I was a boy of 14, my father was so ignorant I could hardly stand to have the old man around. But when I got to be 21, I was astonished at how much the old man had learned in seven years.
>
> —Mark Twain

In evolutionary terms, older adults provided necessary wisdom for survival. While slower than their younger counterparts, in many cultures older adults are revered for their wisdom and insights, and younger family members will care for them out of love, respect, and obligation. As Jared Diamond outlines in his 2012 book, *The World Until Yesterday*, older people can no longer spear a lion, but they can contribute importantly by advising younger people about how to set traps and are a resource for information about the history of hunting. In both tribal settings and more contemporary American life, grandparents also act as babysitters, freeing up time for their children (now parents) to forage, or find jobs and work outside the home. Grandparents may actually be overqualified babysitters; one study showed that the children cared for by a grandmother have half the risk of injuries (and fewer trips to the emergency room) than children cared for at daycare, by other relatives, or even the child's own mother.[24] This finding is important, as it may illustrate the benefits of wisdom that grandparents can utilize when taking care of children.

In addition to babysitting, grandparents can provide a source of wisdom and more formal teaching to grandchildren, which can be a valuable and enriching relationship for both parties. Sometimes the parents get in the way of grandparenting, as parents may view their own parents as not being qualified for the job of watching their children. In some cases this is justified, if it involves physical limitations, such as running after energetic children or implementing rules that are not clearly articulated or understood to be important by the grandparent. In many cases parents are just not aware of the benefits of having grandparents involved in child development.

Grandparents can also unlock children's learning potential, as frustrated and harried parents may not be able to appreciate how to best teach their own children (and feel frustrated with teaching their own children). A good example of this comes from Dr. Nate Kornell, who wrote about the wisdom of his children's grandparents[25]:

> Yesterday my daughters (ages 6 and 3) went for a bike ride with their grandfather. I have been trying to teach the six-year-old how to bike without training wheels, with such disastrous results that I had given up for the summer. I would have said the chance that she would ride home without training wheels was about 0.00%. That's exactly what she did. Saba (her grandfather) taught her to ride. It took him seven minutes.

Sometimes grandparents, and not parents, can be the best teachers in their family.

Family Wisdom and the Stories That Bind Us: Learning More about Your Family from Your Older Family and Mistakes They Made

Do you know where your grandparents grew up and the jobs they had? Do you know about an illness, crime, or something really terrible that happened in your family? Do you know the story of your own birth? Learning about family history can be important and formative for people of any age. Older people turn to genealogy to better understand their family history, but younger people may also benefit from knowing more about their own family, especially early in their life. In one landmark study, researchers asked children these types of family-based questions (and the researchers also taped some dinner conversations to assess overall family dynamics). The researchers then compared the children's knowledge of history to their performance on a variety of psychological tests that assessed a sense of control and self-esteem. The children who knew about their family's history had a stronger sense of control over their lives, had higher self-esteem, and believed their families functioned more successfully. This set of questions, labelled the "Do You Know?" scale,[26] was also a very strong predictor of children's later emotional health and happiness, especially after challenging traumatic events.

Why does knowing where your grandmother went to school help a child deal with the emotions associated with spilled milk, a skinned knee, or a terrorist attack? One suggestion is that a child with knowledge of his or her family history is able to develop a better sense of being part of a larger family. This also doesn't just involve knowing the amazing and great things one's family did, and family recipes that have been passed down, but also knowing about how one's family struggled and what they overcame. The more I know about my family's struggles in the past (e.g., how only some survived World War II and the Holocaust, as told to me by my grandparents, and my mother's difficult battle with cancer, as told by my aunts and uncles), the better I am at appreciating what I have and the opportunities I have been given. These stories make me better able to take on my own challenges, which often seem minuscule compared to those from my family's history.

My daughters' favorite bedtime stories are my own failures, stories aptly titled "Mistakes You Made When You Were Little." These likely reassure them that even their own parents made (and will continue to make) mistakes; that is what living and learning is all about. Children may fear mistakes, but they also want to learn from them and not make the same mistake twice. Often older adult family members can be the best providers of this information. It may be that parents are not discussing blunders or mistakes with their children, out of fear or embarrassment, or wanting to set positive role-model behavior. However, there are clear benefits to knowing the history about mistakes and perseverance, as this is often later related to many positive outcomes. This can also allow for important family stories that can be readily recalled and enjoyed as a form of family tradition and history. In addition, sometimes the communication between grandchildren and grandparents will be more honest and open than the communication that children have with their own parents.

The When of Wisdom: The Opportunity of Giving Advice with Timely Lessons

One reason I was able to interview older adults for this book is that they were readily interested in passing along whatever they had learned along the way. They didn't have secrets to their successfulness in the business of aging, but they were happy to provide some perspective and insights about their lives, and not just about aging. Learning about the journey can provide great insights about successful aging. At the start of an interview with the comedian Bob Newhart, he confessed, "I am at a point in my life where I am trying to empty my brain. I should just put a hose right here. There are things that I have learned that I want to share with other people, especially younger people!"

While I was an avid listener to Newhart's insights and jokes, in general, imparting knowledge onto a younger generation can be a challenge. A parent once told me he read a poem to his 4-year-old child. He wanted his child to learn it, understand it, and see and feel the important lessons that could be gleaned from this work, like he did when he was young. After reading the poem to his son several times, he asked him, "What were you thinking when you heard this poem?" The child said, "I was thinking about how I want you to play with me." Sometimes parents want children to learn more than they need at any given time, and providing lessons has to come with context—such as an actual learning experience, and not just imparting a poem onto a small child, especially a child who just wants to play. As parents and adults, we forget when or why we learned a poem, remembering only that our children should learn it. Children might be better guides about what they want to learn about and when we can impart our wisdom. We can't force wisdom on people—they need to want it, and we need to know when it is needed.

Parents and grandparents often attempt to impart knowledge and enriching experiences, the essence of wisdom. This can range from sage advice by passing on poems and classic books to more direct orders, such as wash your hands before dinner, don't pick your nose, and don't eat from off the floor (does this tell you the ages of my children?). The comedian and actor Billy Crystal might have said it best when he said we should give up on trying to get our kids to stop picking their noses. Children will do it when you aren't looking anyway, so focus on the bigger issues that might have more practical relevance to a child's life.[27] Pick the big battles, not the nose battle. That is the practical wisdom that is learned with age.

Summary

It is challenging to define wisdom, but we tend to know it when we see it. Wisdom is more than information from Wikipedia and can also have an emotional and creative component. Patience can be an essential part of wisdom, especially in older age, but often wisdom involves thinking on your feet, and improvising. Older adults can draw upon life experiences that allow for both wisdom and creative insights. As stated in a birthday card, "What does 'with age comes wisdom' really mean? The answer: 'After all these years, you had better have learned something'." Wisdom can make someone a better teacher and a clearer communicator, sometimes by being slower and more selective. Sometimes wisdom involves knowing what to say, and when and how to say it.

Staying Sharp: What Is an Active Lifestyle?

Whatever you do in life, surround yourself with smart people who'll argue with you.

—John Wooden

WHAT DOES IT MEAN TO BE "ACTIVE," AND WHAT ARE the benefits of an active lifestyle? To keep our brains sharp, is it more important to be mentally active than physically active? Can being around other people keep you sharp? If or when I retire, how do I stay sharp? An active lifestyle doesn't mean running around all the time and constantly being on the go—but it does involve a certain amount of challenge or stimulation that can make one feel fulfilled, from being around people to reciting poetry.

As we age, we are all concerned about how to stay sharp and ways to improve our memory. Many people have opinions regarding what activities are best for this, or what they enjoy and feel has benefits. It is important to know if our beliefs match what research says can actually help us maintain and improve our intellectual ability, and what research is needed to support the latest claims about how to train the brain. This chapter discusses what activities might keep us sharp; the next chapter addresses the advances of computer-based brain training.

How can we stay sharp in middle and old age? Jared Diamond, the Pulitzer Prize–winning author and geographer, says there is no single secret to successful aging. He states the Anna Karenina principle: the one thing is not to look for the one thing that can lead to better memory and successful aging. Based on that principle, perhaps we should also look for a set of things to avoid. There are many important things we can do, and often we don't consciously do these things to succeed at successful aging. Diamond told me he walks and hikes, and he memorizes the many birds he sees during his outings. At night, before he falls asleep, he recalls seeing the birds as a form of relaxation and cognitive exercise.

Identifying activities that keep the mind sharp has been a topic of interest for many years, but the main challenge is to find ways to show that certain activities actually help mental acuity. For example, people who do crosswords might be "verbally sharp" to begin with and gravitate toward these sorts of games. It may not be that crosswords actually lead to improvements in cognition. Thus, just because two things are related doesn't mean one causes the other. To establish cause and effect, experiments are needed. These experiments would typically involve randomly assigning some people to do certain activities while having others not do the activities, or having them do other different but somewhat comparable activities. The issue is that some people like crossword puzzles, some people get frustrated by them, some have experience doing them, and others find them boring. There has been no conclusive study that can accurately assess any causal relation between doing crossword puzzles and memory improvement or ways to prevent dementia, partly because it is hard to tell people who aren't interested in crossword puzzles to do them for long periods of time. This same challenge is true for many of the activities that people claim maintain mental acuity, making the causal contributions of engaging in certain activities unknown. Showing correlations, even without evidence for a clear causal connection, can still be informative to determine how a link might exist between engaging in certain activities and improvements in cognition and a reduced likelihood of developing dementia.

What Do We Do to Keep Sharp? Identifying the Cognitive and Social Aspects

When people comment on what activities they do to stay sharp, the list can be quite diverse, yet it often focuses on mental games, including crosswords, Sudoku, Scrabble, Boggle, Mahjong (the addictive and ancient Chinese game played in group settings around the world), backgammon, chess, writing poetry and poetry recall, playing musical instruments, reading, painting, learning languages, quilting, photography, cooking, keeping a handwritten calendar, and writing in a journal. Some involve a more physical aspect, such as dancing, gardening, walking, hiking, swimming, bird watching, golf, lawn bowling, or shuffleboard.

There are a variety of studies that have examined the impact of these activities, using different methods and approaches. One study found that among people ages 75 to 85, those who engaged in a variety of leisure activities, such as reading, playing board games, playing musical instruments, and dancing, had a reduced prevalence of dementia.[1] Another study found that in people with early stages of dementia, those who played the game Mahjong over a 4-month period improved their memory, and this benefit lasted 1 month after people stopped playing.[2] A study of brain development found that extensive piano practicing was related to development in areas of the brain's white matter.[3] Another study showed that older professional musicians were found to have better spatial memory, as well as better listening skills.[4] But even if you don't play music, simply listening to music can enhance your mood, which may then also help your memory. There are also benefits of bilingualism, in that those who speak more than one language are less likely to develop dementia.[5] In addition, the brain challenges and cognitive complexity of one's job can also be protective in terms of warding off dementia.[6]

One reason people think they can't retire is because they believe their job keeps their brain active. For example, active older professors maintain certain memory abilities well into older age,[7] and retired accountants are more likely to remember numbers relative to verbal information.[8] Finally, variety might be important, as one study found that participating in a wide range of activities reduced cognitive impairment later in life, more so than any one specific activity.[9] Very few of these studies can allow for random assignment because people select what they choose to do early in life, which can lead to specific interests and focus later in life.

People usually say that these activities keep them sharp by "exercising the brain," stimulating mental activity, and keeping the creative juices flowing. Young adults often report using memory strategies to optimize their memory ability, whereas older adults are more likely to focus on cognitive exercise and maintaining physical health.[10] However, very little attention is given to the context in which these activities are carried out, meaning we often think of doing the task, and not the people we interact with while doing these tasks. Some games involve multiple players, whereas others are more solitary. The social aspect of these games can play as much a role in gaining potential beneficial effects as the more cognitive aspects. This can also be true for jobs and occupations, as one study suggested that jobs that have a "people-oriented" component, meaning one interacts with people often and in challenging and rewarding ways, may actually help lower one's risk for later developing certain types of dementia.[11]

Thus, as Maya Angelou said, "I recite poetry all the time, and I also teach poetry, but I think everything keeps you sharp—talking to another human being keeps you sharp!"[12]

Use It or Lose It? Hard to Evaluate It

Our jobs often provide the stimulation that keeps us working hard—using our brains in ways that keep us busy and might also keep us sharp. What happens when we stop working in a demanding profession, or retire without a plan in place to keep our brains active and stimulated? This brings up the "use-it-or-lose-it" hypothesis—if we keep our brain active through intellectual pursuits, we can maintain our brain reserve and buffer against potential cognitive decline later in life. Of course, tackling this question is difficult—it is hard to randomly assign people to different types or levels of intellectual engagement and then to observe long-term changes, but a few studies have addressed this issue with some success.

In a longitudinal study, researchers examined the hypothesis that maintaining intellectual engagement through participation in everyday activities may provide a buffer against cognitive decline in later life.[13] They found a relationship between changes in intellectually related activities and changes in cognitive functioning such that when people did fewer intellectually related tasks, there were negative changes in cognitive skills. These results are consistent with the hypothesis that intellectually engaging activities serve to protect individuals against decline, but again, an alternative hypothesis is that high-ability individuals lead intellectually active lives until cognitive decline in old age limits their activities. Thus, it is hard to know what causes what—there could just be people who are good at seeking out activities that help their brain, not necessarily that the activities are themselves brain training.

In an analysis of the "use-it-or-lose-it" perspective, Professor Tim Salthouse, who has studied cognitive aging for over 40 years, suggests that while it is widely believed that keeping mentally active will prevent age-related mental decline, there is no direct evidence to support this notion. What would be needed is a long-term study that had people do stimulating mental activities for several decades and compared their later-life mental acuity to that of people who didn't do stimulating activities during this same time period. This type of study has never been done, and it would be difficult to conduct, as it is near impossible to ensure that people never engage in stimulating activates over a several-decade period, or to have control over what activities people do over this time period. Despite the lack of this type of large-scale, rigorous research design, there may be benefits in endorsing a view that mental exercise can help. Salthouse[14] suggests that people should continue to engage in mentally stimulating activities, because even if there is not yet evidence that they have beneficial effects in slowing the rate of age-related decline in cognitive functioning, there is also no evidence that such activities have any harmful effects. And if the activities are enjoyable they thus contribute to a higher quality of life, and engagement in cognitively demanding activities serves as "existence proof": if you can still do it, you know that you have not (yet) lost it. In addition, some research[15] suggests that if you have the "use-it-or-lose-it" perspective, then you are more likely to engage in cognitive strategies and activities to keep your mind sharp. Thus, our beliefs may guide us to work at keeping sharp.

Large-Scale Training Studies: Short-Lived Benefits, Need for Challenge and Creativity

One of the largest studies on cognitive training was aptly titled the "Advanced Cognitive Training for Independent and Vital Elderly (ACTIVE)" study.[16] Over a 10-year period, this study enrolled almost 3,000 volunteers (mostly in their 70s) divided into three training groups: one group that received memory training, another that received training in reasoning and speed of processing, and a control group that did not receive any training. The training groups participated in 10 hour-long sessions over 6 weeks. The study measured effects for each specific cognitive ability trained, immediately following the sessions and at 1, 2, 3, 5, and 10 years after the training. After 10 years, all groups showed declines from their baseline tests in memory, reasoning, and speed of processing—something that often tends to be seen with age on these types of tests. However, the participants who had training in reasoning and speed of processing experienced fewer declines than those in the memory and control groups. There was no difference in memory performance between the memory training group and the control group after 10 years. Thus, training in a variety of cognitive "laboratory-based" tasks did not seem to have any long-term benefits for things like finding one's keys, remembering names, or remembering where one put one's glasses, concerns we all have as we age.

How about more stimulating, mentally demanding skills, like learning about photography for the first time, compared to less demanding or more familiar activities, such as listening to classical music or completing word puzzles? Working outside your comfort zone might yield benefits. In one large-scale study,[17] researchers randomly assigned people ranging in age from 60 to 90 to engage in a particular type of activity for 15 hours a week over the course of 3 months. This is a substantial time commitment, much like a part-time job, in which some participants were assigned to learn a new skill—digital photography, quilting, or both—which required active engagement and challenged memory and other high-level cognitive processes. Other participants were asked to engage in more familiar activities at home, such as listening to classical music and completing word puzzles. In addition, to account for the possible influence of social contact, some participants were assigned to a social group that included social interactions, field trips, and entertainment. After 3 months, the researchers found that the adults who were productively engaged in learning new skills showed improvements in memory compared to those who engaged in social activities or non-demanding mental activities at home. The study is particularly noteworthy given that the researchers were able to systematically intervene in people's lives, putting them in new environments, training them with new skills, and exposing them to new relationships. Thus, the key seems to be trying something new that is challenging—there can be benefits over simply doing things your brain is familiar with, such that a new challenge can lead to far-reaching cognitive benefits (not to mention better photos and some nice quilts).

What if you don't like quilting or photography? One of the more creative ways to provide cognitive stimulation was developed by Professor Elizabeth Stine-Morrow. Her work examined how our choices about what activities we pursue and how we approach problems can determine the fate of our cognitive functioning as we age.[18] The program, called the "Senior Odyssey of the Mind," was built off the Odyssey of the Mind program, which gives younger students the opportunity for creative problem-solving in friendly, team-style competitions. Adapted for older adults, the Senior Odyssey program consisted of teams of adults over the age of 60 who took part in creative problem-solving over a 20-week period. In addition to measuring memory and cognitive performance at various points, there was also a tournament at the end of the season for the teams, who as a group were challenged to come up with creative solutions to ill-defined problems. After 2 years, people in the control group (who did not engage in creative problem solving) tended to show declines in cognitive abilities, whereas people on the problem-solving teams tended to show an increase in various cognitive tests of memory and reasoning. The Senior Odyssey approach combines creativity and social interaction and examines potential cognitive benefits from the experiences during the program. Engaging in creative activities, ranging from reading to debates, can have far-reaching benefits for older adults, and also can lead to greater openness to experience in old age.[19]

When Was the Last Time You Tried to Improve at Something?

> Unless you try to do something beyond what you have already mastered, you will never grow.
>
> —Ralph Waldo Emerson

Trying something new, and building on your prior expertise, can have many benefits, including changes in your brain. One study[20] found that "superagers," those in their 70s but whose memory abilities were like those of people 40 years younger, had preserved brain networks that supported attention and memory, as well as regions involved in emotional processing. Emotional processing might be needed to reach new goals and get past the conflict and frustration associated with trying new things. What is unclear is how these people became superagers. When asked about their cognitive and mental health, many reported that they worked hard at their job, as well as in their hobbies and other pursuits. Interestingly, often this hard work was not always pleasurable but quite challenging, leaving people feeling tired and frustrated. Some researchers[21] suggest that it is exactly this discomfort and frustration that means you are challenging yourself in ways that will pay off in the future, whether it is mental frustration or physical challenges that lead to brain and body benefits.

We always have the capacity to improve, and later in life we often have plenty of time and room for improvements. We can pick up music or sports that we played years or decades ago and try to become better at them. In his book *Late to the Ball*, former editor of *New York Times Magazine* Gerald Marzorati describes how he tried to become a better tennis player in his 60s, by learning the science of aging and through sheer practice, practice, practice.[22] As Marzorati writes in his summary of his book in the *New York Times*[23]:

> I took up tennis in my mid-50s. The nest was about to empty, and the weekend afternoons were beginning to yawn. I'd always been a tennis fan. With personal time on my hands, and a career winding down, I wanted to do . . . what? Something different and hard. Something that could counter the looming extended monotonies and

unpromising everydayness I imagined awaited me in retirement. Something that did not transpire in my head and at a desk, which is exactly where most of our lives unfold these days. I wanted to learn and get better at something that embodied life.

Many Steps to Successful Aging: Walking Rebuilds the Aging Brain

There is no one secret or silver bullet that protects us in old age from cognitive decline. However, probably the most surprising thing we can do to keep sharp is physical exercise. This has been repeatedly shown in over a decade of new research in a variety of settings. In one of the most rigorous and large-scale studies,[24] older adults were randomly assigned to a walking group (walking for 40 minutes, three times a week) or a stretching group (muscle-toning exercise for the same amount of time, but these activities are not highly aerobic). After 6 months and again 1 year later, the walking group outperformed the stretching group on various tests of memory and cognitive functioning. In addition, after 1 year, the older people who walked 40 minutes a day, three times a week, showed a 2% increase in the volume of the hippocampus, one of the main brain structures involved in memory. Typically, the volume of the hippocampus declines about 1% a year after the age of 50, so walking actually appears to even *reverse* the effects of aging. By getting large amounts of oxygenated blood to the brain (and circulating all of the body), one provides the nutrients that memory needs in large quantities. Whereas other activities, such as puzzles or video games, involve bringing blood to small and specialized areas of the brain involved in these tasks, walking or physical exercise brings waves of oxygenated blood to refresh the brain, leading to improvement in both brain activity and brain volume.

Another study found that these brain benefits were specific to older adults, as younger adults did not show similar improvements.[25] One reason is that older adults begin to show declines in the hippocampus, so they are the ones that need this training. Given that the hippocampus' volume declines by about 1% every year after the age of 50, an increase of 2% is a big deal. When people hear that walking can improve memory and leads to volumetric changes in the brain, they are often surprised. If the brain is like a muscle, then shouldn't brain exercises help? How can walking lead to changes in the brain? The simple answer is blood flow, although there are likely many reasons why walking helps. Any form of cardiovascular exercise leads to greater blood flow to the brain, bringing oxygen and nutrients; walking, biking, swimming, and dancing are all wonderful ways to reap the benefits.

For most people, walking is easy to do, and you don't need to be an athlete. That is also one reason it attracts research interest—the researcher can randomly assign people to a walking group (or a stretching group, which does not lead to the same benefits as walking), but perhaps not to an extreme biking or marathon running regimen! So, walking helps, as does any other cardiovascular form of exercise. Also, walking can have a social component if one walks with a partner or group or even a pet. Having someone to walk with can lead to greater motivation to walk, and talking while walking can lead to enhanced mental health, social support, and friendship. The comedian Ellen DeGeneres made this joke about the benefits of walking in older age: "My grandmother started walking five miles a day when she was sixty. She's ninety-seven now, and we don't know where the hell she is."[26]

There has been a lot of recent attention on how walking 10,000 steps a day can have health benefits, with people wearing electronic devices to monitor their steps. But you don't need to start with this large number of steps (which is about 5 miles). Barring any disability, there are relatively few impediments to walking, even bad weather. For instance, if you go to the local shopping mall (and especially in a city with colder weather) at 7 a.m., you won't see many shoppers, but you might see older adults walking. Mall-walking is a popular social and physical early-morning activity for many people who live in cold-weather climates. It has huge benefits and can be a great way for older adults to stay active safely, especially when there is snow and ice outside.

Walking Well into Old Age: Some Moving Keeps You Sharp

One commonality of many of the older adults who are in top mental shape is that they report exercising in various ways early in their life, in older age, or both. Often this involves walking, and this activity is well supported by the research discussed earlier. While coaching at UCLA, John Wooden would walk 5 miles a day around the track in the morning.

John Glenn, when in his mid-90s, told me that he walked often. He said:

> I prefer to do it every day and maybe take 1 day a week off. But I'm not breaking any speed records—I used to jog every day but I don't do that anymore. I've had a knee replacement and the other knee is still okay. But I do try to walk every day. And I don't do 2 miles every time but that's my goal and I usually do 2 miles. But it's not very fast. But it's enough that when I come back, if I have a light perspiration, my systems have all had to respond to that exercise. That's what you're trying to do, is keep your body limber and open and the tubes running.[27]

The author Jared Diamond regularly hikes while looking for birds, but the hikes are not as challenging or as long as they were when he was younger. The author and therapist Dr. Ruth walks a lot, but she also takes a car service. When it comes to sex, she says you should be as active as you can, but to also know your limits. As she has said, "You don't need to be hanging from the chandeliers."

The bottom line is that walking, one of the most primitive forms of movement and exercise, can improve your body and your mind, and may actually help you remember where you put your keys. So, the best way to find the fountain of youth may be to walk, and that will help you stay both physically fit and mentally sharp. If you need another reason, poor physical fitness ranks second only to smoking as leading risk factors for an early death. One large-scale study[28] with over 100,000 adults in middle and older age found that those in the higher levels of fitness had a 21% lower risk of death over 45 years of follow-up, even after taking into account other risk factors such as smoking, blood pressure, and cholesterol levels. Walking doesn't just help your memory, it helps you live longer.

Language as a Ladder: Scaffoldings to Build Up New Learning to Stay Sharp

Maya Angelou and Jared Diamond both reported learning new languages later in life. They found this to be a stimulating challenge, as well as having useful rewards if travelling to a new country. If you are already bilingual or multilingual, there is some evidence that this can offset dementia by 5 years,[29] although other work has not found substantial benefits of bilingualism.[30] The idea is that if you have access to multiple languages in your brain, you are constantly doing various mental gymnastics, or inhibitory tasks in which you access one language while inhibiting the others—this can be viewed as a useful mental exercise. For example, my multilingual father, when excited or tired, would yell or swear in his native French (which is how I learned French words that are not appropriate for print) as he struggled to quickly recall the needed English words. For him, it is nice to know there might be long-terms benefits from his language struggles over the years.

Learning a new language might be easier when you are young, as the critical period perspective would suggest, but this type of frustrating challenge may help older people stay sharp. For example, in his book *Flirting with French*, William Alexander writes about his struggles to learn French at age 57.[31] These challenges can have important benefits, even if you never become fluent, and in older age, learning a new language can be a building-block process. One effective method to learn aspects of a new language later in life involves connecting the new terms with the language you know well. In addition, being around people who speak another language can challenge you to learn. As I have several coworkers who are Japanese, I recently learned to count in Japanese. The first few numbers in Japanese sound to me like certain English words: *one* sounds like "itchy," *two* sounds like "knee," *three* sounds like "sun." So, now impress your friends by saying that you are learning Japanese, easy as itchy knee, son.

Down with Crosswords? The Case for and against Crosswords

One of the most common activities that people think should keep them sharp is mental word games, and the first one that people mention? Fill in the blanks: Cr_ssw_rds. However, few studies have directly examined this hypothesis, and these studies did not involve random assignment where some people are "forced" to do crosswords and others do some other comparable task, in order to determine any causal effect of doing crosswords on memory in older age. One study[32] found that people who had some lifelong experience doing crosswords developed dementia about 2.5 years later than those who reported not doing crosswords, but another study[33] found that reading, playing board games, playing musical instruments, and dancing were associated with a reduced risk of dementia, and crosswords had little impact.

Crossword puzzles can be very challenging, but with more experience at reading and solving word puzzles we get better at them. By doing more crosswords, you might become better at something you're already good at—so you are strengthening a strength, of recalling words that are often not used in conversation. As a result, some research suggests that doing crossword puzzles doesn't really challenge the aging brain to come up with novel insights or use reasoning skills and, for that matter, doesn't even help improve memory.[34] So, what might be happening is that one is strengthening an already strong area of cognition—word retrieval and vocabulary.[35] Compared to learning the name of a new person (a new association), crosswords give fragmented clues or cues to retrieve an already known word. So, if you really want to improve memory, crosswords may be low on the list if you are already doing well in this area. If you enjoy crosswords, that is the important thing, but you don't need to start doing them to ward off dementia, as a lot of other activities can help.

Can Playing Music Keep You ♯ Sharp?

As described earlier, listening to and playing music can elevate mood, and there is some evidence that music can help keep you sharp (pun intended). There are many examples of older musicians who rely on music to keep them stimulated, such as Arthur Rubinstein, a well-known pianist who performed until he was in his 90s, and Dave Brubeck, the jazz musician who could never retire. Conductors may have the most challenging job, as they need to read and anticipate the music, as well as coordinate the other musicians via hand gestures. Some research supports the notion that the demanding challenges experienced by leaders of an orchestra can have an effect such that older conductors perform as well as much younger adults on memory tests.[36]

In terms of musical instruments and training, playing the piano can lead to faster fingers (my 80-year-old father can still catch flies with his bare hands, likely because of his piano playing) and also better memory. Several studies have shown that people who have played a musical instrument at any point in their lives for a prolonged period show better memory for verbal material, as well as spatial skills.[37] In addition, playing a wind instrument, like the clarinet, can improve cardiovascular health in older adults, and the skills necessary for playing other instruments might also lead to health benefits. Making music social can have additive benefits. My father, who spent 65 years playing mostly classical piano, recently joined a jazz trio that makes him learn new styles and pieces, and this motivates him to meet with his group weekly to play.

Music can influence one's mood. Music is now used as a tool for therapy in a variety of settings. Jared Diamond reports that listening to the Bach cantatas (having played and memorized them) is a very stimulating but also relaxing experience. In one study, when older adults listened to classical music (an excerpt from Vivaldi's *Four Seasons*), they later performed better on a memory task, compared to older adults who listened to white noise or no music.[38] Music and dance can lead to improvements in memory as well, via the same mechanisms that result in the benefits of walking. Incorporating social aspects, such as playing music in a band, listening to music in a social setting, or dancing, can be beneficial, instead of listening to music while sedentary or in solitude. Thus, there are a variety of ways in which music can keep us sharp, improve our mood, and enhance memory.

Is Lifelong Learning a Path to a Sharper Mind?

If you ask a college student why they are in college, answers would likely include "to learn," "to get a good job," or "to become a lawyer or doctor." However, it is unlikely that they will answer, "to ward off dementia when I am older" or "to keep me sharp when I retire." Research has often shown that there is a strong link between level of education and cognitive performance, as well as the likelihood of developing Alzheimer's disease.[39] Basically, the more education you have, the less your chance of developing dementia. Again, this is a hard question to address experimentally, as you can't randomly assign some people to get a PhD and others to drop out of high school. There are many reasons people do or do not continue with their education, but the findings are very clear, even after taking into account differences in people's income, parental achievement, gender, physical activity, and age: people with more education are less likely to get dementia. Also, over the last few decades, the rates of Alzheimer's disease have actually been on a slight decline, according to a large-scale 2017 study conducted in the United States with over 20,000 Americans.[40] While the reason for this surprising decline is unclear, one possibility is that people are obtaining more education. In this large study, the older Americans had one more year of schooling than older Americans in 2000, and years of education were associated with decreased dementia risk in this study, as has been found in many others.

While formal education matters a lot, one can also make up for earlier life educational disadvantages by engaging in stimulating activities or jobs. One of the largest studies surveyed more than 7,000 people ranging in age from 25 to 74. The researchers found that into middle age and beyond, people could make up for a lack of schooling in various ways.[41] Those who said that they regularly challenged their brains, by reading, writing, attending lectures, or doing puzzles, performed better on tests of intelligence.

What may be most promising is that it was those people with the fewest years of schooling who showed the greatest benefits. The middle-aged people who had left school early but began working on keeping their minds sharp in other ways had substantially better memory and faster calculating skills than those who did not report doing cognitively challenging activities. These middle-aged people who worked hard at learning, reading, and writing performed as well as people up to 10 years younger than them, and in some cases, their scores were comparable to those of college graduates. Thus, formal education matters, but a desire to learn can make up for lost time in school.

There were some common themes among those older adults who had higher education and performed well into old age. These people said that they exercised frequently and were socially active; they frequently met with friends and family and volunteered; they were better at remaining calm in the face of stress; and they felt more in control of their lives. This research shows that a desire to learn may slow the negative aspects of aging by a decade. In addition, there is no deadline for completing a college degree: in 2007, Nola Ochs became the oldest person to complete a college degree, at age 95. She was able to graduate at the same ceremony as her 21-year-old granddaughter, Alexandra Ochs.[42]

Basketball coach John Wooden once said, "When I am through learning, then I am through." This illustrates his lifelong commitment to education and learning for his players, himself, and his family. As a proud grandfather, he hung old report cards from his grandchildren on the walls and enthusiastically talked about various great-grandchildren pursuing undergraduate and graduate degrees. Former astronaut and Senator John Glenn took great pride that his grandson Daniel had completed a PhD in clinical psychology. Glenn even read his thesis, but told me that there were a lot of terms and jargon that he wasn't familiar with.

Today, we are entering a golden age of self-directed learning, as evidenced by many online learning platforms. Self-guided learning can keep people active, and the Web enables us to learn a lot on our own, with sources ranging from YouTube videos to the more structured Khan Academy and Duolingo. But what makes us want to learn, and does this change with age? Older adults often use various learning platforms to learn new languages, whereas younger adults tend to want to learn for specific goals (such as travelling to a foreign country, or learning skills for a job). While people often report interest in learning a new language, having an upcoming trip to a foreign country where one actually wants or needs to learn some new vocabulary will make one learn it. According to one report,[43] those people who studied languages because they had an upcoming trip to a new country learned the most, whereas people studying simply for personal interest learned the least. So having a plane ticket for an upcoming trip can be good motivation to learn.

The Bigger the Better? What Is the Effect Size of Beneficial Activities?

While there is a long list of what people can and should do to stay mentally sharp, it is unrealistic to actually do all of them. It is important to know just how much some certain activity will help.

The key is to focus on the effect size—how much of a relative impact each of these activities might have on brain health. The impact something has on one's day-to-day life can be related to the effect size. We need to consider just how much of an effect something has before we adopt it as something that might work.

People often look to new research to guide them, especially if this involves consuming something they enjoy already. Red wine would be a great silver bullet, but the long-term effects of prolonged alcohol consumption can be deleterious to one's general health. Blueberries sound good—a healthy fruit, full of antioxidants, and we can consume them while sitting on the couch—too good to be true? However, unless you are missing key nutrients in your diet, this will likely not have an appreciable benefit, meaning it won't make you find your keys in the morning or help you remember names of people you just met. Again, the key is to focus on the effect size—how much of a relative impact, in this case, blueberries might have on your brain health. For example, the health benefit of eating organic food versus nonorganic food is likely minute if you are already smoking a pack of cigarettes a day. The benefits of crosswords might be small if you already have an impressive vocabulary. So it might be best to strengthen a weakness, and if you do, take on something that can pack the biggest punch in terms of helping your brain.

By and large, physical exercise has had the most meaningful observed effect on memory. Walking has been shown to have a large and lasting effect, and there may even be a dose–response curve, such that the more you do it, the bigger the effect (to a certain point), something that is likely not the case for crosswords, drinking red wine, and, sadly, eating more chocolate (something we can predictably say would lead to weight gain). Walking also has many other benefits: reducing heart disease, diabetes, and cancer, not to mention being a way to keep weight in check. The same approach can be true for things that might improve sleep and nutrition, as these areas can affect brain health in meaningful and substantial ways. Thus, the effect size—the magnitude to which the activity can actually help you—is important to pay attention to so you can reap the sizable benefits and not get caught up in smaller effects.

There are studies (mostly using mice) showing that the flavonoids in red wine and chocolate can be beneficial for memory, but you would need to consume large amounts of red wine, or seven bars of chocolate, a day[44]—clearly not a practical thing to help you in general. And sometimes the news is just too good to be true, but people will want to believe it, like the idea that chocolate can lead to weight loss.

A journalist (who also holds a PhD) made up a bit of fictitious "junk" science (with a headline of "Chocolate Can Make You Lose Weight") just to see how the media would react, and react it did.[45] Thus, you need to be a critical consumer of science (and chocolate), otherwise you might just be eating too much chocolate without much benefit.

Social Support (not Web Support) Can Influence Longevity

One of the best ways to stay active is to have a social network. With age, our social networks tend to shrink in size, but this doesn't necessarily lead to loneliness. Instead, older adults are more likely to invest in more meaningful relationships. In 1965, a classic large-scale longitudinal study[46] followed residents in Alameda County, California over a 9-year period. People who lacked social and community ties were more likely to die during this period than those with more extensive contacts. More impressively, this study accounted for self-reported physical health at the start of the survey, socioeconomic status, and health practices such as smoking, alcoholic beverage consumption, obesity, physical activity, and use of preventive health services. Loneliness may be a silent killer, such that chronic loneliness poses as large a risk factor for long-term physical health and longevity as cigarette smoking.

Rates of loneliness among older adults are growing, and loneliness can lead to depression. While some people might suggest that phone calls, Skype, social media, or email can fill this void, research[47] has shown that "real person" contact is needed. Researchers found that only face-to-face interaction forestalled depression in older adults. Phone calls made a difference to people with a history of mood disorders but not to anyone else. Email and texts had no impact at all. However, how often people got together with friends and family was the _most_ telling factor, and the more in-person contact there was on a day-to-day basis, the less likelihood there was of developing future depression. Most critically, those older people who reported that they had face-to-face contact with their children, friends, and family only every few months had the highest levels of depression, whereas those who met with people in person at least three times a week had the lowest rates of depression. Though children and grandchildren may provide loving social support, sometimes the best support comes from friends who are of similar age with similar age-related challenges and pleasures in life. In addition, being around others who have different opinions can lead to lively debates and useful social interactions and can enable new learning. Staying sharp involves staying connected—and not to the Internet. Facebook can give the illusion of having hundreds or thousands of online friends, but face-to-face contact keeps us alive and well at any age.

Volunteering in Older Age: The Benefits of Giving and Being Connected

> It is one of the beautiful compensations of life that no man can sincerely try to help another without helping himself.
> —Ralph Waldo Emerson

While we often focus on what we can do to improve our own cognitive health, ideally, these energies can also be directed at helping others, leading to mutual benefits. Volunteering can connect people with their community (a key social component) and involves both physical and cognitive challenges. Surprisingly, older adults are less likely to volunteer than their younger counterparts, but when seniors do volunteer, they commit more time to their volunteer activities than all other age groups. In the United States, almost 25% of people over the age of 65 said that they volunteered, spending on average 85 hours a year volunteering.[48] Volunteering can bring people together to accomplish something bigger than themselves, something people like John Glenn said are critical in terms of keeping active.

Research on the effects of volunteering on older adults can take many different forms. Studies often compare groups of people who have chosen to volunteer with those who do not volunteer, or have self-report measures that do not allow for random assignment. Many of these studies report beneficial effects such as feeling like part of a community, helping others, and contributing to the next generation, but they also report improvements in physical health.[49] One major study examined Experience Corps, a large volunteer program, to examine the benefits of volunteering among older adults.[50] Older adults were randomly assigned to either be on a wait list or volunteer, by working in public elementary schools across the country. On average, the volunteer commitment was

15 hours a week in kindergarten to grade 3 classrooms. The activities involved helping students with reading and teaching children conflict resolution through problem-solving and play. After several months, volunteers reported many positive benefits, such as greater happiness and life satisfaction. The active volunteers in this Experience Corps program showed improvements in various forms of memory. Also, volunteers said that they had met other volunteers, made new friends, and increased the number of people they could turn to for help. What may matter most is finding something where you feel you are needed, appreciated, and making a difference for other people.

Summary

There is no single activity that keeps us mentally sharp. We should do what we enjoy (and enjoy what we do), be it social interaction, physical movement, or mental challenges, as long as there is some benefit. Recalling poems can be relaxing. While we don't know if they ward off dementia, if proving that you can memorize poems lessens your anxiety and relaxes you, these might be benefits in themselves. Crossword puzzles may have similar effects, but there is no need to start doing them if you do not enjoy them. Music, learning, reading, and social connections are often an important element of staying sharp. Volunteering provides a connection to something meaningful and allows us to be part of something bigger than ourselves. Often, you are the best guide in choosing these activities. Choose something you are passionate about, as the challenge of doing something enjoyable can change your brain. The brain can produce a release of neurotransmitters when rewards are present, so if you find something rewarding, doing it can keep your brain sharp. The most effective activities combine being active, being social, and having some level of stimulation. Walking or other physical exercise is likely the best method to ensure brain and body health. Thus, while people tend to emphasize the ways in which the brain needs to be exercised, the best activities may involve physical exercise and social interactions, mixed with any cognitive activity that is rewarding and provides some challenge to stimulate your brain.

Brain Training:
Can Computer Games
Really Make Me Smarter?

I F YOU WANT TO GET YOUR BODY IN SHAPE, YOU MIGHT join a gym, go jogging, or maybe even get a personal trainer. But if you want to train your brain, what do you do? Practice mental gymnastics, do crossword puzzles, memorize poetry, or learn a new language? About 50% of all Americans believe games like Sudoku and crossword puzzles keep their brains healthy,[1] but as discussed in the previous chapter, there is not enough evidence to show that these types of puzzles help train the brain for more general types of memory challenges.

You might sign up for the latest computerized brain-training program that is tailored to your specific needs to maximize your brainpower. However, what if the answer to training the body was the same for training the brain? Despite the intuitive allure of stimulating computerized brain training, a large amount of research shows that physical exercise (such as walking) increases brain power, memory abilities, and even the size of the parts of the brain involved in memory.

People often say, "The brain is like a muscle, and it needs exercise," but this is only somewhat accurate. We know that there are no muscle fibers in the brain that actually need toning or strength training, but working the brain has its benefits. A more accurate saying might be, "The brain is an oxygen-hogging organ that needs oxygen, and physical exercise helps the brain get the fuel it needs." Although the human brain represents only 2% of our body weight, it receives 15% of the cardiac output, 20% of total body oxygen consumption, and 25% of total body glucose utilization.[2] Our big, demanding, curious brains are addicted to problem-solving, glucose, and oxygen. Our brains do amazing things, and how we use them matters. Getting better at one type of spatial computer game might not make us better at other spatial challenges in our lives, such as finding our keys or where we parked the car.

Today, when people refer to "brain training" it usually involves the latest virtual reality game or computer-based simulation that is adapted to a user's level and challenges the person, all while he or she is seated on their couch or at the computer desk. The user gets feedback about their performance, sees what level they could achieve, and becomes addicted. Despite the evidence that physical exercise can improve brain health, many people feel that mental activity, in the form of computer-based brain training, can, and should, yield big benefits. But what is the evidence?

People spend billions of dollars on various brain-training tools. Given that the stakes are high, and finding an effective (if not simply popular) brain game is much like the pharmaceutical industry finding ways to prevent dementia, we need to be critical consumers. What did we do before brain-training technology like this was available? The more traditional (and likely less expensive) activities might be just as effective, such as birdwatching, balancing a bank account, or even just reading a book.

Why Is Brain Training Considered the Future?

The use of computer technology and the Internet can help provide training programs and techniques that in the past were not easily available. As a result, there has been an explosion of computer-based brain games, many with claims that playing them can improve your memory and even your intelligence, and make your brain younger.

The promise of all of these brain game products, either implied or sometimes quite explicit, is that this type of brain training can make you smarter. But again, what is the evidence? While brain training may be the way of the future, many scientists are very cautious about interpreting what little evidence might support this endeavor, and there is wide debate about brain-training efficacy in its current state.

A statement released by the Stanford University Center on Longevity and the Berlin Max Planck Institute for Human Development said that there is no solid scientific evidence to back up this promise.[3] Signed by 70 of the world's leading cognitive psychologists and neuroscientists, the statement is very clear in its message:

> The strong consensus of this group is that the scientific literature does not support claims that the use of software-based "brain games" alters neural functioning in ways that improve general cognitive performance in everyday life, or prevent cognitive slowing and brain disease.

Recently, the U.S. Federal Trade Commission (FTC) fined the company behind the brain-training program Lumosity $50 million (eventually settled for $2 million) for deceptive advertising.[4] Lumosity sold game subscriptions to its 70 million customers (ranging from monthly payments of $14.95 to lifetime memberships for $299.95), and marketed the games as tools to keep the brain sharp and healthy. But the FTC said the program "preyed on consumers' fears about age-related cognitive decline," and it "simply did not have the science to back up its ads." People are very drawn toward a game that can help them avoid memory decline, but the effectiveness still needs to be shown.

Some suggest that brain training may work, and some scientists feel that it is not constructive to be overly critical of the brain-training endeavor as a whole. In response to the Stanford–Max Planck Institute statement, a letter signed by many leading scientists (many of whom are deeply invested in brain-training research industries and start-up companies) was issued. This response letter states that we should remain open-minded about the results and promises that brain training may be able to deliver in the future. As a result, there may be considerable funding from brain-training companies to find ways to support the claim that brain training is scientifically proven.

Brain Training Studies: Some Failure to Find Transfer (or Where You Put Your Keys)

The Holy Grail for brain-training programs is to improve memory and attention enough to make a marked difference in your life. The goal is to first train people on simple and engaging puzzles, have them advance gradually to more complex puzzles, and then demonstrate improvement in performance on these puzzle tasks. Finally, if they are really training memory, they should see improvement in other memory-related challenges, such as remembering names, where they put their keys, and to take their medications. So far, brain training works for getting a person better at the task they are doing—the game aspects. But if brain training is actually training memory, and not just making you better at the specific game you are playing, then there should be transfer of memory improvements to other games. This means that after you get better at the brain-training puzzles, other aspects of memory should also be improved, such that you are also better at remembering names, where you put your keys, and taking medications, and in general you feel sharper. Interestingly, people do report "feeling" sharper. As of yet, there has been no evidence of real transfer to other tasks that people really care about. And there have been a lot of very large and expensive studies that have looked for such a result.

In one of the largest studies,[5] conducted in the UK, over 11,000 people were trained in a 6-week online study. They engaged in the brain training from home several times each week, by doing various computer-based cognitive tasks that were designed to improve reasoning, memory, planning, visual spatial skills, and attention. People got better at these tasks and showed improvements in every one of the cognitive tasks that they were trained on, but no evidence was found for transfer effects to untrained new tasks, even when those tasks were cognitively closely related. While other approaches and programs suggest some evidence for the efficacy of brain training for older adults,[6] it is still unclear whether these benefits lead to improvements in everyday memory challenges.

Although most brain training focuses on memory and attention, a skill that may respond well to brain training is the ability to ignore distractions, or filter out irrelevant information (like that annoying fire engine siren I hear as I type this sentence). In one breakthrough and highly publicized study,[7] researchers led by professor and entrepreneur Adam Gazzaley trained a sample of older adults in a custom video game called "Neuroracer." Neuroracer is designed to strengthen the ability to filter out distractions while driving. Using a video game platform, the player's goal is to steer the car on a windy road with one hand while using the other hand to shoot down only signs of a particular color and shape, ignoring other signs. This is certainly a challenging and engaging task. Participants played Neuroracer or a control task several hours a week over a month-long period—a lot of driving practice in a very challenging video game. Demonstrating practice and training effects, participants in the study showed improvements in the driving-and-ignoring-distractions game, to the point that some of the older adults improved to the level of a 20-year old, a very impressive training effect. Gazzaley explained that the long-term goal for this type of game training is to "become the world's first prescribed videogame."[8]

While substantial training is needed to see any improvements, many of the improvements are seen only on tasks that are similar to the ones people were initially trained in. This is known as "near transfer": our skills only translate to other video game–based tasks of a similar variety, but we don't become better drivers in the real world as a result of playing these types of driving games. Also, we need to spend our time wisely: if I have been driving a car for hours, I would hope that at the very least I would arrive at the Grand Canyon, or some other interesting destination, to reward me for the long drive!

Although it is likely still too early to know if there are any benefits of brain training in its current state, there are perhaps certain skills that people can learn through brain training that are useful in the real world. In terms of real driving behavior (an activity that can decline with age simply due to sensory changes and slower reaction times), researchers have shown that the amount of information one can attend to in one's visual environment, a measure known as "useful field of view," can improve through training on various visual-attention and driving tasks in older adults.[9] More recent work has shown some long-term benefits of training in divided attention, to help make older adults better behind the wheel.[10] In some ways, this may be the type of thing we want to be able to train, to improve safety for people of all ages (until we have self-driving cars, something that will be extremely helpful for older adults).

In general, we need to ask ourselves if there are costs to playing these brain games, especially if the benefits are unclear or unsupported. The challenge of all of these games is that they are often sedentary and involve large amounts of screen time, factors which then present a trade-off with time for physical exercise, which has been proven to lead to cognitive benefits. More screen time necessarily requires the sacrifice of the proven benefits of non-sedentary physical activity, such as walking. A large review of all the past and current relevant research came to a similar conclusion[11] and suggested that more research is needed to determine just how computer-based brain training can lead to any observable memory benefits.

Beliefs about Brain Training: Why They Might Help and Hurt Us

As it turns out, most of us are quite optimistic about the promise of brain training. A recent study[12] found that even highly educated and critically minded people have relatively high expectations about the potential of brain exercises to improve cognitive functions such as memory, concentration, and performance in everyday activities. These high expectations do not necessarily decrease with adverse reports. Older adults may be especially prone to this favorable bias and report that their own intuition is the primary factor guiding their positive beliefs and attitudes regarding brain training.

What might be influencing these expectations? Optimism surrounding brain-training software may stem from the "technology effect," where people generally expect technology to generate success. One study[13] showed that people are more likely to invest in technology industries and that they implicitly associate technology—particularly new technologies—with success. The brain-training industry fits well within this concept and draws on the relative novelty of neuroscience and the idea that the brain's structure and activity can change in response to lifestyle activities. These findings gave birth to the term *neuroplasticity*—a favorite catchphrase of brain-training companies—and encouraged the development of technology-based interventions that showed initial success in certain populations, such as children and adults with attention deficit/hyperactivity disorder (ADHD) and some older adults. Mostly, we seem to believe in the promise of brain training because we wish it to be true.

Expectations motivate us and may account for at least some of the benefits that are achieved through computer-based brain training. Recent work has shown that people perform better on intelligence tests if they expect brain-training games to help them. Some studies showing that brain-training games are effective may be inherently biased, due to selecting participants who want or *expected* to get smarter by playing brain games. Researchers designed a study[14] to test whether expectation for a positive effect can lead to a positive outcome—namely, whether a placebo effect may be at play in many brain-training programs. The researchers put up flyers around their campus inviting students to take part in a research study. Half of the flyers were highly descriptive, stating that the study was about "Brain Training" and "Cognitive Enhancement." The other half were standard, generic ads that simply said "participate in a psychology study." All of the people who participated in the experiment first took a pre-test to measure their baseline intelligence (similar to an IQ test). They all then played a challenging game that was designed to engage and train memory, as had been shown in prior research.[15] The next day, the participants returned to the lab for a second intelligence test. The participants who had responded to the suggestive flyer advertising "Brain Training" and "Cognitive Enhancement" showed improvement on the second intelligence test amounting to a 5- to 10-point increase on a standard IQ test. The group who responded to the more bland and benign advertisement, however, showed no improvements, even though *both* groups did exactly the same testing and training task. The enhanced performance of the clearly labeled "Brain Training" group shows the powerful nature of a positive placebo effect. Thus, the manner and message used when recruiting people for these types of studies can influence how people perform in them. It may often be the case that brain-training studies attract the type of people who expect benefits from brain training (like most of us would hope for if we were spending our time in one of these studies). This is another example of how our expectations can influence our brain abilities, and there might be good reason to have hope that brain training really works.

In general, our beliefs can play a big role in whether we see benefits—having a positive mindset makes a big difference. If we think we can improve, then we can and will, especially if that is what we expect from a study or training program (even if we don't enjoy transfer or near-transfer to other tasks). It is important to note that this study was conducted on a college campus with younger adults, so it remains to be seen if a similar finding holds true for older adults. I would believe it does in many settings. At UCLA, many older adults come to our memory lab to stay sharp, and our studies may seem to them to be stimulating and a form of brain training. These studies are not designed to actually improve memory but simply to test people on various memory and attention tasks. The testing component in and of itself may make people believe in the powers of brain training. In our studies at UCLA, almost all of the older adults I talk to want to do something to boost their brain power, and that is one reason why they come and participate in our research on memory.

Can Brain Training Be Brain Draining?

Despite many research studies showing that physical exercise improves memory for all ages, most people still believe that they will improve their memory with computer-based brain training. It certainly can help to learn a new language or become better at certain tasks that involve vigilance or attention. But there could also be a huge cost, and not just the financial cost of choosing these games over exercise.

As mentioned earlier, the biggest cost of computer-based brain training may be an increase in screen time. Playing computer-based brain games could come at the expense of doing other important activities, some that might actually help you, like physical exercise. In fact, the more you play these games, the less likely you are to have time to be physically active, and the end result could, in fact, be poorer memory and mental fitness—exactly what one wanted to avoid in the first place. There are other benefits of reducing screen time. A recent study[16] showed that sixth-graders who spent 5 days at outdoor camps without using or seeing a smartphone, TV, or other digital screen were better at reading the emotions of others around them (something that older adults are quite adept at) than kids who had constant access to electronic devices. The irony is that engaging in brain training might reduce your time for other activities that could train your brain more.

So, in terms of keeping our brains sharp, which do *you* think is more important, stimulating brain activities or physical exercise?

Some research[17] has tested these two choices in mice. One group was raised in a cage with lots of stimulating toys to play with, such as tunnels, balls, and mirrors. The other mice didn't have the toys but had a running wheel in their cage, which they used regularly and on a voluntary basis (perhaps they were that bored). Most people would think that the stimulating environment would lead to much more brain development, compared to the sparse environment that only had an exercise wheel. After several months of living in these very different environments, the mice that had access to the running wheels showed large improvements on spatial memory tests, as well as the creation of new brain cells (neurogenesis), in some cases more so than the mice raised with all the toys. One view of how these two different environments or lifestyles influence brain health is that the stimulating environment helps to protect and maintain current brain cells, whereas physical activity actually aids in the creation of new brain cells. This doesn't happen just for younger mice raised in different cages. Older mice showed similar benefits of physical exercise on the creation of new brain cells, which suggests that getting physical exercise in older age can actually reverse some of the age-related decline in older brains.[18] Having a running wheel had an important effect on the mice in terms of new brain cells and better memory. When told about this research finding, one older adult jokingly exclaimed: "Where can I find such a wheel!"[19] Thus, while having lots of stimulating toys and games can be very stimulating and appealing, physical exercise can make a big difference for both your brain and your body.

Now Read This: Reading Makes Us Sharper and More Socially Aware

> Reading is to the mind what exercise is to the body.
> —Joseph Addison (English essayist, poet, playwright, and politician)

Mystery novels and television shows capture audiences' attention and can provide useful exercises for the brain. Reading detective novels such as *Sherlock Holmes*, listening to a baseball broadcast on the radio, or watching *CSI: Crime Scene Investigation* or *Murder She Wrote* (depending on your generation) might have been the precursors to modern-day brain training. While many older adults are curious about video game–based brain training, the more common brain training they engage in is reading, often done over a lifetime. John Wooden was an avid reader of biographies, such as those of Benjamin Franklin and Winston Churchill, and often read books as a treat for his brain. Recent research supports the notion that reading influences our thought processes and is a very potent form of brain training. Professor Keith Oatley, an expert in the field of reading, compared reading to being in a flight simulator: "You experience a lot of situations in a short span of time, far more so than if we went about our lives waiting for those experiences to actually happen to us."[20] While reading may be a solitary activity, unlike many video games, reading may, in fact, make us more socially aware. Oatley suggests that books are much like life simulators in that they allow us to see ourselves in someone else's position, to take other people's perspectives and figure out why certain characters in books behave the way they do, and to consider what would happen if we did the same in our own world.

Some studies have linked how much people read (as measured by the number of authors they know) with empathy and the ability to interpret the mental states, feelings, and emotions of others when shown photographs of faces in different emotional states.[21] These studies suggest that those who read more are better at interpreting social cues in their environment and, ultimately, better at understanding others. While we might think of people who are bookworms as some sort of stereotype (a loner wearing glasses, sitting in the corner reading while others are playing), reading as brain training might lead to better emotional processing of situations. Thus, a lifetime of reading can have benefits in terms of social intelligence— something that can often get better with age.

Warren Buffett estimates that he spends as much as 80% of his day reading.[22] Lifelong reading, especially in older age, may be one of the secrets to preserving mental ability. Reading this book may actually help you, though fiction may be better for social intelligence. In one study,[23] researchers tested almost 300 older adults' memory and thinking ability every year for 6 years, and the participants answered questionnaires about their reading and writing habits, from childhood to their current age. After the participants' deaths (at an average age of 89), the researchers examined their brains for evidence of the physical signs of dementia, which typically include lesions, plaques, and neural tangles, the brain abnormalities often associated with memory lapses. Those people who reported that they read were protected against brain lesions and tangles and self-reported memory decline over the 6-year study. In addition, remaining a bookworm into old age reduced memory decline by more than 30%, compared to engaging in other forms of mental activity. Those who read the most had the fewest physical signs of dementia (of course, it could be for this reason that they kept reading later in life). However, those who read less often later in life did much worse, as their memory decline was almost 50% faster than that of people who spent an average amount of time reading. Reading challenges your brain, and now you have another reason to keep reading this book!

Reading is a form of brain training that begins early in life, and growing up in a household that has books can lead to big benefits. Books can be both enjoyable and powerful learning devices, especially for children. One large-scale study[24] conducted over 20 years found that people who grow up in a house that has books are more likely to achieve higher education, something that is related to higher income and better cognitive function later in life. This study found that regardless of income or education level, parents who have more books in the home will have children with higher levels of education, relative to parents who have fewer books in the home. Children growing up in homes with many books average 3 years more schooling than that of children from bookless homes, independent of their parents' education, occupation, and class. Also, while having a large, 500-book library at home was associated with children achieving more education, even having a small collection of books made a difference. The point is not simply to have many books but to read them, and having access to books leads to reading. Thus, starting at an early age, exposure to books and reading can lead to good things for your brain later in life.

Returning to Our Roots: Reading, Writing, and Typing?

I often joke that the most important class I took in high school (way back in 1990) was typing. I was part of perhaps the last cohort to use a typewriter to learn to type, and that skill has served me well.

Learning to type helps us use computers (a reason many children now learn to type), but learning to write by hand helps us even more. While learning to write using a keyboard has practical value, learning to write with a pen, using printing or cursive, has personal value (a handwritten note conveys more appreciation and better identification of a handwriting style) as well as cognitive benefits in terms of both creativity and comprehension. While many people might not write as fast as they type (surprising but not uncommon in today's university students), taking notes by hand may challenge you much more to write down the more important information, instead of the rote recording of a court stenographer, typing word for word what a teacher is saying without trying to first understand it, digest it, and then selectively write down the main points. Some renowned writers, including Pulitzer prize–winning author and geographer Jared Diamond, will often abstain from typing and computer use and write by hand in order to write more coherently and creatively.

While there are many stereotypes of older adults who avoid technology and computers, many older adults are computer literate and Internet savvy, using email and searching the Web. On the other hand, there are also many older adults who are intimidated by the Internet and don't use it in the same manner as younger adults. As middle-aged adults get older, new technology will replace what they have learned—often in work environments—making it harder to incorporate the usefulness of more modern technology. Also, some apps and websites aren't useful for an older adult, who may not find the need to use Twitter or Facebook, or find them to be an overly informal or impersonal way of communicating. And yet John Glenn, who travelled into space at age 77, described how, in his older age, he enjoyed using Internet-assisted devices on long road trips or his OnStar service in his car to find hotels and for travel assistance.

As we age, we certainly shouldn't avoid using computer technology. Some research[25] shows that older men who use computers have a lower risk of developing dementia, although there is not yet any evidence for a causal connection. In addition, other work shows that older adults who are familiar with the Internet show significant brain activity when engaging in Internet searches, above and beyond the activity that is present when simply reading books.[26] Younger adults often have jobs that involve sitting in front of a computer and conducting Internet searches, and as a result may overuse computers for both professional and personal and social purposes. This overuse can lead to being sedentary and having a Facebook-fueled illusion of social activity.

Older adults are also using the Internet, as recent statistics[27] suggest that 6 out of 10 older adults go online regularly, and 3 out of 4 have cell phones. Among the older adults who use the Internet, 71% go online every day or almost every day. Older adults may report that the Internet enables them to search for vast amounts of information and find old friends, but to also reminisce about the days of hard-copy encyclopedias. But older adults also don't know whether to trust everything on the Web, such as rapidly updated blogs, and many don't understand the constant need to download new software and updates. In addition, emails and websites can be the source of many scams for older adults.

Older adults will also actively seek to connect with family using the Internet, often through FaceTime or Skype, but may still enjoy the simplicity, familiarity, and genuine nature of phone calls over a barely readable "txt msg." Keep in mind, the computer world recycles terms that may initially confuse an older person; for example, *window, tablet, cookie,* and *mouse* all had different meanings 40 years ago. Older adults may experience interference or confusion as to what these words' new meanings are, as they might actually know what a tablet was historically (or the pill form of a tablet), not just the computer version that my children only know about. In some instances we may even be turning back the clock, finding benefits to not having laptops used in classrooms, or banning the use of cell phones during school hours. Some schools that have banned cell phone use have done so in order to see better academic results.[28] Technology isn't bad, if we use it to make us better, not just lazier. In general, and especially in older age, using technology in an appropriate manner is the key, in terms of both time and money well spent.

Competition Can Fuel Us: Compete against a Friend, Yourself, or Your Age Group

People often enjoy a little friendly competition, even when it may simply involve competing against themselves. Competition can motivate people at any age. We often make social comparisons, comparing ourselves to others in our social class, in terms of jobs, income, and other forms of productivity or levels of happiness. We also make personal comparisons—I weigh more now than I did 10 years ago, and I would like to lose weight; I don't run as fast as I used to, but I would now to like to run a marathon with a friend. We can also compare ourselves to our parents at the same age and set goals of being like them, or not, in order to achieve health. While many people engage in activities for their sheer pleasure or enjoyment, often we need a goal or some friendly competition to motivate us.

Today, there are many ways we can set goals coupled with technology, such as measuring how fast we run, or heart rates, and the number of steps we take a day. Right now, I can run faster than my children, although I still sometimes let them win. But there will come a time in my life when they will run faster than me—and this is a good thing. We should not always compete against our younger selves or counterparts but rather our current cohort, and we should only seek maintenance or improvement in our own ability when using our current selves as a comparison. Albert Bandura, the famous Stanford University social psychologist who studies self-efficacy, told me that when training for a marathon, we should compare ourselves to others in the same age range, not self-comparisons to our younger selves. Winning within your age group in a running race is a more realistic and meaningful goal than trying to win the entire race. He suggests we also should have some balance and engage in activities that we enjoy; he says he now spends a lot of time gardening and growing tomatoes. He said that he feels he is doing pretty well for his age, considering that he is now over 90.

It's only natural that we make social and personal comparisons. Often, older adults will say that their memory isn't as good as it used to be, but on the whole, they're doing pretty well compared to their friends of the same age group. In general, the best comparison may be to others in your own age cohort, and not against a younger generation. One reason computer-based brain training is popular is that it provides these types of comparisons. Brain training can sometimes take advantage of this by giving feedback about how well you are doing compared to people your own age, and also possibly reducing your brain age, sometimes even giving some estimate of your current "mental age." We would like to feel younger, or perhaps have our memory function like it did 20 years ago. This feedback can be compelling and rewarding, especially if it is a 75-year-old who is told that he is performing like a 55-year-old. However, I think that at age 40, I have more knowledge and insight than I did at age 20, so saying that you have a younger brain should not always be interpreted as a compliment.

Another form of comparison is to our own family history, a reason why so many people invest both time and money in brain training. We often will compare ourselves to our parents when thinking about our health as we age and envision our own future health. Knowledge of family history can motivate people to change their behavior. For example, my mother passed away at age 39 as a result of skin cancer. While I feel grateful to celebrate my fortieth birthday, this family history of skin cancer has made me concerned for my children growing up in sunny California. My father, who recently turned 80, still bicycles around the small city where I grew up, plays the piano, and works full-time. Looking at our own family can make us aware of the things we need to do to stay mentally sharp, and it can also make us realize how fortunate we are for every year that we are healthy.

We may know that avoiding things like extensive sun exposure or smoking can prevent cancer. We know that regular exercise can prevent cardiovascular disease. However, awareness of one's family history can make people engage in brain training to keep their brain sharp. This may be especially true if a family member suffered from dementia. They have seen what has happened to senile parents and loved ones and want to know what they can do for themselves today to stay sharp. This comparison and concern may make some people more inclined to seek out a healthier lifestyle, but at the same time, also more prone to engage in computer-based brain training that may not always be effective.

Brain Training around the House: Dinner, DIY, or Call Someone Who Can Help?

There are no shortages of brain-challenging things to do every day, so we don't need to seek out video games to stimulate our brain. While we have many routines and habits in place in our daily lives, often we encounter new challenges. For example, we notice that the car is making a funny noise, or that the roof is leaking, or that we are hungry and need to figure out what to have for dinner. These are all challenging problem-solving tasks, some more routine than others, but each requires rules and reasoning to solve a problem. Sometimes this involves calling someone who knows more about a specific domain (e.g., a mechanic or handyperson).[29] Sometimes we seek out resources to solve these problems ourselves, finding a good takeout restaurant we like, or making dinner with whatever we have in the refrigerator. Even if you aren't handy and know you are better off getting someone else to fix things around the house (sometimes that in itself is a sign of wisdom), knowing whom to call, getting a set of estimates, and figuring out the various options and ways to cut costs without compromising quality or what you want can all be challenging and a form of brain training.

Simply figuring out what to make for dinner or, on a grander scale, a kitchen renovation (even if you don't touch a single tool) can be a demanding activity to plan and see through from start to finish. In many cases, these activities of daily living can challenge our brain, so we should feel accomplished if we are successful in completing some simpler ones, like making dinner, but the more challenging ones (a new kitchen) should be especially rewarding.

Beyond around-the-house challenges, there are also a variety of social challenges that train your brain, such as figuring out whom to invite to a party, who gets along with whom, or even just incorporating the appropriate etiquette at various social settings. Thus, while we typically think of video game training or crossword puzzles as the elixir of brain training, there are plenty of challenges around the house and in your social world that could use your attention and brain time. The results are practical, useful, and sometimes very satisfying.

Brain Training, Blueberries, and Red Wine: No Big Benefits on Their Own?

Science has yet to deliver the silver bullet to stop cognitive decline, but if and when it does, people seem most responsive to discoveries that involve something quick and simple, preferably something they can do while sitting down and enjoying themselves: taking a pill, playing a game, eating something good, or drinking something they already enjoy. Blueberries, brain training, red wine, and chocolate might all fit this bill.

The notion that red wine consumption offers health benefits has come under fire, as some of the research was found to be "too good to be true." One prominent researcher actually fabricated the findings of red wine's "benefits" (or maybe the person had drunk too much red wine). While some studies found that mice who were given large doses of resveratrol were healthier and lived longer, an article in the *New York Times* pointed out that the average 150-pound person would need to drink 750 to 1,500 bottles of red wine a day in order to get the equivalent beneficial dose![30] One small study[31] found that when healthy people (between the age of 50 and 70) drank a mixture high in cocoa flavonols for 3 months, they performed better on a memory test than a control group of participants. My daughters love this study, and whenever I forget something they cheerfully say, "Daddy, we should eat some chocolate to help you remember." Clearly they are firm believers in this research finding. However, most commercial candy bars do not actually have enough real cocoa, or are processed so that the beneficial flavonols are rendered inactive.[32]

There certainly are good things in blueberries, chocolate, and red wine that, in theory, can help memory. However, in order to really show appreciable benefits, you would have to consume large amounts (almost seven bars of chocolate)—something that is appealing in some ways but, of course, would have other undesirable consequences (such as weight gain, or possibly detrimental effects of large amounts of alcohol consumption). Most of the studies do not actually give people chocolate or red wine but rather a concentrated cocoa drink or resveratrol pills. The truth is that preventing cognitive decline will likely involve a number of factors and treatments.

Simply because one thing may enhance memory or reduce the likelihood of dementia doesn't mean that that thing is counteracting the causal agent, unless it has a substantial impact on preventing cognitive decline. Even then, there likely is no way to know if this is what is causing dementia in general. The advice that exercise is good for your brain and your memory may be surprising to some people. We often think brain games should help our brain, whereas exercising our bodies is something that helps just our body. People also don't like hearing that they should exercise more. Nothing new there, as doctors recommend exercise often, although not specifically for staying sharp. Getting more exercise doesn't sound like a major scientific breakthrough, compared to discovering a new nutrient or treatment for remembering where you left your keys. Exercising your brain can be as simple as adding more physical exercise to your life.

Easy Learning = Fast Forgetting: Creating Challenges Can Have Long-Term Benefits

Sometimes a good challenge can be just what our brains need for training, and that challenge doesn't always need to come in the form of crossword puzzles or computer brain training. Brushing your teeth with your nondominant hand, or using the mouse with your nondominant hand can be very frustrating at first but also challenges your brain. The idea is that introducing small challenges can slow us down, but this can result in better learning. This notion is the basis behind what Drs. Robert and Elizabeth Bjork refer to as "desirable difficulties."[33] In the context of learning, beginners' errors and slowing down the learning process can challenge the learner, leading to more reinforced long-term memory. For example, first having to guess the answer to a trivia question before being told the answer can better ensure that you will remember the answer later. Desirable difficulties can help us to get better at something, but this approach can seem somewhat counterintuitive. Typically, we want learning to be fast and easy, but often *easy* learning leads to *fast* forgetting. Creating challenges or obstacles that can be conquered can be a useful way to train the brain and challenge us in various domains, such as learning a language, how to play a musical instrument, or how to play a sport. The desirable-difficulty approach has also been incorporated into balance training so that encountering more challenging terrain, such as slightly uneven floors or cobblestones,[34] may be beneficial training for better balance.

Try Everything? Put It All Together for Big Benefits

Since physical exercise has been shown to improve brain health and memory, are there benefits to simultaneously combining exercise with brain training? This approach, referred to as "exer-game training," has been tested in an innovative study[35] in which older adults played interactive physical-activity video games that were designed to engage both mental processes and physical activity together. After 24 one-hour sessions, older adults showed benefits in measures of both physical function and several cognitive measures, which suggests that this approach may be a useful avenue for improving brain health. Although it is unclear what led to the benefits of this "exer-gaming," this hybrid approach holds enough promise that it has already been adopted in several older adult community settings.

One "combination-platter" approach capitalizes on the already known activities that may reduce cognitive decline. A small exploratory study[36] exposed a group of middle-aged patients who were experiencing early signs of dementia to over 20 types of treatments over the course of several months. These treatments were tailored to the specific needs of each person to target various things such as diet, lifestyle, exercise, sleep, and metabolic functions. The patients did activities including computer-based brain training, walking, yoga, and fasting 3 hours before bed. They also took vitamins, drugs, probiotics, resveratrol, and coconut oil and followed an anti-inflammatory diet. Many were able to reverse signs of dementia over a 6-month period, a finding suggesting that a dedicated and multifaceted approach may be the future of dementia prevention. Thus, there likely is no *one thing* to do to help your brain stay sharp. There are, in fact, many, and in the right combination, they might provide the best overall approach to brain fitness.

A Balanced Approach: Balance Training May Often Be Overlooked

In the first year of life, a new baby struggles for balance and the ability to take steps on their own. But it doesn't end there, as the rest of our lives are spent trying to find balance in various ways. We should balance out activities—long, 8-hour blocks of computer-based brain training a day, sitting at a desk, or working at one specific task may have negative outcomes. Probably the safest and yet most complicated bit of advice we hear again and again is "everything in moderation." Balancing work with family activities can be a constant challenge. Physical balance is often something we take for granted, but this form of balance can be especially important as we get older. A toddler learns to balance early in life, through trial and error, and bounces back from many falls. As we age, we especially need to maintain our physical balance in order to prevent falls, which are a leading cause of death for the aged.

John Wooden, an American icon as a basketball player and coach, at age 92, one night was making his usual way from his bedroom to the bathroom, a trip he had taken many times. Wooden vividly recalled the incident[37]:

> I was just going into the bathroom before going to bed, and going in I got my walker stuck on the rug and I fell over. I tried to catch myself, but I couldn't—I was flat on the floor and in pain. For a few minutes, I was kind of in shock. I had pain from the breaks. I was awake the whole time. I was cold. In that time, I was between laughing and crying, but that was all. More than anything else, I got cold. I couldn't crawl and get to a blanket or anything. I just had to stay there.

Wooden lay on the floor from 9 p.m. that evening until 7 a.m. in the morning (a full 10 hours, when most of us are sleeping) until his friend and caretaker arrived at his usual time in the morning. Wooden was immediately taken to the hospital and treated for a broken arm, collarbone, and wrist, but he survived the fall and the long night he spent lying on the floor, waiting for help.

Each year, more than 2 million older Americans go to the emergency room because of fall-related injuries.[38] Falls can be fatal or signal the beginning of the end of life. Falls and fall-related injuries, such as hip fractures, can have a serious impact on an older person's life and make it impossible to live independently. While we are often obsessed with brain training to keep us sharp, balance exercises, along with certain strength exercises, can help prevent falls and keep us walking. Unlike many brain training regimens, balance training can be done almost anywhere, at any time, and is free. As long as you have something or someone sturdy nearby to hold onto if you become unsteady, you can do simple exercises that keep your brain and body in line, and prevents falls. In the beginning, using a chair or the wall for support will help you work on your balance safely. There are many simple programs for balance training that can take less than 10 minutes a day to do. Parts of the brain involved in balance, such as the cerebellum, one of the most primitive parts of the brain, can benefit immensely from balance training. Practicing good balance can train both the brain and the body to prevent falls.

Balance is important for many daily tasks, such as getting up out of a chair—a challenge you face multiple times a day, although you probably never it gave much thought. One study[39] showed that people who could complete this getting-up-from-a-chair task more than 30 times in a minute were less likely to develop dementia and were also more likely to live longer than those who could not meet this criterion. Another simple task that may predict dementia and having a history of strokes (sometimes small ones you didn't even know you had) is standing on one leg. Surprisingly, it is also a good predictor of your longevity. This simple exercise involves trying to stand on one leg, with your eyes open, for up to 60 seconds. Being able to do this for more than 10 seconds is an indicator of good balance. Those who did poorly on this test were later found to be at greater risk for stroke and dementia. In addition to his impressive feats of strength and stamina, fitness pioneer Jack LaLanne also had an exercise program for seniors, called "Better Balance for Life." Even better than doing solitary balance exercises would be to go enjoy social interactions in one of the many classes that focus on balance. In our busy lives, sometimes balance involves doing less, such as not multitasking, so that we can focus on being safe.

Unlike computer-based brain training, which may or may not help our brains become better at important activities of daily life, balance training is proven to prevent falls. The point is that we should be focusing our resources, whether time, money, or motivation, for exercising and improving our brain, on good balance—both in the form of balancing many different activities and in improving our balance to prevent falls. Unlike memory, which we tend to notice when it fails, balance may be an overlooked issue until we suffer a traumatic and life-changing fall. It is only when we experience a fall that we become aware of the need to train for balance.

Summary

Computer-based brain training holds tremendous promise as a way to challenge our minds. It can adaptively challenge the brain with different puzzles and feedback about one's brain age. Currently, there is not enough evidence that computer-based brain training can help us improve memory, help us to remember names better, or find our keys. Using computer-based brain games and searching the Internet are activities that stimulate and reward our curious brain, but can also come at a large cost in terms of replacing other more tried-and-true activities, such as physical exercise. Brain training can be beneficial if you believe it works, and such placebo effects can be powerful. Brain training can also lead to additional screen time, being sedentary and less socializing with others, so the off-setting costs may be greater than any actual benefits. Trying any form of brain training can be a novel and challenging activity, but improving balance may be the most essential training activity for older adults. There are many simple, low-cost brain-training activities that can help us in meaningful ways to develop emotional skills and physical benefits, such as reading or walking.

Habits and Hobbies:
Old and New Friends

An old man went to the doctor and asked what he could do to live longer. The doctor said, "Give up alcohol, quit smoking, and stop eating any desserts. You may not live longer, but your life will *seem* longer."

You can live to be a hundred if you give up all the things that make you want to live to be a hundred.

—Woody Allen

O NE MAY THINK THAT, AS WE AGE, OUR HABITS AND routines become more ingrained and become harder to change. While this is true in some ways, older adults also have more experience changing habits, simply by having lived longer and adapted along the way. This suggests that we don't just get more "set in our ways" as we age. Often, overriding a habit can lead to the use of creativity and can open doors to new adventures. For example, many older adults will take a much-wanted trip as a reward after retirement, after not taking a vacation for many years.

Changing lifestyle habits can yield positive results at any point in life. Some habits, such as drinking soda and playing video games, can start in the teenage years and can have long-term effects on our physical and mental well-being, but we can also modify these behaviors substantially as we age. Simple behavioral changes that lead to better diet or avoiding excessive alcohol or tobacco use can have long-term benefits. There are a wide range of habits and hobbies people have as they age. For example, quilting, painting, walking, playing chess, yoga, mahjong, backgammon, birdwatching, or sports can be hobbies and habits that lead to cognitive stimulation and social engagement, as well as providing joy and personal fulfillment. Maintaining healthy habits in old age, from exercise to napping, can be important for physical and mental health.

We also have adaptive routines and habits that we don't want to change. For example, leaving our car keys in the same spot at home can help us to find them when we rush out of the house in the morning. Set routines are usually helpful, but anger and frustration at a violated routine may be quite harmful. Some research suggests that a strong preference and need for routines can make older adults more vulnerable to anxiety, depression levels, and cognitive complaints.[1] Thus, adaptive flexibility is needed, such as in situations where we need to alter a routine (e.g., eating unfamiliar foods when travelling). As frustrating as it can be, changing routines, even for brief periods of time, may be adaptive and beneficial.

Are Older Adults More "Set in Their Ways"?

One stereotype of older adults is that they are more set in their ways, more stubborn, and less open to new experiences. In fact, many older adults are often more open to new experiences. For example, often shortly after retirement, older adults seek to take trips to foreign countries, to experience new cultures, and to enjoy the adventure of travelling. Older adults often enroll in various classes in different areas than their professional domain to satisfy interests and curiosity in fields they are not overly familiar with—again suggesting an interest to learn new things and meet new people with similar interests.

As for day-to-day activities, older adults may prefer familiar restaurants instead of trying a new restaurant every week, but that does not mean older adults are not interested in seeking out new experiences. I dine out with two older adults who are often interested in trying new restaurants. But when we go out to one that we know well, I am tempted to try something new on the menu, often being disappointed that I didn't go with the tried-and-true option. The older couple usually sticks with the tried-and-true house favorites. This may be some form of wisdom. Although they seem to be happy to see me trying something else, and they will sample what I ordered, they are usually happy they didn't order it. This same couple loves ice cream and has for years. Lately, they have been going to a different ice cream shop in their neighborhood—one that has flavors such as cucumber and saffron rose. Instead of ordering standard chocolate and vanilla, they are excited to satisfy their curiosity by trying new flavors. In fact, two-thirds of today's retirees say they prefer trying new things in their leisure time over doing things they've already done.[2] However, many older adults often are brand loyal and choose the familiar brand they have used over the years (e.g., Bayer for their aspirin).[3]

Exercise Habits and the Benefits of Walking

Joining a gym can be costly and frustrating if you never go, while going to a seniors group exercise class or meeting with others to walk or exercise can be empowering and have social benefits. Jack LaLanne's main message about successful aging can be captured in this simple statement: exercising little and often, eating right, and having a positive mind set. His book, *Live Young Forever*, outlines all of his secrets and motivational approaches to live longer and healthier.[4] While he exercised 2 hours a day 7 day a week, he said that was for "his ego." His advice for people was to exercise 30 minutes, three to four times a week, and every 30 days to change the exercises to something slightly different. Thus, exercise routines don't always have to be routine. As also stated in his book, "The only way you can hurt the body is not use it," he liked to say. "Inactivity is the killer, and remember, it's never too late." While LaLanne engaged in various forms of fitness, simply walking is a good start. A recent study[5] found that it is never too late to start walking as a form of exercise, and it may be that those who are the most sedentary get the most benefits. To educate and encourage seniors to exercise, the National Institute on Aging has developed the Go4Life program,[6] which is designed to help people fit physical activity into their daily life.

Sometimes learning about the benefits of exercise can be particularly motivating. For example, in one study,[7] older adults who were informed about the *benefits* of walking walked more than those who were informed about the *negative* consequences of *failing* to walk. While younger adults were unaffected by the emotional manner or framing of the message, older adults responded more to the positive message—perhaps one reason this book focuses on the potential bright side of old age. The positivity conveyed in a message can be critical for making people engage in new healthy habits. Thus, a positive message emphasizing the health benefits of walking will make older people walk more, compared to a negative message stating the harms and unhealthy consequences of not walking and having a sedentary lifestyle.

Some people, even doctors, may think exercise is most appropriate for athletic people and fit younger adults. Ageism sometimes contributes to doctors not suggesting walking as a useful way to stay fit and sharp in older age. Physicians are less likely to recommend physical activity to those with arthritis who are 65 and older than to those who are younger than 65, despite evidence suggesting that all age groups may benefit substantially from exercise.[8] Thus, even some doctors may have attitudes that are biased against prescribing some of the best free medicine that is available to older adults: a simple dose of walking several times a week.

Healthy habits can pay off, by reducing the number of trips a person needs to take to a doctor. Insurance companies know this, and they spend a lot of time and money encouraging older people to stay in good shape, via newsletters and even paying for free gym visits for seniors. Through a program known as Silver Sneakers, older adults can visit participating gyms where they live and, when travelling, go to other "in network" gyms, which allows for flexibility beyond a single gym membership and means there is no excuse not to exercise. This form of encouraging healthy habits is considered preventative medicine. I spoke to one grandfather from New York who was visiting his adult children and grandchildren in Los Angeles, and he enjoyed taking advantage of a free and flexible gym membership, with a chance to meet new people. His family also noted the benefits of getting him out of the house during his month-long visits. Sometimes a free offer of a gym membership can't be refused, although simply walking outside with a friend might be the best form of free medicine, as it includes both physical and social aspects.

Walking can be a healthy habit, but also modifying habits is an even better way to exercise. Variations on a good habit can challenge you and can reduce the repetitiveness that can be both boring and cause excessive wear and tear on your body. "Retro-walking" involves walking backwards while clapping your hands. One needs to be careful walking backwards, and while it seems simple, after several steps one notices how challenging it can be. Walking backwards while clapping brings walking to a whole new level—a challenge that involves the coordination of several simple exercises. One study has found that walking backwards for a short period of time led to benefits on tests of thinking and concentration.[9] Adding hand movements while walking backwards can make for a whole body exercise experience. Performing this exercise activity while walking up a mountainside is said to have originated in ancient China. Although this practice may seem challenging, it focuses one more on the need to be present and in the moment when walking, something that can tone the brain while at the same time leading to more in-the-moment mindfulness.

One of the more common habitual exercises is running or jogging, as it can be simple and convenient and often is very rewarding and challenging. People do it regularly, some with goals of competing in races or marathons, but many simply for the sake of exercise. However, even though running is popular, it may not be a good habit to keep in old age. A recent study[10] examined whether running alone, in lieu of other forms of exercise, was enough to maintain general fitness in older adults. Over a 5-year period, the runners (most of whom were in their late 50s) actually lost knee strength. Too much running can have a negative impact in terms of joint pain and injuries and diminishing returns of the benefits of running.[11] Some famous older adults (John Glenn, John Wooden, and Bill Clinton) who spent time running in their middle age later traded running for walking, since the lower impact of walking limits the wear and tear that comes with running. At work, "walking meetings" or "walking conferences" can be set up so that people walk together for a stimulating meeting, for both the mind and the body.

Some core strength training can also be done at home if you have the stamina and patience. Cher, the singer famous for her cat suits and voluminous wigs, recently said that in her 70s she regularly practices core body strengthening. She said she does a 5-minute "plank exercise." Plank involves maintaining a push-up position, with the upper body held off the ground by the forearms and toes. Most people (myself included) struggle after holding this position for a minute. But that is not all; she says she works out 5 days a week with a trainer who doesn't let her "play the age card."[12] Cher, famous for the songs "Believe" and "Turn Back Time," shows how a commitment and belief in the benefits of exercise may actually help your body turn back time.

Eating Habits at Every Age: New Foods with Old Habits

Eating habits and eating behaviors develop when we are children, but they also change substantially over the adult lifespan. Younger children and teenagers might crave sweets, soda, and sugar and are encouraged to eat more vegetables; as we age, we are aware of the need to eat healthier, and sugar and soda might give way to coffee habits and alcohol consumption.

Jack LaLanne said that as a boy he was addicted to sugar and junk food. He had violent outbursts and described himself as "a miserable goddamn kid . . . it was like hell." Besides having a bad temper, he also suffered from headaches and bulimia and temporarily dropped out of high school at age 14. The following year, at age 15, he heard health food crusader Paul Bragg give a talk on health and nutrition, focusing on the "evils of meat and sugar." Bragg's message had a powerful influence on LaLanne, who then drastically changed his habits and focused on his diet and exercise. In his own words, he was "born again" with his new focus on nutrition, and he began working out daily.[13]

Some older adults will invoke drastic changes in their eating habits. For example, Bill Clinton was famous for his jogging and his love of cheeseburgers. Often the two activities would go hand in hand, as Clinton was photographed going to McDonald's during an exercise outing. After coping with heart disease and having several surgeries, his eating habits changed drastically. He is now a vegan. In older age, he managed to change his diet and eating habits, to lose more than 30 pounds, and now feels more energetic. Clinton said,[14] "I just decided that I was the high-risk person, and I didn't want to fool with this anymore. And I wanted to live to be a grandfather. So I decided to pick the diet that I thought would maximize my chances of long-term survival." Once a week, as suggested by his doctor, he will eat salmon or an omelet, to maintain iron, zinc, and muscle mass. In addition to his dietary changes, Clinton also walks 2 or 3 miles a day, outdoors whenever possible, works out with weights, and uses an exercise ball for balance drills. He continues to play golf, always walking the course without a cart. Replacing jogging and McDonald's with walking and a mostly vegan diet can allow Clinton to enjoy life as a grandfather and to keep up with his wife.

On the other hand, Warren Buffett regularly discusses how he eats junk food and drinks several cans of Coca-Cola every day. He feels that changing these habits won't make him live any longer. "There's no evidence that I will any better reach 100 if I had lived on broccoli and water," says Buffett. With billions of dollars at his disposal, you might think Buffett would be having gourmet meals. Buffett said, "I checked the actuarial tables, and the lowest death rate is among six-year-olds. So I decided to eat like a six-year-old. It's the safest course I can take."[15] This contrasts with fitness guru Jack LaLanne's famous saying that "if man made it, don't eat it."

One common habit we all have is our morning routine, which often involves breakfast or coffee or both. Breakfast can be more than just nutrition. For many years, when he was retired and widowed, John Wooden went regularly to a small local diner in Encino, California, for breakfast. Everybody knew one another by name, he made many friends, and it was very close to his condominium. Wooden almost always ordered the same thing: two eggs, two hotcakes, and two slices of bacon or sausage.[16] Wooden would always sit in the same booth and read the morning newspapers while talking to the regulars seated at the counter near him, usually about current events. Many of them knew next to nothing about sports. They would talk about politics, religion, and upcoming elections, and almost never about last night's games. Of course, Wooden also had other eating and exercise habits earlier in his life. Many years earlier, while coaching at UCLA, in the early mornings Wooden would walk 5 miles around the track next to Pauley Pavilion. He would also frequent Stan's Donuts for what is now known as the "John Wooden" donut: a glazed blueberry buttermilk classic.[17] There might be something about being a "regular" that allows for consistent social interaction, good food, and often long-lasting friendships.

A habit of having bacon and eggs for breakfast every day can't be healthy, or can it? Coffee, green tea, or orange juice? A diverse diet can be essential, but knowing what to eat can be confusing: avoid fat, eat fat, low fat, trans-fat, good fat, full fat and egg whites, egg yolks, raw eggs, organic free-range eggs? Many of the latest diets and scientific findings may be the opposite of what an older adult has been hearing for the past 50 years. Is fat good or bad, and what about carbohydrates? How about butter versus margarine and the link to high cholesterol? What are the benefits of organic and grass-fed beef? Today, it is unclear if you should eat your bread without the butter, or your butter without the bread. These might be confusing times for people of any age, but especially if they go against years of already established habits.[18] After all, for many years, asbestos and smoking cigarettes were considered safe. In terms of remembering what is good to eat, and what is now considered bad for you, living a long life can lead to complete confusion about the latest health and diet advice. Perhaps it is easiest to follow what food author Michael Pollan says: "Don't eat anything your great-grandmother wouldn't recognize as food.'[19]

Sleeping: The Benefits of Good Sleep and Naps in Older Age

Sleep disruptions, which are more common as we get older, can have dramatic negative effects. These effects range from impaired memory to weight gain, not to mention irritability if you have a poor night's sleep (as any new parent can attest to). As we get older, the quality, not just the quantity, of sleep can also decline. We may not be as aware of the quality of the sleep as we are of the disruptions and nighttime trips to the bathroom. Typically, older adults will experience more frequent sleep disturbances than younger adults, and a healthy older adult may wake up several times a night without it being due to a disease. Older adults will spend less time in deep sleep, waking up earlier and often throughout the night.[20] This interruption in sleep can be caused by many factors, including lack of exercise during the day, consumption of alcohol or caffeine, the frequent need to urinate throughout the night (nocturia), or sleep disorders such as sleep apnea. Some research[21] shows that sleep disruptions in older adults lead to memory impairments and sleep disorders, such as sleep apnea, a potentially serious sleep disorder in which breathing repeatedly stops and starts often without people being aware of it, which can have pronounced effects on cognitive abilities during the day.

However, old age doesn't have to include poor sleep, as there are many things we can do during the day to enjoy better sleep at night. Making some of these a habit, and having a consistent bedtime routine, can facilitate getting a good night's sleep. Some research suggests that spending daytime outdoors and in nature and fresh air can lead to a better quality of sleep at night.[22] Having set routines during the day, such as regular mealtimes, set meetings with friends, and regular exercise times, can also be a key to sleeping well. In one study,[23] both good sleepers and insomniacs did various activities throughout the day, but it was the good sleepers who did these activities on a set schedule, which suggests that a regular routine can set your biological rhythms so that your body is ready for bed at a consistent time. Another study[24] found that performing basic activities such as eating, dressing, and bathing at the same time every day was associated with improved sleep quality. People who followed daily routines most closely took less time to fall asleep, spent more time asleep, reported less tossing and turning, and rated their sleep as being of higher quality.

An often understated habit is napping. Stan Berman has been the owner of Stan's Donuts for over 40 years. He always gets up early, and then takes a nap after lunch. This is part of his routine, and he hasn't missed more than a day of work due to sickness in 40 years. While some people might view napping as part of a lazy, relaxing day, more research shows that short naps can enhance not only productivity but also how long you will live.[25] In addition, the concept of "beauty sleep" may not be a myth, as during sleep our body releases a growth hormone that helps restore collagen and elastin, the essential building blocks of young, healthy skin. Also, studies have shown a connection between insomnia and the onset of dementia.[26] As my father always told me as a child, "sleep is the best medicine." Or as Benjamin Franklin said, "Early to bed, and early to rise, makes a man healthy, wealthy and wise."

SuccesSEXful Aging: Sexual Activity and Enjoying Sex in Older Age

Sexual activity and other forms of intimacy can be an important part of old age. While there can be a decline in health and physical ability that allow for an active sex life and many medications can interfere with sex drive, older adults are still very interested in sex. In addition, it isn't a necessity to have sex as often or as much as one did when younger. Some research[27] suggests that over 60% of older women aged 40 to 99 are generally happy with their sex lives, regardless of whether they had a sex partner or even sexual activity. Satisfaction also increased with age, as the oldest women in the study were nearly twice as likely as the youngest women to report being "very satisfied" with their sex lives. Despite some suggestion that older people are less interested in sex, many older adults consider sex to be important for maintaining a healthy and long-lasting relationship.[28]

While one may not necessarily consider sexual activity a habit or a hobby, it is something that many older adults seek and engage in quite frequently. When asked about sex, Jack LaLanne had a standard joke, saying that despite his advanced age, he and his wife still made love *almost* every night: "Almost on Monday, almost on Tuesday, almost on Wednesday . . . " Dr. Ruth Westheimer, the renowned sex therapist and author of *Sex After 50*, is well known for encouraging couples to break out of habits or routines that might not have a spark. She outlines her tips in her book.[29] She herself finds having a massage to be a very relaxing and important way to have physical contact, commenting that she feels 6 feet tall after each massage (she is 4 foot 7). While Dr. Ruth herself doesn't divulge much about her own sex life at age 87 (twice divorced and a widow), she says that one habit that keeps her active is walking fast and walking while talking on the phone, also noting that she skied until the age of 80. She says that curiosity plays a big role in staying active. "I am still very curious to learn. I am still teaching. I taught at Yale and Princeton. I go to lectures. I am not satisfied by standing still. I still want to learn. I go to concerts. It's very nice to be Dr. Ruth. I am now a widow for more than 16 years. If I could find an interesting older gentleman who can still walk and talk, that would be very nice. I would be very happy."[30]

Driving Habits and Aging: Knowing When to Focus and When to Get Off the Phone or Road

Driving is a skill we often learn as teens, and we develop many driving habits over the years. Older drivers may experience sensory declines, contributing to poorer night vision and slower reaction times that give rise to accidents. There certainly have been some horrible and highly publicized cases involving seniors. While these events likely contribute to the stigma of older adults as unsafe drivers,[31] it is individuals in the least experienced and youngest age category (ages 16–19) who take the most risks on the road and who actually have the highest number of accidents. Compared to younger adults, older adults are more likely to wear seat belts and to take familiar routes. Older adults are also less likely to drive at night, in bad weather, and while impaired.[32] In addition, over the past 20 years, the rate of fatal car crashes has declined more for drivers over 70 than for those ages 35–54 (many of whom are often distracted drivers). That might be one reason why Uber and Lyft have many older drivers, as older adults feel they have the necessary experience to drive and also to enjoy the social interactions.

Driving allows for independence as we age, but in older age it becomes more difficult to multitask. Using a phone while driving can be a dangerous behavior at any age, but likely especially so for older adults. Older adults may be more aware of this and so are less likely to use cell phones and text in general. When my daughters are driven by their grandfather who is healthy and driving at age 88, he tells them not to talk to him while he drives. He is aware that they can distract him from driving. Older adults may have learned how to avoid risks on the road. For example, when I spoke to Jared Diamond about his commute to and from UCLA, he told me how he reduces risks by avoiding a dangerous left turn on his daily commute by taking several safer right turns, which increases his drive time by 2 minutes. Reducing these risks can be the small routines that lead to greater awareness and safety in older drivers.

Secrets to Successful Aging: Are Unusual Habits a Secret to Successful Aging?

We often see stories about "centenarians," people who have lived to be over 100 years old. When asked, "What is the secret"? or

"What have you done that makes you live so long?" the replies are illuminating. Here is a selection of various responses from a few different centenarians as reported recently in the media: "drinks 3 Dr. Pepper's a day for the past forty years," "eats sushi regularly and sleeps well," "smokes a pack of cigarettes a day, and is a childless bachelor," "be nice to people every day, worship God, and eat pig's feet." While there is certainly no scientific study that would encourage people to smoke regularly, drink Dr. Pepper daily, or eat pig's feet, all of these individuals have lived past the age of 100. It is also important to note that these people are lifespan "outliers," meaning that they have lived well beyond the norms of life expectancy in old age. As a result, they may represent oddities more than examples of what to do to live a long, healthy life. What is clear is that there is considerable diversity, some contradictions with the science of aging, and some habits that go against conventional wisdom. Thus, it is hard to glean any specific secrets. Since some habits go against what science would endorse to promote healthy living, there may be even more complex interactions among genes, epigenetics, and environmental factors that influence aging, especially in older aging.

Some people have the perspective that we should enjoy life, even if this includes bad habits that may go against advice about longevity. For example, Leonard Cohen (the singer, songwriter, poet, and novelist), when celebrating his 80th birthday, announced that he would resume smoking. "It's the right age to recommence," he explained.[33] He died 2 years later from a fall at night. While research shows that, at any age, taking up smoking is not sensible, Cohen's plan presents a provocative question: When should we set aside a life lived for the future and, instead, embrace the pleasures of the present?

Winnie Langley started smoking 1 day after the first World War broke out in June 1914, when she was just 7 years old. She said she has smoked about five cigarettes a day since then. There is a famous picture of her lighting a cigarette from the candles of her 100th birthday cake—but what may have helped her is that she never really inhaled. She said she smoked cigarettes to help calm her nerves during the World Wars. She was finally persuaded to stop smoking at the age of 102, when her eyesight prevented her from actually seeing the end of her lit match. Somewhat ironically, she died about 7 months after she stopped smoking.[34]

There is some research suggesting that moderate consumption of alcohol and coffee is associated with longer life. A study of people over the age of 90 at the huge retirement community, Leisure World and Laguna Woods in Orange County, California, asked these older-old adults to list various habits they had in their older age, to see what was associated with longevity.[35] Researchers found that there was not much of a longevity benefit in taking vitamins or calcium supplements. Drinking tea and drinking soda did not have a positive or negative effect, either. Somewhat surprising was that people who drank modest amounts of alcohol—from one or two drinks a week to one daily drink—seemed to live longer, on average. Perhaps there is a social and stress-reducing component to drinking alcohol with others that has lasting benefits. And if you are a coffee drinker, often another social activity, you might enjoy this: those over the age of 90 who also consumed one small cup of coffee a day lived longer on average than those who didn't drink coffee.

To add to the advice of centenarians, at our lab at UCLA, we recently had a 103-year-old woman participate in our memory study. Before she came to the study, she asked if she could come with her son, who happened to be 79! After testing her memory, my graduate student, Alex Siegel, politely asked about her keys to successful aging. This is what she said:

- It is important to keep active physically (she takes dancing classes).
- It is important to care about fellow citizens and stay involved in politics.
- Try to do a little bit each day to reach your ideal.
- Take care of your health (no smoking and very little alcohol).
- Be kind to your fellow man, don't be judgmental.

So there we have it. The recipe to living life beyond 100 years, and still participating in memory studies!

Socializing Can Be an Often Underappreciated Good Habit

In my neighborhood, I notice a regular group of older adults who meet at the local coffee shop for backgammon. One group meets in the morning and another meets later in the afternoon. There is evidence that people with more social support tend to live longer than those who are more isolated.[36] A habit of socializing has been the inspiration for the Red Hat Society, a group of older women who meet regularly to enjoy each other's company, all while wearing fashionable red hats and purple dresses. The male offshoot is known as the ROMEO Social Club, where ROMEO stands for Retired Older Men Eating Out—a group that meets at various restaurants with lively social behavior. The Red Hat Society and the ROMEO Club both provide regular structured ways to socialize, to spend time with people you know well while also meeting new people. Regular social engagement is associated with a stronger immune system, especially for older adults, which can be critical when you are trying to avoid catching a cold or the flu. Some research also shows that social engagement can help in terms of improving your mood, and there is evidence that people who lead active social lives are less likely to develop dementia than those who are more socially isolated.[37] Thus, having socializing routines can be beneficial in many ways, including healthy aging and longevity.

Rituals and Family Traditions as Habits

Family traditions such as regular trips or celebrations of holidays often are important repeated occasions that bring family members together. Some families have dinner together on Friday nights or have a large Sunday brunch. They remark that these are regular times to be together with family and friends, providing social connections as a result of these family-wise traditions and habits. Simple family traditions may involve grandparents picking up kids after school, playing chess together, going fishing, watching baseball, or even watching the neighborhood garbage trucks (something my son and I do weekly with other children, parents, and grandparents on our block).

Taking family vacations can also be an important habit. People of all ages remark that they remember their family vacations very fondly and are amazed at how those events stand out in life. Some research[38] suggests that vacations can be thought of as "memory assets," since they are remembered quite vividly for a long time. Ironically, some people "forget" to take vacations, don't use their vacations days, or feel they don't have the time and money. However, vacations can be the best way to free yourself from bad habits that accumulate over the year, and a vacation can be something that is remembered by young and old alike for years to come. Some families may have "time-shares," ensuring that they use their 2 weeks off a year, often in a similar location, bringing family together. Even a short drive to a new hotel can serve as a memorable vacation and a way to escape habits and routines while staying close to home.

There are many reasons to enjoy holidays, but one common theme, especially as we grow older, is that holidays often bring families together with specific traditions. Older adults will report that religious rituals and Thanksgiving rituals are some of the most important traditions to maintain.[39] Even if they are not religious, parents and grandparents say that celebrating religious events (e.g., Christmas, Hanukkah, Easter, Passover) brings family together and allows for enjoyment and understanding of the traditions that are passed down through generations. Early in life, children view these holidays in terms of things like Santa, gifts, dreidels, long dinners, and Easter egg hunts. Later in life, people become more aware of the cultural significance, the need to disengage from regular day-to-day busyness, and the joy of bringing family together. Dave Brubeck, the jazz pianist and a proud grandparent, remarked that one of the most pleasurable events for him was a large Easter egg hunt when all of his children and grandchildren visited. These family gatherings become traditions even if only practiced to bring joy to children and to connect with family. I know one family who has large annual family golf vacations. Older adults can often be the vehicles for maintaining and passing down family traditions.[40] One study[41] found that 65% of grandparents noted that rituals now practiced by their children and grandchildren had roots in their own caregiving to their own children, which suggests the passing down of these routines and habits as family traditions.

When Habits and Routines Collide: Young and Old on Different Schedules

Nap time, mealtime, playtime, snack time and bedtime may all be important times of the day, but they are experienced very differently for people of different ages. Take, for example, a situation in which grandparents are visiting their children and grandchildren. This can be a pleasurable time, but when routines and habits come into play, groups will differ in terms of when and how to carry them out. A baby needs two naps a day, and a parent needs to feed children at certain fixed times to prevent unruly behavior, while an older adult may be on a very different schedule. This can lead to conflict, and grandparents may feel that accommodating routines for younger family members involves an unnecessary imposition. Development trends for routines mean that older adults may not have the same routines at the same time as younger people. When we are older, a nap can occur whenever we are tired, but allowing a 2-year-old to skip a scheduled nap can destroy the rest of the day for the entire family.

At my memory lab at UCLA, when we schedule older adults to come in for an appointment, they often arrive 30 minutes early. Usually this is because they want to make sure they have enough time to find the place or beat traffic, and they don't mind waiting after they arrive early. Often early birds, older adults value being on time. Perhaps this is a generational thing, as many younger people might find it adequate to send a text saying that they are running late. While younger adults may claim to be busier or have fluctuating schedules, older adults also report being very busy, but may be punctual because they have a more structured schedule, plan to be punctual, and also expect punctuality. For example, meeting my father-in-law for dinner at 6 p.m. means that he will get there at 5:45. Allowing extra time can also allow for anticipated challenges for older adults, from parking to navigating unfamiliar roads. This can also be useful when travelling to medical appointments, when planning trips, or for mundane things such as returning library books on time. However, there certainly are punctual people of all ages. My daughter hates being late for anything (she's clearly related to her grandfather), so much so that on the night before her first day of kindergarten, she decided to sleep in her clothes, just to ensure she would be on time for her first day of school.

Variability and Altering Habits Can Help Us Learn

We often start a book on page 1 and begin playing music at the start of a piece. Through habit, I know the first eight bars of many piano pieces from memory. I always start practicing at the beginning of each piece, but often don't make it to the end of the piece of music. As a result, I spend much more time practicing the first part of the music and much less time on the other parts. If I started in the middle or the end, then I would know more of each piece. When we learn, we often rely on habits, such as starting at the beginning, learning the easy things first, avoiding making mistakes, and studying similar things at the same time. Suppose you were a birdwatcher and wanted to learn more about different birds types. Typically, we spend a lot of time learning what a sparrow looks like, make sure we know it, and then move on to studying what a lark is like, then a blue jay. The better way is to mix them all together so that we see one, then another, then another type, as that is often how we find them in nature. As a desirable difficulty, learning the birds in a mixed-up manner would feel slow and frustrating, but it would lead to less forgetting.[42]

The habits we have in place for learning are sometimes the easiest ones, but not always the most effective, so incorporating desirable difficulties (discussed in Chapter 6) can lead to benefits by making learning more challenging. Routines allow us to accomplish things, often without thinking. When I go to the gym, I do the same weight-training activities, almost without thinking. When we read a book, we usually start at the beginning, thinking we might read from start to finish. However, there are benefits to breaking these habits, of starting in the middle, skimming, reading overviews, then being more thorough. These might be useful habits if you are short on time, not sure if you are interested, or want to get better at some particular skill. Sometimes a good way to retrain your brain is to do a variation on something you do regularly. Hiking a familiar trail in reverse order, walking your dog on a new route, or even shopping at a different market can challenge your brain and break up familiarity. The novelty may make it more interesting and rewarding. You may notice things you hadn't noticed before or improve in ways you didn't even know you were able to change.

Summary

We often focus on "bad habits" that we have or are constantly trying to break, but habits help us in many ways and may be especially important in old age. Learned habits and predictable routines can also provide an important safety mechanism in both professional and personal settings. Older adults can rely on habits to ensure structure, to reduce uncertainty, and to provide important guiding principles that allow for a productive lifestyle. However, older adults are often open to new experiences, and also have a lifetime of changing their habits with age. Maintaining healthy habits in old age, ranging from engaging in exercise to meeting with friends, is important. As we age, our habits can be surprisingly modifiable and adaptive, responding to needs and interests. This flexibility of routine is crucial for successful aging.

Retiring and Rewiring:
The New "R & R" of Old Age

Retirement at 65 is ridiculous. When I was 65, I still had pimples.
　　　　　—George Burns, comedian, who died at age 100

Retirement: That's when you come home from work one day and say,
"Hi, Honey, I'm home—forever."
　　　—Gene Perret, writer and producer for the *Carol Burnett Show*

TODAY, RETIREMENT DOES NOT HAVE A CLEAR DEFINITION. To show how fuzzy the term *retirement* really is, according to a recent survey,[1] 83% of adults ages 65 and over describe themselves as "retired," but the word clearly means different things to different people. Many who claim to be retired from full-time work report they are actually semi-retired, work part-time at new jobs or, despite being officially retired, are still connected to their profession as a consultant, member of a professional association, advisor, volunteer contributor, or mentor. Retirement can also lead to many challenges, as illustrated in these quotes:

Retirement kills more people than hard work ever did. (Malcolm Forbes, entrepreneur)

A retired husband is often a wife's full-time job. (Ella Harris)

If and when you retire, what will you miss most? For those who have yet to retire, the most popular answer is "the income." However, for those who have already retired and have a better idea of what retired life is actually like, the answer is quite different. In a recent survey, retirees said they missed social connections the most. If you combine the answers of "missing social connections," "lack of having purpose," and "less mental stimulation," then these responses account for over 65% of the most pressing issues retirees experience.[2] That shows another paradox of aging: the glaring contrast between what we *think* is important in retirement while we are still working and what is *actually* important when we reach that stage.

While some studies show that people who retire earlier in life are more likely to die, it is very hard to determine if they retire because they are unhealthy or if their retirement itself has led to unhealthy behavior. Researchers[3] found that healthy adults who retired 1 year past the age 65 had an 11% lower risk of death from all causes, even after taking into account demographics, lifestyle, and health issues. Also, they found that adults who described themselves as "unhealthy" were more likely to live longer if they kept working, which suggests that factors beyond healthfulness may affect mortality.

People may spend a lot of time thinking about their future or far-off retirement. When retirement becomes a closer reality, we may experience some hesitation and resistance, often because we don't feel ready or old enough to retire. Some people and cultures consider retirement a flawed or outdated concept. Even the word *retirement* can be loaded. AARP is no longer referred to as the American Association of Retired People (they are now just AARP, which rhymes with "sharp"), because some people object to the term *retired*. In fact, AARP no longer requires that members be retired, simply over the age of 50.

Sometimes we worry what will become of us when we retire—only so much golf and Mahjong can keep us busy, entertained, or happy. In addition, some have seen how others' health and well-being have deteriorated after retirement, and research supports this observation. Albert Camus, the French writer and philosopher, said, "Without work all life goes rotten. But when work is soulless, life stifles and dies."

What goals will you pursue when retired? How will you stay connected and not be irrelevant? This again presents a paradox: we work many years so that we can enjoy retirement, only to then be worried and apprehensive about the transition to this next stage of life. Comedian and TV star Bob Newhart told me he tried golf, but it didn't work for him. He didn't feel the need to retire, his stand-up comedy routine is a form of motivation. Being nervous before a show is almost addictive for him, a good form of stress, as he needs to be prepared to get people to do one of the most important things in life: laugh, smile, and find humor in the little things.

What Are We When We Are a "Retiree"?

We may not only miss social connections but also experience a change in our core identity when we retire. Over time, people develop a strong bond with their jobs, have considerable expertise and knowledge and have forged social connections with others in the workplace. My 80-year-old father is unable to retire. He loves his work, and it defines him. His greatest stress in life is when he, or someone around him, contemplates his retirement. There may also be differences in how men and women view retirement and how they define themselves before and after retirement. The quality and quantity of social support can differ for men and women, and this can be important when one retires, especially for someone whose friends are mostly from their job. A respondent to a study on retirement[4] said, "Before retirement, I defined myself by my work. Now, I define myself by what I do with my leisure—I'm now a grandmother, a French student, a cook, and a volunteer. I seek out new ways to define myself, to become who I want to be."

Legendary basketball coach John Wooden had many friends from his years at UCLA—other coaches, former players, and other celebrities. His most cherished times were their visits when they would stop by his Encino apartment. He formed a long-lasting friendship with his former players Kareem Abdul-Jabbar and Bill Walton, who visited at his bedside when he was dying in the UCLA hospital. These two players differed from Wooden in many ways, but in their retirements they formed a close social bond.

One's profession can have a lasting impact on how one thinks and observes the world around them. For example, a retired doctor may immediately recognize that a child on the playground has signs of a cold or flu or worse. Simply being retired doesn't mean you stop doing your job, or thinking the way you have been thinking for the past few decades. My 88-year-old father-in-law is a semi-retired real estate agent, which doesn't stop him from assessing a home's value, or helping someone to make a decision about buying a house. Our expertise doesn't just fade with age, as often it is related to our interests in life. For example, accountants may pay special attention to numbers later in life because of their past experience working with numbers. This attention to numbers may lead to better memory for numerical information.[5] Research has shown that professions that place high demands on language and math may preserve parts of the brain involved in these processes in older age.[6] Thus, what you have been doing for the past 30 years as your occupation changes your brain, and will play a role in what you do, and how you think, in your retirement.

As we retire from professions, we often transition into more familial roles—roles we may have maintained throughout our working life. We never really retire from roles such as being a mother or father, an uncle or aunt, or a grandparent. In fact, these important roles sometimes become how we define ourselves as we age. As one transitions into retirement, one may identify less with a former job title or occupation. Others may retain a strong attachment to their working identity, but also emphasize their new roles and leisure activities.

Stages of Retirement: Similar and Different Steps to Greater Life Satisfaction

Some theories of retirement[7] suggest that workers approaching retirement go through stages. At first, we have vague ideas and fantasies about what retirement will entail, while we are still active in a job or career. As retirement becomes more imminent, our plans become more concrete. Once formally separated from the workforce, a "honeymoon phase" ensues, where one may take a much-wanted trip, and engage in activities that one could not do when fully employed. Often this honeymoon phase is followed by an emotional disenchantment phase, in which one realizes that their retirement may lack structure or satisfaction. One then needs to find regular activities and make necessary adjustments that leads to a more stable day-to-day enjoyment of life. There are also cultural differences in how people envision and experience retirement, and retirement may remind people of the finite nature of life.[8] While one may take specials trips, family visits, grandparenting roles, volunteer or work part-time, the pace is less frantic than when one was working full time. While this is a model of how retirement may work for many, it doesn't mean everyone goes through every stage—in fact, retirement can involve reinventing stages as needed, sometimes for financial reasons, but often for greater life satisfaction.

Loneliness: The Scariest Part of Retirement, and the Silent Killer of Retirees

> Count your age by friends, not years. Count your life by smiles, not tears.
>
> —John Lennon, singer, songwriter,
> and co-founder of the Beatles

Retirement can be a surprisingly difficult transition, sometimes associated with depression and changes in physical health. You leave behind a job, a social circle, a sense of status and satisfying needs. Researchers have found that complete retirement is associated with increases in illness and difficulties in mobility and daily activities, as well as with a decline in mental health, over a period of 6 years.[9] In addition, other studies have found that lower levels of adjustment to retirement are associated with increased use of alcohol and smoking.[10] However, one of the most overlooked factors that contribute to an unhappy retirement is loss of social connection. In fact, the negative effect of loneliness on overall health in older age has been compared to smoking 15 cigarettes a day, being an alcoholic, and not exercising, and may be twice as harmful for retirees as obesity.

One retired person said,[11] "I was very interactive with people all day and I missed that when I retired from work. It was important for me to replace that social interaction. Through new activities, I now have my church friends, my yoga friends, and my travel friends who fill that void."

It is difficult to directly study the effects of retirement on well-being, because people retire at different times and for different reasons, and often only partially retire. Some research[12] has shown that self-esteem remains stable over the course of pre- and post-retirement and that rates of depression and anxiety actually decline, possibly because of less workplace-related stress and more time directed toward activities of leisure. In general, having high levels of social support, being able to enjoy vacations, having a strong marriage, and participating in enjoyable hobbies have been shown to be related to higher retirement satisfaction.[13]

While making new friends can be a useful way to combat loneliness, people may also rely on friends they've had for a lifetime. Sometimes older age is a time people seek to rekindle their past friendships or to attend reunions. Friendships are one of the best formulas for preventing loneliness, especially during a life transition such as retirement. As an example, a group of seven men have been friends for over 76 years. They have been meeting monthly for decades. These men have been together since they were 8 years old, attending the same schools with the same teachers. They certainly have a lot in common, as they all enjoy sports and movies and all served in the Navy. Even more impressive is that six out of the seven are still married to their original wives, who were credited for nurturing these long friendships.[14] While it is unclear how retirement can affect overall marital satisfaction, there is some evidence that when one initially retires, having more time at home as a couple can lead to conflict. However, research suggests that this often dissipates after a year or two as new routines, travel, or a part-time job become part of retired life.[15]

Retirement can often mean a change in the social circles developed out of work interactions. Men and women differ in terms of nurturing social connections. Women are more likely to seek out social connections, whereas men may not be as aware of the need for friendship in older age.[16] The Retired Old Men Eating Out (ROMEO) Social Club facilitates regular social interactions among men, as older men often say that they miss the interactions in their former jobs. Friendships among men improve their physical condition and well-being, increase their sense of belonging and purpose, boost happiness, reduce stress, and improve self-esteem, as well as steering them away from unhealthy lifestyles such as smoking, gambling, alcohol, or drugs. Regular meetings at a senior center or for morning coffee can be highly beneficial, but nothing is more important than having a friend you can turn to, talk to, and meet with often. Some research suggests that adult men seem to be especially bad at keeping and cultivating friendships.[17] Sadly, the number of Americans who say that they have no close friends has roughly tripled in recent decades. "Zero" is also the most common response when people are asked how many confidantes they have in their life, perhaps because today we often spend more time in front a screen than with people.

Idleness Aversion and a "Busy Ethic" in Older Age

Some people want to relax in retirement and enjoy taking it easy. However, many people feel driven with a need to keep active and stay busy and to engage in activities they didn't have time for while working. Although retirement is often thought of as unlimited free time, paradoxically, being idle actually concerns people who consider retirement. A common phrase among many retired older adults is "I keep busy" or that retirement is a "good type of busy." Arthur Conan Doyle, author of the Sherlock Holmes detective novels, captured this, saying, "I never remember feeling tired by work, though idleness exhausts me completely."[18]

Coach John Wooden's simple advice for successful aging centered on being busy, staying active, and having some variety in life—and he was successfully retired for over 30 years. Some research has shown that retirees who do not work in paid jobs are actually very busy people, and that these people report being busier in retirement than when they were employed.[19] However, the quality of this busyness is different in retirement. People have more control over what they choose to do as a retiree. The need and enjoyment of being busy has been referred to as a "busy ethic." Wooden, at age 98, had a full hand-written calendar, and he carefully picked what went into that calendar—similar to Dr. Ruth, Phyllis Diller, Mara Angelou, Frank Gehry, Jared Diamond, Bob Newhart, Jack LaLanne, and Dave Brubeck. In the process of my writing this book, many busy older adults made a point of scheduling time with me, as it was something they wanted to do, and because they felt their input was important, even if it added to their busy schedules. Recent work shows that those people who report having a busy schedule have better memory and stay sharper in their older age than those who report a less busy and idler lifestyle.[20] As Bob Dylan wrote, in the song "It's

Alright, Ma (I'm Only Bleeding)," "He not busy being born is busy dying."

Indeed, at almost any age, we often strive to stay busy and active, despite our tendencies toward procrastination. Partly because we feel overwhelmed, we will often fill up our time with small tasks, like answering piles of email and deleting spam. Simply keeping busy is not the key to retirement, unless the activity we choose has meaning or inherent importance. Retirement is a time to pursue personal goals without the constant pressure of other commitments—and it may be important to keep it that way. One man told me that his retired father, once a busy executive, now reads every piece of spam in his inbox because he finally has time to read all of his email. Thus, there is still a need to balance and focus on what is important, maybe even more so when one has more time on one's hands.

Older adults may feel they need to justify their retirement, by being perceived as busy by their adult children or friends. For example, a "busy ethic" may exist when older adults feel they need to defend their leisure time, telling others they are "keeping busy" and so don't have time for mundane tasks. As captured in her book *No, I Don't Want to Join a Book Club*, Virginia Ironside discusses why people may think or want to do very little in old age, whereas she herself chose to write a book at the age of 60.[21]

Of course, one doesn't know what retirement will actually be like until one is retired. People may consider or avoid retirement for many different reasons. Architect Frank Gehry still actively pursues new and challenging architectural projects, but he is more selective about what he does, whereas earlier in his life he took whatever he could get, because that is what makes one successful. John Wooden, by contrast, walked away from being the head coach of a dynasty basketball team with an inspirational and surprising (even to his wife) announcement 2 days before the 1975 championship game, one that likely motivated his team to win an unprecedented 10th national championship title. Coach Wooden was 65 at the time and wanted to enjoy his legacy rather than cling to it. He had a large social network of family and an even larger UCLA and athletic community that allowed him to enjoy his retirement. However, when I spoke with him, at age 95, Wooden said he wouldn't mind working as a consultant who could help players and mentor new coaches.

While many of the luminaries of successful aging say they won't retire, they also display effective ways of prioritizing what they enjoy about their jobs and minimizing the negative aspects—perhaps a privilege that comes with aging, seniority, and respect in a field. During her retirement, Phyllis Diller turned from comedy to painting, playing the piano, and hosting lively parties where she featured her paintings for sale. To keep her mind active, she did crosswords and read the newspapers, but said she most enjoyed being social. Sully Sullenberger, the pilot who was hailed a hero for successfully executing an emergency landing in the Hudson River, retired soon after the event and enjoyed the success of being acknowledged as a hero and piloting expert. He gave inspirational talks all over the country, as well as addressing Congress regarding airline safety and pilots' working conditions. However, after a few months off, Sullenberger returned to US Airways in a new role, consulting on safety management for the airline. In his retirement, Sullenberger has said that his advocacy for aviation safety and the piloting profession will continue.[22]

While retirement is often a goal for many, it can be also be a trying and challenging time of reconsidering goals from differing perspectives. It can allow one to select new paths or to realize that the intense and constant pleasure of certain livelihoods, in fact, keeps one lively. For example, in the case of jazz pianist Dave Brubeck, a doctor once advised him not to retire from live performance because he plainly looked to be in better shape *after* performing than *before* he got up on stage. Brubeck agreed: "I have more energy at the end than I do at the beginning. You can be so beat up that you can scarcely walk on stage but when you get to the piano the excitement kicks in, you forget about being tired."[23] In his older age, Brubeck regularly performed live on stage with his oxygen tank.

Bob Newhart shared a similar perspective, and he still tours the country doing his stand-up comedy. While he gets nervous and anxious before every show, this is what keeps him going. Newhart said,

> I stay active, by still doing my stand-up shows. It is a muscle, so you have to use it. Also, I would go nuts if I didn't stay active. I can't retire. I played golf, but I can't do that all the time. I went to a psychiatrist, and he said you just don't retire, you have to plan it 20 years in advance, have things to do, like bookbinding. I didn't do that, and I can't stop what I am doing because I enjoy it.[24]

Writer and professor Jared Diamond switched careers in a sense, from a wet-lab scientist who studied the physiology of the gall bladder to a global field researcher and writer—and the reasons were clear to him: he didn't want to study the gall bladder for another 30 years and had other aspirations to pursue.

The key to retirement may be to remain curious about what you are most interested in and pursue those avenues and adventures while reducing commitment to other forms of work that provide little stimulation or reward. Leisure activities do not have to be crossword puzzles, as there are many other activities that involve social interaction that can strengthen the brain and memory in significant ways. While joining a book club can engage both intellectual and social communication, many other stimulating activities involve both thinking and socializing. Following sports can involve updating information, emotional connections to both the teams and the fans who follow the sport with you, as well as gatherings with others and lively and informed conversations about sporting events.

Sherry Lansing was the first woman to head a major Hollywood studio (Paramount Pictures), and she played a large role in developing movies such as *Forrest Gump*, *Braveheart*, and *Titanic*. She at first found it very challenging to retire. However, now retired and at age 72, she says, "I am busier than I've ever been. And I am so happy with what I am doing because it all comes from my heart."[25] Since here retirement, she has devoted herself to many philanthropic endeavors, serves on the University of California Board of Regents, and co-founded the nonprofit Stand Up for Cancer. One of her most important roles now is that she is a mentor to young women.

When John Wooden retired, he still wanted to stay active and connected to UCLA. The athletic director at UCLA was J.D. Morgan. Morgan wanted Wooden to have an office in the athletic department so that he could stay connected to UCLA during his retirement. Morgan suggested he share an office with the new, incoming head basketball coach. However, Wooden realized this would infringe and put pressure on the new coach, so he asked instead to share offices with the then first-year baseball coach, Gary Adams, as baseball was, in fact, Wooden's favorite sport. Gary Adams went on to become head coach of the UCLA baseball team for 38 years. The two coaches became very good friends, and this arrangement allowed for many valuable professional and personal interactions between these coaches.

Actor Dick Van Dyke, in his 90s, said in his book, *Keep Moving: And Other Tips and Truths About Aging*, that the most important thing is to keep moving, to dance and sing, and to stay positive. As he did in *Mary Poppins, Chitty Chitty Bang Bang*, and the *Dick Van Dyke Show*, he still enjoys dancing and singing. He says, "Everyone should dance. And everyone should sing. People say, 'Well, I can't sing.' Everybody can sing. That you do it badly is no reason not to sing."[26]

A Growing Natural Resource: Policies about Retirement, and Why Retire Now?

Older adults represent one of the fastest-growing natural resources, a comment made by many who study the demographics of aging and know just how valuable older adults are in the workforce. Jared Diamond says it is important to use old people for what they are good at and like to do, rather than require them to put in long, 60-hour work weeks similar to work weeks of ambitious younger people. In his book, *The World Until Yesterday*, he also considers the opposite extreme, mandatory retirement at 65 (like in some countries) to be "stupidly imposing policy."[27]

Diamond, who sees Guiseppe Verdi as one of his role models for successful aging, notes that Verdi intended to end his musical career at age 58, after writing *Aida*. Verdi was persuaded by his publishers to write two more operas, *Otello*, at age 74, and *Falstaff*, at age 80. Both operas are often considered his greatest works. Thus, sometimes we ourselves are not the best judges of our retirement. Diamond is now working on his next book as he approaches the age of 80. He is also finding time to take an important family vacation to Africa with his wife and two grown sons, something he hasn't done in over 7 years. This suggests that older age is also a good time to balance work and family vacations.

Getting "rehired" in older age can be challenging, especially in domains where the hurdle of ageism (age discrimination) is prevalent. However, some companies make special efforts to recruit and hire older adults, many of whom have had careers in fields that can lend themselves well to their future employment. For example, Uber has a partnership with Life Reimagined (a non-profit subsidiary of AARP) to recruit older adults as drivers. Despite what many people might think, older drivers are actually safer on the road than younger drivers. Overall, older adults are involved in fewer accidents, partly because they don't take as many risks while driving, aren't speeding, and are less likely to text while driving. The first ride I ever took in an Uber car was with a 72-year-old retiree, who turned to driving as a way to have more social interaction. I was in Irvine, California, and had never been to Irvine before. Instead of calling a taxi I decided to try Uber. Arriving in minutes, with an eager smile on his face, the friendly driver gave me a guided tour through regions that he recalled were orange groves when he was a child. As I was new to Uber, he also showed me many helpful aspects of the Uber app, and tricks of the trade that he had picked up over the 2 years he had been driving. He told me he only worked when he wanted to, and that he had complete control over his schedule. He also said that his wife had encouraged it; she sometimes tells him to get out of the house and go drive his car.

Home Depot is another company that hires many older adults. Managers say that seniors are reliable, bring decades of work experience, and can mentor other employees. In addition, older adults are much less likely to move, get pregnant, or depart after a few months. One manager noted that the turnover rate for employees 50 and older was one-tenth that of workers under 30.[28] Many customers come to Home Depot with questions about their projects—I have done this many times myself. I will often seek out an older adult employee who will be patient with me while I ask for advice for my "do it yourself" handyman jobs around the house. Many of the older employees have had years of home repair expertise, as well as customer service experience from previous careers. Professor Timothy Salthouse notes, "Some jobs require rapid problem solving, where people are always performing to the limits—professional athletes and air traffic controllers, for example. But many jobs are like crossword puzzles. Novel problem solving is less important than experience."[29] Thus, older adults can put their years of experience to good use in these types of part-time jobs.

Vin Scully, the legendary baseball announcer, worked with the Dodgers for over 65 years, starting in 1950 in Brooklyn and then for 66 years in Los Angeles. He retired as he approached his 90th birthday. In his last few years as a broadcaster he intentionally limited his travel and only worked the home games. When asked what he was doing on his first days of retirement, with the Dodgers playing at home and him not doing his broadcast, he said he was just doing normal things, like getting his car washed, and that he was engaged in that other national pastime, paying bills. "My wife Sandi told me that I should tell you I spent the day doing something like studying Mandarin," he said. "But I told her, people know me better than that."[30]

David Letterman, television host of *Late Show with David Letterman* for over 30 years, retired in 2015, at age 70. Reflecting on this he said, "I can remember the first day that Stephen Colbert took over—put his new show on the air. I thought I would have some trouble, some emotional trouble, or some feeling of displacement, but I realized, hey, that's not my problem anymore. And I have felt much better."[31] In retirement, Letterman wanted to try something new, to be part of a National Geographic series on the impact of climate change. Illustrating the need to be part of something bigger, Letterman now sees environmental issues as an important challenge for the next generation (he also has a 12-year-old son). In contrast to his clean-shaven look on late-night TV, he has grown a large beard and feels less concerned about what others think of him, after spending so much time worrying about whether his TV shows would get popular ratings. In his retirement, he enjoys skiing with his family and devoting his time and energy to climate issues, recently travelling to India to learn more about the world's energy future. However, like for many other retirees, his complete retirement was short-lived, as 2 years after retiring from late-night TV he agreed to do a six-episode talk show for Netflix, a job that doesn't require the nightly grind of late-night TV. Regarding what he learned from his retirement, Letterman said, "Here's what I have learned, if you retire to spend more time with your family, check with your family first."[32]

Some people take on new jobs because they don't want to retire, even in their 90s. At 93, Betty Reid Soskin is a park ranger at Rosie the Riveter–World War II Home Front National Historical Park in Richmond, California. She writes frequently on her blog and has been interviewed by NPR and *People* magazine. She has become so popular that the park's tour audiences have doubled, tours are now booked months ahead, and the park has added tours to keep up. Hired as an interpretive ranger at the age of 85, she works 5 hours a day, 5 days a week. She says that when one has lived through nine decades before entering the park service, holding many roles—wife, mother, artist, caretaker, merchant, administrative aide, field representative in the state legislature, research project administer, chief of staff for the City of Berkeley—all that adds wisdom and insight to her current career. And she has no plans to retire.[33] Of course, there is a middle ground, such as when professional athletes retire (sometimes several times) from their playing career and then return as managers, coaches, and owners. Hockey star Wayne Gretzky and basketball icon Magic Johnson illustrate these paths of multiple retirements during their playing careers, while never really retiring from professional sports and the sports that they love.

Stan Berman, age 87, has owned Stan's Donuts, in Westwood, near UCLA, for over 50 years. He has reduced his hours over the last 5 years, but he would not consider himself retired. He still comes in almost every day, early in the morning, has a donut, talks to regular customers, and will even make a few donut deliveries. He told me that it is in his blood, and when he is not travelling (taking the vacations he always wanted to take) he rarely misses a day of work. Jack LaLanne, John Glenn, Dr. Ruth, and Frank Gehry all said they almost feared retirement, because their work was their passion. They all said that they had seen some friends and colleagues deteriorate shortly after retirement, and that they read some of these people's obituaries a few years later. These observations likely fueled their desire to remain active, to not retire completely, and to find ways to stay connected.

Kareem Abdul-Jabbar played professional basketball for 20 years, from 1969 to 1989, and retired at age 42 as the all-time leader in points scored in the National Basketball Association. He has now been retired more years than he played professionally. He says[34] that his retirement years have been the most exciting and rewarding of his life—a striking statement given his illustrious collegiate and professional basketball career. He has now written many books on various subjects, including children's literature, African American history, and mystery novels. He outlines three ways to enjoy retirement:

(1) Don't think of it as retirement, as it is not the end of something, and don't let that term make you feel like you are no longer able to contribute.

(2) Go from being a success to being significant. (He is currently writing a series of novels for middle-school children, a completely new avenue for him.)

(3) Possibly the most important: maintain relationships by having a presence in people's lives.

Abdul-Jabbar says he frequently calls and visits his friends and family, staying updated on what they're doing, even though he says he is "not an overly chatty person," and he goes out to meet new people. He notes that his writing time is fairly solitary, so he does a lot of volunteer work, such as visiting cancer patients, visiting other countries as a U.S. global cultural ambassador, or visiting schools to promote science, technology, engineering, and math education. He says that meeting people of different ages and backgrounds makes life more meaningful and fulfilling.

There may be a variety of physical reasons for seeking out retirement. For example, if you are in a job that requires substantial physical labor, such as in construction, the aging process may not allow you to work long hours or lift heavy objects. However, there are also many professions that may get better with age, when wisdom is accrued and valued, making it difficult or unnecessary to consider retirement. For example, some professors and politicians may reach the height of their career in their 60s or 70s. Jared Diamond, who is nearly 80, still regularly teaches small undergraduate classes, and enjoys interacting with younger students and younger colleagues such as myself. He uses the books that he authored for his undergraduate classes and tests out ideas for future books, getting feedback and insight from the students.

Some older people also feel that working with younger people keeps them active, stimulated, and, in many ways, feeling younger if not wiser. Interactions between generations can also enable an important transfer of knowledge and information. Younger adults can teach older adults about new-trending technology, while older adults and parents can serve as role models and mentors in many ways. Professors Jared Diamond and Bob Bjork, among others, have played an important mentorship role during my career at UCLA.

Off to Work We Go (Sometimes Too Often): Retire or Work Less and Enjoy It More

Many times older adults who partially retire find that they then enjoy their job more because they work less and have more leisure time, while still having an income and job satisfaction. Why should this only happen in older age, once our children are grown or when we are faced with some age-related physical challenges? One innovative idea, proposed by Laura Carstensen in her book *A Long Bright Future*, is that people might actually take a "mini-retirement" earlier in life, before having a full-time job, career success, and associated professional responsibilities. During this "partial retirement" time one might have young children and other responsibilities or interests, but then return to full-time work later in life, given that lifespan for most people continues to be extended. This unique form of partial retirement and later re-entering the workforce would allow parents to spend more time with children, which can have many benefits. While our culture emphasizes and expects a working life until age 65, there are other cultures, or even similar countries, that may work less and have a comparable or better quality of life.

Americans spend a lot of time working, averaging about 1,800 working hours per year. People often do not, or cannot, take their allotted vacation days, which suggests we are not well positioned to transition into retirement if we can't even find time to vacation or just relax before retirement. This is true not just in the United States. For instance, Greeks average over 2,000 working hours a year. In comparison, Germans tend to work about 1,400 hours each year, but German productivity is still very high. France seems to take all of August off, without huge negative consequences on overall productivity.[35] In older age, working less can pay off, both in terms of health and quality of life—and semi-retirement may be a way to implement the "work less, do more" approach. Life transitions can encourage efficiency. Having young children has certainly made me more efficient in how I spend my time. Older workers may, in fact, work in a more efficient manner. The "father of economics," economist and philosopher Adam Smith, stated, "The man who works so moderately as to be able to work constantly not only preserves his health the longest, but in the course of the year, executes the greatest quantity of works."[36]

Recently I got a letter from my dentist, which stated the following:

> After 46 years in my dental practice, I have decided to slow down. My new main focus will be following my passion: making high quality wine. It has been a pleasure to care for you and your family, and you have made my professional career extremely rewarding, and surprisingly fun.

While I was disappointed that I was no longer going to have him as my dentist, I was also impressed that he was following his passion. I learned that while he was turning over his newer patients to his associates at the same office, he would still be seeing a select few older patients (ones he has had for over 30 years), working in a manner that would keep him still tied to the practice while directing more time to his passions.

One common observation about retirement is that although some very successful people avoid retirement, when they do take up some form of semi-retirement, it usually involves doing *more* of the work that they like and less of the work they don't like. As one older adult said, "I am now in my declining years. When people ask me to do things I am not interested in doing, I decline."

Being Part of Something BIGGER in Retirement

After logging many years working in a specific job or field, people often seek to make a contribution to something "bigger than themselves," sometimes becoming more involved with a religious group, a charity, a community organization, a social group, or focusing on family. This can also involve blending professional pursuits so that they better fit with *generativity*, defined as a stage in life in which one focuses on making the world better for the next generation. One study found that being part of a volunteer group that involved intergenerational civic interactions led to stronger feelings of connection and contributions to the next generation.[37] For example, shortly after the miracle landing on the Hudson, Sully advocated for better aviation safety, an issue he was interested in well before the incident. After retirement, he has taken on additional roles advocating for improvement in aviation safety, such as presenting these issues to Congress and becoming an aviation and safety expert for CBS News.

Making the world a better place can also involve mentoring younger people and contributing to a better understanding of our world. Many older adults are happy and pleased to serve as mentors. Writers, comedians, and professors represent some professions that see mentoring as a way to connect and provide direction to the future of their field. Some people may write a memoir documenting their life and important contributions. A surprising number also turn to writing children's books, teaming up with younger family or friends, to pass on a message and story to the youngest generation. For example, John Wooden, John Glenn, Dr. Ruth, Bob Dylan, Keith Richards (with his daughter), and Kareem Abdul-Jabbar have all authored children's books. Dr. Seuss's last book published during his lifetime, *Oh, the Places You'll Go!*, outlines the journey of life, unknown adventures, and challenges of new beginnings in life.

Jackie Robinson was a pioneer in the Civil Rights Movement and became the first African American to play Major League Baseball in the modern era. After an exceptional 10-year playing career in the major leagues he retired at age 37, noting, "The game of baseball is great, but the greatest thing is what you do after your career is over."[38] Robinson went on to become the first African American television analyst in Major League Baseball, and the first African American vice president of a major American corporation, to name a few of his many other accomplishments and contributions to society after he retired from playing professional baseball.

John Glenn was selected in 1959 by NASA as one of the United States' first astronauts. After officially retiring from the Marine Corps and NASA at age 45, John Glenn ran for Senate in 1974, serving until 1999. In 1998, at the age of 72, and while still a sitting senator, he became the oldest person to fly in space. Thus, he has had many "encore" careers. He was heavily involved with the John Glenn College of Public Affairs at The Ohio State University, something he helped found in order to encourage public service. He and his wife would often give lectures there in small seminars. Glenn also remained active as a Freemason, in the Masonic youth organization, and is an ordained elder in the Presbyterian Church.

Grandparenting and Contributing to the Next Generation

Many adults who are retired are very involved in grandparenting, and some have scheduled retirement to coincide with this endeavor. However, the average age at which many Americans become first-time grandparents is on the rise. For a variety of reasons, people put off having children until later in life, leading to challenges in fertility, as well as a large generation gap between grandparents and grandchildren. This is often a concern for many older and retired adults, who may be anxiously awaiting grandchildren.[39]

In general, people who enjoy being grandparents report feeling younger, believe that people become old at older ages, and hope to live longer than those who do not enjoy grandparenting.[40] Becoming a grandparent often motivates older people to be healthier. However, many people are not in a rush to become grandparents. I had one friend whose mother would remind her when she went out on a date in high school and in college, "Be home by midnight; I don't want to be a grandmother yet." While becoming a grandparent at a young age may accelerate aging in a sense, positive interaction with grandchildren can lead to a younger age identity.

Comedian, writer, and actress Rita Rudner once quipped, "Have children while your parents are still young enough to take care of them." Grandparents often do more than simply babysit here and there or call on birthdays. In the United States, almost six million children live with their grandparents. Half of these grandparents have legal custody of the grandchildren, often because parents are unable to care for the child or are under financial hardship.[41] For example, the gymnastics multiple–gold medalist Simone Biles was raised by her grandparents while her parents struggled with drug and alcohol addiction. Simone's grandparents stepped in at an early age and adopted her and her sister. In many families, grandparents often make major financial contributions to grandchildren; they may pay for schooling, clothing, and music lessons, give or buy their grandchildren a car, and pay for college. Given our longer lifespan, it is possible for several family generations to interact and help with children, although there are still many older adults who are waiting for grandchildren.

Most retirees say spending time with grandchildren is as much or even more enjoyable than spending time with their own children.[42] The attraction to grandchildren is often so strong that retirees say that the top reason they would move in retirement is to be closer to their families. Older people learn to use technology, such as FaceTime and Skype, to be better connected to their grandchildren. Other than the joy (and sometimes worry) that often accompanies being a grandparent, there may be mental health benefits to grandparenting. Some research has shown that grandmothers who care for a grandchild 1 day a week are less likely to develop dementia.[43] However, to illustrate just how taxing it can be to take care of a child, caring for a grandchild 5 days a week was associated with memory impairments in grandmothers. Gene Perret, the comedian and writer, said, "My grandkids believe I'm the oldest thing in the world. And after two or three hours with them, I believe it, too." As for grandfathers, some research has shown that grandfathers who have meaningful relationships with grandchildren are less likely to develop depression.[44] Seeing and being around grandchildren may give more meaning and motivation to live a healthy life. Grandparents also may not act like they did when they were parents. Grandparents may have more time, money, or both for grandchildren than when they were busy working, and this may be a way to compensate and focus attention on the next generation.

There may be benefits for grandparents beyond simply helping their busy grown children who are now parents: grandparenting may contribute to higher levels of happiness and life satisfaction for all. One reward is more connectedness within three generations of family. Being around grandchildren can make grandparents feel young, recall times when their own children were young, and share these stories and impart knowledge. My mother-in-law has recently taken on the role of both Latin and math teacher to her grandchildren once a week. These interactive classes include field trips to the thrift shop or toy shop to study business and applied math, and presents of toys and clothing. Grandpa will proudly show pictures of his six grandchildren to virtually anyone—which often leads to a common connection with other grandparents. He also yells and cheers at their basketball games. One of the rewards of retirement is that it allows for greater flexibility to be closer to grandchildren, something that can benefit the children, parents, and grandparents.

Summary

Even though many people see retirement as having a lot of free time, it doesn't mean not being busy. People can focus on what really matters and invest their time wisely, without spending time on the mundane. We can spend more time on what we enjoy and less time on tasks we don't take pleasure in or don't find meaningful. Retirement is not a finish line, and fully retiring is not always an option. Some form of retirement can allow time for more leisure and focusing on what is important, whether it be family, professional interests, or hobbies. However, retirement can also be a leading cause of mortality and a time of mental unrest and confusion. We often don't consider the psychological aspects of retirement and instead focus on financial concerns, only to report that it is the social connections that are missed most once we retire. Today, many older people take on encore careers, often to satisfy the need to be busy, to apply expertise and interests in a less stressful and more enjoyable job, and to have social connections. It is common for older adults to be working in some capacity in their 80s, often by choice, and sometimes this involves taking on the important role of grandparenting. Retirement can be both a challenging and gratifying time in life, and it may take time to learn how to retire and enjoy it.

It Gets Even Better with Age:
Start Successful Aging Now

Old age is full of enjoyment if you know how to use it.
                    —Seneca (the Younger), 4 BC–AD 65

OLD AGE IS CONSTANTLY GETTING OLDER, WITH THOSE
90 and over representing one of the fastest growing age groups.
What is important is the quality of these years, as dementia, diabetes, and various physical disabilities can be major challenges for
older adults both today and in the future. The phrase "Adding life
to years, and not just more years to life" is especially relevant given
increasing life expectancy. While some think the reason we live long
lives is simply "good genes," it is clear that our behavior and beliefs
can have a substantial impact. What can we do now to better prepare,
both physically and psychologically, for successful aging?

This book is meant to provide some insights regarding how
successful aging can begin at any age, and can be accomplished in
many different ways. Being aware of the myths, paradoxes, and psychology of aging can have an impact on how we experience aging.
As jazz musician Eubie Blake said, and many others have echoed, "If
I knew I was going to live this long, I would have taken better care of

myself." We can be better informed about aging earlier in life, often through exposure to older family and friends and other role models of aging.

Aging Is about Attitude: Our Attitudes Change as We Age

What do you expect to be when you grow up? When we are children, our parents, teachers, peers, or role models set up expectations. Children respond to those expectations, and it may be no different when we are middle-aged and contemplate what old age will be like for us. Astronaut and Senator John Glenn reinforced this idea:

> I think that people respond to expectations—and this starts when we're kids. Kids tend to rise to what's expected of them. I think as we get older, maybe we set expectations of ourselves in addition to what other people expect of us. The general public thinks, once you're about 70 you're going downhill, 80 you're really downhill, 90 you're just lucky like Annie (my wife) and I are, and very few reach 100. But whether those expectations go down or not, I think your own expectations of what you can or cannot do and what you want to do, your own expectations of yourself guide you.[1]

Kareem Abdul-Jabbar, the basketball star who recently battled leukemia and is now in his 70s, said in an interview with *The Rotarian*:

> Age is about attitude. As we get older, it's natural that we think more about death. But knowing that the end is on the horizon helps us prioritize what's important in our lives and motivates us to do more to enjoy those priorities. Knowing that my time is limited makes me cherish my friends and family more intensely and encourages me to make sure they know this. I no longer put off doing things that are important to me.[2]

He also quoted Yoko Ono, who had just turned 80: "I do feel that I am starting a new life at 80, a second life that will have so many things I didn't have in the first life." Abdul-Jabbar then said:

> That's a good way to look at this new era in our lives—as an opportunity to express those parts of ourselves that we ignored or overlooked in our youth. These days, when I'm forced to choose among several

options, I ask myself which choice will bring the most joy to my life and the lives of those around me. This has encouraged me to try new things, forge new relationships, and seek new ways to contribute to my community.

Abdul-Jabbar wrote a book entitled *Coach Wooden and Me: Our 50-Year Friendship On and Off the Court*, showing how important dynamic lifelong friendships can be as we age. He discusses what an enormous impact Coach Wooden, who was 37 years older than him, had on his time at UCLA and on life well after his basketball-playing days were over.[3] Abdul-Jabbar references Ernest Hemingway when describing how he thought of Wooden in his older age: "As you get older, it's more difficult to have heroes, but it's just as necessary." As we age, we might reflect more on those older role models providing some guidance for how we experience old age. In general, when we are younger, we are fairly naïve regarding the aging process and what life is like in old age, until we actually experience it. Our experiences may be far different from our expectations earlier in life. However, our expectations in middle age may dictate or influence our experience later in life, which suggests that attitudes about aging are extremely important.

What to Expect in Old Age Is Not What You Get: Expectations versus Experience

As outlined in Chapter 2, levels of happiness and levels of life satisfaction can be quite high in older age, often higher than in middle age. This represents what is known as the "paradox of well-being."[4] Older adults report high subjective well-being despite facing various challenges associated with changes in health and declines associated with aging. Younger people may not accurately predict older adults' feelings in old age, or even their own, once they reach old age. In fact, often younger people's expectations about aging don't match up with what older adults report. A large-scale study[5] showed that among those over age 75, more than 80% reported being happy or very happy. Most rated their own experience of old age more favorably than what the younger adults would expect of themselves in old age. Thus, there is an illuminating age gap in terms of expectations and what older adults actually experience. While memory loss, not being able to drive, and struggling to pay bills were all concerns, the older adults reported them to be less of an issue relative to what the younger adults would expect in old age. This discrepancy between expectations and actual experiences suggests that certain issues in old age aren't as bad as younger people might expect.

What are some of your expectations about aging? On a scale of 1 to 10, with 1 being "I don't agree at all" and 10 being "I strongly agree," how much do you disagree or agree with each of the following statements?

- The human body is like a car: when it gets old it gets worn out.
- I expect that as I get older I will spend less time with friends and family.
- Being lonely is just something that happens when people get old.
- As people get older they worry more.
- It's normal to be depressed when you get old.

This survey, known as the "Expectation Regarding Aging" survey, has been used to measure the degree to which people think of aging in a positive or negative light.[6] If you disagreed with most of the statements listed, then you have a fairly positive outlook on aging. Our beliefs about aging predict a number of important health behaviors. For example, having low expectations about aging, as measured by having a low score on this survey, was associated with not believing it was important to seek healthcare in older age. In addition, doctors who had more positive views about aging were more likely to provide counseling and preventive medicine to older patients than to simply prescribe medications.[7] Thus, you might ask your doctor these same questions regarding expectations about aging when deciding on a doctor to see in your older age. It also depends how old we want to live to be, as research has shown that people's preference of either dying young (before age 80) or living longer (more than age 90) was related to either a belief in negative or positive expectations about aging, respectively.[8] Thus, our expectations may influence how we age, how long we live, and what we do in older age.

Lying about Our Age and Other Ways to Avoid
Negative Stereotypes of Aging

Several recent studies have shown how stereotypes about aging can influence our beliefs and how we age. Older adults are under "stereotype threat" when expectations about aging bias one's behaviors, sometimes leading to anxiety and self-fulfilling prophecies about how to act in older age. If you are an older person in a doctor's office, and the doctor says they will now test your memory, there may be an implied expectation of dementia, so people do more poorly when tested. Simply taking a memory test called a "dementia screening" test can be an anxiety-provoking experience. In a study conducted in the UK,[9] 14% of the older adults who were tested met the criteria for dementia when they were *not tested* under stereotype threat, but *when tested* under stereotype threat conditions, a whopping 70% met the diagnostic criteria for dementia. Thus, if doctors use terms such as *dementia* and *Alzheimer's disease*, this can induce a level of anxiety in patients, making older adults behave like they may have these conditions.

Stereotype threat can be induced in a variety of ways. It could be that simply seeing a younger doctor who asks about your memory and asks your age can lead you to forget things. In this clinical setting it can cause you to perform poorly on a test designed to assess the onset of dementia. There are ways to avoid stereotype threat, by simply believing less in the negative stereotypes about aging, feeling younger than your actual age (which is sometimes why people lie about their age), not being around others who believe in the negative stereotypes, or not finding the stereotypes all that terribly concerning or surprising. For example, 80-year-olds might not be overly concerned about forgetting some things as they have been doing this for many years, so they do not experience the anxiety of the stereotype threat, whereas 60-year-olds might be much more concerned about possible decline or dementia, despite the fact that some forgetting naturally happens to people as they age.

Just reading or talking about successful aging might not make you think about aging in a positive light. You might think that cases of successful aging are rare or unique, and you might in general hold negative beliefs about the aging process. In one study,[10] two groups of older people viewed a computer screen, looking for a dot and pressing a key. On the surface, this was quite a mundane task. However, unbeknownst to participants in one group, sometimes positive words about aging (e.g., *spry, active*) were presented subliminally on the screen so that people could not consciously notice them, whereas the second group had no subliminal words presented. Simply the rapid presentation of these words made an impact on later behavior. Upon testing several weeks later, when the first groups had the positive stereotype activated "implicitly" or subliminally, these people had better attitudes about aging several weeks later. In addition, these participants also had greater physical abilities compared to those who didn't see the positive words, as measured by how often the participants could sit down and get out of a chair in 1 minute. Thus, activating positive stereotypes about aging can benefit physical health and can have long-term effects on successful aging. Just a few subtle or simple reminders can be a good way to promote successful aging.

As aging parents, we have the responsibility to teach our children about life. One important lesson involves setting a good example of how life can be good in old age and challenging them to prepare for their old age. Holding positive stereotypes about aging doesn't just lead to successful aging, it is also associated with the amount of time it takes to recover from various disabilities as an older adult.[11] Thus, the mind–body connection can be important when one encounters the various physical challenges that are associated with aging.

Role Models of Old Age Can Help Us All Learn to Age Successfully

Who is your old-age hero or role model? Try to name five people whom you admire for how they have aged, and take your pick of qualities and traits you would like to embrace in your own way.

When I ask students in my classes at UCLA to name people they think illustrate successful aging, there are a variety of answers, ranging from grandparents, political figures, teachers, librarians, and actors to the "they are never going to retire" accountants, professors, coaches, and family friends.

Thinking about role models can help us all age better, but having clear goals is important. Research in goal setting has shown that simply writing out or clearly articulating a goal can make you more likely to achieve it.[12] Often this involves being specific. So, "eat healthy" might help generally, but a more specific goal of "eating fewer cookies after 7 p.m." is more likely to cause a real change. "Get more exercise" is a general goal, but saying you will "walk 4 days a week before breakfast with a friend" is a more specific goal. "Maintain friendships" is a good general goal, but having a standing date to "call a friend or family member every Friday morning" is more specific. Having specific goals makes things happen, as it gives the brain a clearer and simpler direction in which to act. By outlining these specific plans in your head or on a calendar, you can better achieve what you want to do, and who you want to be, in old age.

It is important to know that successful aging can be the norm. In fact, some researchers[13] suggest that almost 90% of the population can be considered successful agers to some degree. Most ordinary people who do not achieve lasting fame can achieve successful aging. Many older adults provide inspiring life stories or narratives for their family and future generations. Successful aging involves meaningful aging, such as having a purpose in life, whether it is a job, a hobby, being a mentor, having connection to family, or a spiritual conviction.

When I told people about my interviews with older people and my interest in aging, they often came up with many more people I should interview. The list got very long, illustrating just how many impressive figures of successful aging are out there in our communities. Successful aging is often hard to define, but there are many examples in the world, and having a role model makes us better at achieving that goal.

Your Life Story

There was never yet an uninteresting life. Such a thing is an impossibility. Inside the dullest exterior, there is a drama, a comedy, and a tragedy.

—Mark Twain

I've learned that people will forget what you said, people will forget what you did, but people will never forget how you made them feel.

—Maya Angelou

We all have a life story. While we might not all write a lengthy memoir, it can be a useful exercise to write about 500 words to describe your life to date—what are the important points? This exercise can be done in as little as 20 minutes, and you might try this for yourself now—I recently tried this and it made me very reflective. I found doing this to be both challenging and illuminating in terms of figuring out what really defines the important journeys and themes in my life. Writing about your life can make you not only think about your past but also about your own future. What things would you hope to do in the next 10 years, building off of your current narrative, or what new things would you like to focus on? This was a formative exercise that changed my perspective and caused me to realize that while my enjoyable professional career was described in the narrative, it was more part of the journey of my life. My family and friends, many of whom were from my professional life, were more of the constant and enriching aspects of my life.

Learning about our family and family stories can have an impact on the next generation. Documenting life stories can be important for family members for various reasons, and there is no time like the present to write and think about your life. One way to get started on this is through a structured program called "guided autobiography." Guided autobiography provides an opportunity to reminisce about experiences in your life, capture them in writing, and share them with a small group. The emphasis is on your story and how to construct it so that others can learn more about you. Guided autobiography was developed by gerontologist Dr. James Birren over the past 40 years as a method for helping people to document their life stories.[14] With the aid of a trained instructor, participants are led through themes and are given questions that can evoke memories of key life events, sometimes ones that have been seemingly forgotten. People are asked to write a two-page story on a particular theme from their life each week, bring the story of their lives to the class, and read it to a small group of receptive classmates. Writing and sharing life stories with others is an ideal way to find new meaning in life and to put life events into perspective. While connecting with one another on their journey of self-discovery, people who take part in this program often report feeling "enlivened by the group experience" and gain a greater appreciation of their own lives and of the lives of others. While not considered therapy, it can be a powerful catalyst for improving self-esteem, self-confidence, and communication within communities and families.[15] In addition, your younger family members might enjoy and cherish the now-documented treasures of these stories and life histories. Often it is easier to understand and appreciate someone's life by hearing their story. Our life stories define who we are, and this form of narrative psychology becomes richer, more apparent, and often important in older age.

Another way to document our lives is to have a younger generation interview an older generation, such as grandchildren interviewing grandparents. This can involve asking an older person about their own childhood, such as what books they liked, toys they had, chores they had, and mistakes they made, and how they look back on their career and family life. Grandparents can also be asked what they expect their grandchildren will do in the future, possibly empowering them through expectations (as John Glenn suggests). Sometimes you learn the most about people by talking to their families. I learned unique things about John Glenn by talking to his grandson, Daniel Glenn, who was a graduate student at UCLA. Daniel shared heartwarming and inspiring stories about his grandfather and family, illustrating how older relatives can be role models in many ways.

We also set an important example for our next generation, first by our behavior and also by describing our lives in a historical context. My children see me writing, hear me say how I need to write today, and it makes them want to write. One is writing a book, another writes letters and emails to her friends, and the youngest is writing on the walls. Sometimes leading by example, even unintentionally, will cause others to follow in their own creative manner. Successful aging can be led by example for future generations.

When the Ages Complement Each Other: Teaching and Learning Benefits

While boarding a local city bus, a well-dressed older woman asked a group of people if they had change for a quarter. The bus fare was 55 cents, and she had three quarters. Eventually someone offered her change, and later on the bus ride, a younger student sitting next to her started talking to this older woman. The conversation they engaged in was illuminating, so I had to listen. First, the student said to the woman that not many people ask for change for a quarter. She laughed, and then explained that she also needed the change for her next bus, explaining the logic behind her request. The student said that she admired the older adult's courage to ask for change. The student told the woman that she was a new UCLA student, majoring in ethnomusicology. They discussed the student's major and what she wanted to do. Then the older woman revealed more about herself, saying that she had been a nurse for the past 40 years and was a student at UCLA before that, and told where she was going today. In fact, they appeared to become quick friends in the 20-minute bus ride and exchanged contact information. Since it was the student's first week, she did not know where to get off the bus to find her building at UCLA. She got detailed directions from the older woman, who admitted that some things might have changed since she was last on campus. As I silently observed this interaction, I was impressed at how the younger student took such interest in the older woman, and how they both seemed to benefit from this interaction.

Watching grandparents at the park taking care of younger grandchildren can be very illuminating. Grandparents clearly are responsible, vigilant, sometimes even overly watchful because they feel responsible to report back to the parents. Some parents, by contrast (perhaps not the helicopter parents), may more often be spotted on their phone or texting while their children run free and wild. While we might think that grandparents can't run as fast or react as quickly as younger parents, their years of past parenting experience may be especially valuable when caring for grandchildren.

In American culture, grandparents usually don't live in the same home as their grandchildren, though this is common in other cultures and can clearly have some benefits. When grandparents are involved in their grandchildren's childcare, there may be some conflict, such as debates over the benefits of organic foods: "We didn't have organic food back then" (or it was all organic back then). The focus of parenting also changes over time, which can result in conflict between grandparents, whose perspective is from a different era, and today's parents.[16] While grandparents and parents may sometimes have conflict over a variety of evolving issues, grandparents can leave lifelong impressions and can be the best teachers for both parents and grandchildren.

Younger and older adults can certainly have conflicting schedules, viewpoints, and interests. However, much can be gained through didactic interactions, for both young and old, as well as their audiences. While many of the interviews I conducted for this book were learning experiences, I have had much more interaction via mentoring from energetic and wise older adults. My PhD advisor, Fergus Craik, was over 70 and officially retired from the university while I was in graduate school. He still remains active as a research scientist and scholar (and also as a connoisseur of the best drinks Scotland has to offer). At UCLA, I co-teach a graduate class on memory and learning with my esteemed colleague, Robert Bjork, who is in his late 70s and officially retired but very active both professionally and on the golf course. We have been teaching this class together for almost a decade, each time learning more from each other. Working with a more senior person has many benefits, as does working with a more junior person. Our students love comparing and contrasting our teaching styles and stories. Bjork has far more stories than I do, and I now use those stories in other classes. This is also illustrated in the unique collaboration between 85-year-old psychiatrist Jimmie Holland and 50-year-old clinical psychologist Mindy Greenstein, with additional insights from Holland's 20-something-year-old granddaughter and various older adults from a book club, that resulted in an insightful and inspiring book about the aging process, entitled *Lighter as We Go*.[17]

In general, collaboration between people of different ages, backgrounds, and viewpoints can be an enriching experience and can lead to creative insights. An apprenticeship can connect younger people with older adults, to better understand aging and provide transmission of information and knowledge regarding popular culture and historical events. For example, a new housing program in New York City links older adult residents who have an apartment with a spare bedroom near NYU with younger college students. This housing arrangement provides a unique intergenerational roommate situation. The older adult may benefit from having a younger person around and from having additional income from the rent. The younger adult has a knowledgeable mature person living with them. These types of programs are now popular in many states. One younger student who participated in this intergenerational housing program in Illinois said[18]:

> I have lived with roommates my own age, and it wasn't a positive living experience. Here [living with seniors] everyone gets along. We

watch a lot of *Star Trek* together. Everyone is really laid back. The most important job I have is grocery shopping.

These sorts of intergenerational living environments provide unique benefits for young and old, and are becoming popular in other parts of the world as well. Having a household of young and old may be an ideal living environment for all parties.

Balance, Love, and Not Worrying about What You Can't Control

Balance

John Wooden said that the two most important words in the world were *balance* and *love*. Throughout life, we often struggle with balance: in our social life, our studies, our work, jobs, family, checkbooks, emotions, and, later in life, our physical balance, an issue that vitally affects older adults. Poor balance and falls are one of the leading causes of death in older age. Falls are preventable, and aging itself does not cause falls, as suggested by Steve Kasner, a NASA research psychologist, in his book *Careful: A User's Guide to Our Injury-Prone Minds*. Falling isn't just for frail older people as falls may actually be most common in those age 50 to 60, as this age group is still very active.[19] People are often distracted when walking, talking, and using a phone, so distracted walking can lead to loss of balance and falls. Sometimes simply being careful is not enough, as we have to work at having good balance. Having good balance can save your life. The true sense of the word also encompasses many important aspects of life.

Despite his success as a coach, Wooden said that his most important role in life was being a parent, followed by being a teacher and coach. Finding balance can be one of the most challenging aspects of life, whether we are a high school or college student, starting a demanding career, being a parent, or retiring from a job. Even when we have large amounts of leisure time, we need balance and structure. Often we are not aware of just how enjoyable simple experiences can be when done in a balanced manner. The same can be said for all of the activities that may be associated with successful aging, as we need to fit these activities into a balanced lifestyle. Balance, whether it be physical, mental, or emotional, is crucial for successful aging.

Love

Love is important for people of any age. John Wooden, whose wife Nel of over 50 years died at age 73, insisted that the UCLA basketball court be named in her honor, not his alone. He also spent his remaining 25 years writing letters to her each month and not sleeping on her side of the bed in their apartment. Many older adults will speak openly about finding love, as it can be an important aspect about aging and enjoying life, and the earlier the better. For example, John Glenn met his wife Annie when they were toddlers. They were married for over 70 years.

People look for love at all ages, and older adults join the more youthful in online dating. Emotional expression may also improve in old age, such that people are more appreciative of meaningful relationships and more open to telling people how they feel. Hearing a simple "I love you" can be one of the most important messages. Whether it comes from a spouse, a child, a grandchild, or a more recent meaningful partner, many older adults recognize the value of love, especially in a world where we see a lot of conflict and turmoil in the news. Older adults may become emotionally tender as old age leads to an expression of deeper emotions.[20] As I was finishing my interview with Coach Wooden, my pregnant wife joined me to meet him. He commented that I was lucky to have such a beautiful wife, and that the most important thing in life was to be a good husband, father, and teacher. He gave me a copy of one his favorite poems, "A Little Fellow Follows Me." He then told me that having a loving family is the best thing in life.

Emotional states become even more important as we get older, as is recognizing important emotional events. Just look at older adults at a wedding, bar mitzvah, or funeral. They are often expressive, balanced, and emotionally present, something that may come with age. Older adults may also value these important emotional events more than younger adults, as they are more aware of their significance. Emotional regulation is one aspect that gets better with age, as older adults are better able to communicate their emotions. This doesn't mean simply hiding emotion but expressing it when appropriate, and often being more uninhibited than younger adults when discussing emotions, albeit in more succinct ways.

Sherry Lansing, the former studio head of Paramount Pictures, is now in her 70s. She said she is now aware of the gifts and deficits of aging, commenting that "the losses are more, but there is also more gratitude, more determination not to let the small stuff bother you. You learn to only do what's important and meaningful. The only thing that matters at the end of the day is love and human connections."[21]

Don't Worry, Be Happy

"You worry too much." That is what my father would say to me at various points in my life—keep in mind, he also worried that I worried too much, so look where I got it from. Now in his 80s, he seems to worry less about me worrying and, in general, worries less himself. As I interviewed hundreds of older adults, I was impressed with their sense of calmness, making me more aware of my own need to relax, to appreciate the bigger, and finer, aspects of life. We need to know what we have control over, what to be thankful for, and what isn't worth the worry.

Among the many older adults I interviewed, very few had strong regrets, but many commented on how much they used to worry about what they now feel is the "small stuff." Of course, this might have also been part of the reason they were successful in life, by focusing on details, anticipating future actions, and preparing many different plans, even if only a few were actually carried out. For example, basketball coach John Wooden was an obsessive planner for his basketball practices and implemented various rules and lessons for his players, to the point that some of his players considered him a micromanager of sorts. But his results were impressive, both in terms of player development and numerous championships, and years later former players often speak about how Wooden taught them many important lessons about life. Later in life, older adults aren't simply always living in the moment, as they do make plans and think about the future, but they are less likely to second-guess themselves and fret about things they don't have control over. Mark Twain summed this wisdom up as follows: "I am an old man, and I have known a great many troubles, but most of them never happened."

When we are younger, we worry about finding a job, paying a mortgage, finding a partner, and raising our children. Planning can be helpful, but worrying can often be an endless obsession, and often anxiety can get in the way of enjoying life. Dr. Karl Pillemer, a Cornell University professor of sociology who interviewed thousands of older adults for his books *30 Lessons for Living* and *30 Lessons for Loving*, proclaims himself a world-class worrier.[22] However, his take-home lesson, based on all of these interviews, was that most older adults had a very similar message: "stop worrying." If they had any regrets, it was that they wished they had all the time back they had spent worrying, when they may have spoiled those precious be-in-the-present moments with fruitless ruminating about the future.[23] Certainly, my younger daughter has taken this to heart, and endlessly sings the song "Don't Worry, Be Happy" while skipping around the house. Clearly she is wise beyond her years.

Successfully Avoiding Scams in Older Age

Successful aging also involves knowing whom and what to avoid, and what sounds too good to be true. Older adults are often a target of financial scams and swindles, partly because older adults have time and money, and may have a genuine interest in wanting to help people. Older adults' poorer memory and propensity to focus on positive information (as outlined in Chapter 2 on happiness) can be exploited to scam them into thinking they have won a prize or have a lucky opportunity. There is evidence that some companies provide sales employees with training and knowledge in how to gain the confidence of older consumers. For example, in one case, *Alliance for Mature Americans* was charged with using deception and misrepresentation to sell more than $200 million worth of living trusts and annuities to 10,000 older adults in California, by specifically targeting older adults.[24]

One way to engage in successful aging is to disengage from people you don't trust or don't want to be around and who will take advantage of you. Sadly, sometimes these people are family, friends, or trusted associates. Loneliness can cause older adults to engage with people who are unethical opportunists and are not concerned with the best interests of the older adult. Older adults are often targeted because of their accumulated assets, yet some research suggests that younger adults are just as likely to be victims of scams.[25] Scamming has become an increasing concern, to the point that the FBI's Common

Fraud Schemes Web page[26] provides specific tips on how you can pro-tect yourself and your family from fraud. We are all prey to these predators, many of whom will use proven psychological techniques to get results.

This is not an issue just for older adults, as some research[27] suggests that a "prototypical victim" of financial fraud is a 55-year-old male who is an experienced investor—the middle-age brain may react positively to enticing rewards. Thus, having money can make you a target, as the brain may react to rewards in different ways as we age. While the classic definitions of successful aging often do not consider fraud a core issue, it can be devastating for both the victim and the family, especially if they are repeated targets of fraud be-cause of their financial standing. Older adults may be more trusting in some cases, but there is also evidence that adults of any age can have difficulty determining whom to trust.[28]

It seems that con artists also know about socioemotional se-lectivity theory at some level and will use it to their advantage. Socioemotional selectivity theory suggests that older adults place a priority on emotional goals and maintaining connections with close family. Scams that involve the potential to help or hurt a family member may be most effective with older adults. In one instance, my father-in-law (now over the age of 80) got a frantic phone call saying his daughter had been kidnapped. He heard her desperately screaming "Daddy!" in the background (at least he thought it sounded like her). The capturers demanded that he wire them $5,000 immediately or she would be hurt. By using her Facebook profile, the caller was able to confirm personal details about his daughter to convince him that she had actually been kidnapped. Socioemotional selectivity theory, and even common sense, suggests that older adults will do anything to protect their family. Pressuring concerned older adults in a vul-nerable and stressful situation may make them succumb to this type of fraud without thinking more critically.

One way to avoid scams is to remove yourself from people who want your time and money. My grandfather was good at hanging up the phone on people, sometimes even his own family! He did not want to waste his time or theirs, and as a rule of business, rarely trusted people he didn't know. He would, however, bet obsessively on horses and play the lottery. I am not sure what he would be like today, where email can consume and lure us. If we took every email message seriously, we would be taken for every scam and swindle, not to mention have bought many time-shares, won foreign lotteries, or helped distressed people from other countries who "just need a small donation." Having said all this, not all older adults are frail or easy targets for scams. Recently,[29] a 91-year-old man was assaulted in a Detroit parking lot by a 20-something-year-old robber. First, he told the robber that he had a license to conceal-carry a gun, and then defended himself by drawing his gun and shooting and wounding the younger robber. How we protect ourselves often involves whom and what we are exposed to, and we don't need a gun to protect us from scams. For example, not reading junk mail and not talking to a cold-caller on the phone can be most effective.

Do You Think an Old Dog Can Learn New Tricks? Your Mindset Really Matters

When I ask people for advice on how to age well, sometimes they smirk and smile and simply say, "Pick your parents wisely." The emphasis we place on our genetics can often undermine the great deal of control we actually have over the aging process. One of the most undervalued or underappreciated aspects is the need to joyfully connect with others, whether with family, friends, or caretakers. We appreciate these social connections more as we get older, and for good reason—social support is often directly tied to healthy aging. Thus, a more empowering version of this saying is "Pick your *friends* wisely." You might want to find friends who have a positive outlook on aging, as being socially connected to people that are important to you may be one of the more underappreciated ways to stay healthy and enjoy old age.

We all have an idea of what old age is like, and what it might be like for us. Interacting with older adults, or reading about case studies of successful aging, may be inspirational, or you may regard them as unique but certainly not the norm. In general, our mindset and our expectations can bias and guide our own behavior. For example, do you think older people can learn new tricks and enjoy trying new things? Do you think memory declines with age and there isn't much you can do about it? Psychologist Carol Dweck at Stanford has shown that there are two different perspectives or mindsets that people have about intelligence: "entity theorists" and "incremental theorists."

Entity theorists believe that intelligence is fixed for the most part, despite one's motivation to change, and can't often benefit from engaging in additional practice or learning. Incremental theorists view abilities in a more growth mindset manner, believing that one can improve with motivation and practice and can often benefit from working harder on problems.[30] These two different types of mindsets also hold true when we think about aging. One could think of aging as a clear course of decline (entity theorists), or as a process in which we can find ways to improve our memory and cognitive function (incremental theorists) such that our mindset may control our outcome.

One intriguing study based on the differing mindsets proposed by Dweck shows that your mindset about aging really does matter when you interpret new research findings and how they might apply to you. This study[31] showed that older adults who believed that memory abilities were malleable (and could improve in old age) actually did better on several tests of memory, compared to those who felt that memory abilities are a fixed trait. In this study, participants first read a news article, such as one you might find in the *New York Times*, which outlined how the aging brain can create new connections and neurons, and how walking can lead to improvements in memory in older adults by increasing the size of the hippocampus—all supported by the latest research findings from various studies around the world. After older adults read this short article about the positive findings about memory and aging, they actually did better on several memory tests. This benefit occurred because the incremental growth mindset had been activated in the people who read the news article on the positive findings, but not in people who read the article without these positive conclusions. Just by reading about how the aging brain can get better with age made people do better on a memory test. So, if you think you can, then you probably can, illustrating the role of one's perspective on the aging process. This type of research finding is consistent with John Glenn's perspective on expectations and aging. He said that as we age, we have expectations, and we can rise or fall, based on these expectations about ourselves and what other people expect from us.

Jack LaLanne always had a positive mindset, saying "Anything in life is possible, and you can make it happen," an inspiring message to people of any age. He said he didn't always enjoy exercise, but he needed to do it to survive and eventually it became a passion. Indeed, there is research that shows that people with a younger "subjective" age, such as an 80-year-old who thinks of himself as 65, may actually perform better on tasks that measure physical strength. In fact, one can actually be made to feel younger by getting encouraging feedback about one's own abilities. In one study,[32] older people first did a handgrip strength test and were then told that their test performance was better than the performance of most of their same-aged peers and that they were stronger than most people their age. Compared to those who weren't given this positive social-comparison feedback, these participants then reported feeling younger than their actual age *and then actually showed an increase* in grip strength on a second strength test. Thus, simply being given encouraging news about how you perform relative to others in your age group not only makes you feel younger but also makes you stronger—a Jack LaLanne–like effect linking positive thinking and strength in older age.

The Time Is NOW: Thinking about a Limited Future Makes You Focus on the Positives

> Old age is like everything else. To make a success of it, you've got to start young.
>
> —Theodore Roosevelt

We all know that life is finite, but many younger people don't think of it that way. Older age, on the other hand, may give us more reason to be aware of the limits of life. As we get older, we all know people who fought cancer, have terminal diseases, have life-threatening conditions, or have passed away, and we know that we should be grateful for our good health. This sort of appreciation of life can be very important. In fact, just thinking like an appreciative older adult can actually make you happier.

When we are young, we don't spend much time thinking about old age. Younger adults perceive time as vast or expansive, and this causes them to prioritize future-oriented goals, such as pursuing higher education, exploring career options, and expanding their social networks. Older adults are more likely to appreciate life's fragility and to perceive time as limited. As a result, older adults prioritize present-oriented goals and their emotional well-being.

Thus, with age, people focus more on savoring life and enjoying existing relationships. Research supports the notions outlined in socioemotional selectivity theory, which suggest that we have more survival goals when we are younger, and more emotional goals when we are older. However, there are ways to make younger adults see the world, and their lives, more like older adults. For example, the 9/11 terrorist attacks on the United States in 2001 and the SARS epidemic that spread from Hong Kong in 2003 reminded people of all ages that life is fragile. In response to these fearful situations, younger adults shifted toward goals that were similar to those of older adults, maximizing their emotional well-being, spending time with family, and enjoying the present.[33]

I found that writing this book led to voices in my head. The voices were of the people I interviewed. They provide motivation to exercise, to rise up to my own expectations and to the expectations of others, to eat well and to exercise, to be a good parent and teacher, to challenge myself in areas I feel lacking, to not fear failure, and to surround myself with the people I care about. The voices inspired me to have a positive attitude and to sometimes look at life from the perspective of those older adults who are from what is called the "Greatest Generation,"[34] those who grew up in the United States during the Great Depression and World War II. These perspectives are often supported by research. However, these insights have also led to more questions that research has only begun to address—and the research often isn't the voice of inspiration, people are. Hearing what older adults have to say can provide motivation to better understand ourselves and to identify what is important in life. Learning about old age can be a most illuminating experience, and one that we all can benefit from as we continually embark on the journey to successful aging.

Summary

There are many myths about aging, and various paradoxes of old age—ones that we might not actually come to fully appreciate until we are older ourselves. This book shows some of the paradoxes and myths about aging. In a way, we are all detectives of the aging process, trying to figure out what is good and bad as we get older and what we can do about it. At various points in our life, we may overemphasize the need for youthfulness in order to be happy and healthy, and we may underestimate how our subjective age and attitudes about aging can influence longevity. While successful aging can start at any age, practically speaking, middle age is the optimal time to think about older age. Despite any genetic contributions, there is a lot we can do to make sure that we engage in successful aging. Old age will soon be very "new age," due partly to the sheer dominance of demographics and partly to an emerging public presence in the media. Technological advances have the capabilities to make healthy aging even better and more enjoyable. Greater awareness of the potential benefits of old age can make one at any age better prepared to achieve those benefits to the fullest, and to live a long, productive, and meaningful life.

Closing Comments

Grow old along with me! The best is yet to be.
The last of life, for which the first was made.
> —Robert Browning, poet (1812–1889), from the poem
> "Rabbi Ben Ezra"

IDEALLY, SUCCESSFUL AGING IS A LONG AND ENJOYABLE journey. There is no single or best way to engage in successful aging. As we age, we often have greater perspective and an appreciation of life, the ups and downs, and the challenges in the world and in our own life. While we may often think that our accomplishments define our lifetime contributions, it is our emotional state, how we interact with and make others feel, and how we make those around us better people, that may be our most defining contributions. In reviewing interviews and studies with older adults, it is clear to me that having role models and social connections is what makes us strive to be successful and to live longer and healthier lives.

Jackie Robinson, the pioneer baseball player, said, "A life is not important except in the impact it has on other lives." The older adults I have interviewed have made an impact on other people's lives, including my own. How we make other people feel may be the most important lesson of all. Having a sense of purpose and a set of goals, as a parent, grandparent, worker, or volunteer, can add years to our lives and bring happiness to those around us. Successful aging involves mistakes, paradoxes, goals, and challenges. These are the lessons that the psychology of aging has shown us about how we age. Long live old age.

Epilogue: Are You Aging, or Is It Just Me?

WE ARE ALL *OLDER-ADULTS-IN-TRAINING*, AND THOSE actually in old age have met a challenge. My joke was that I hoped to finish this book before I reached old age. The truth is that I experienced a great deal of aging while working on this book, and I learned a lot about the many paradoxes of aging. This book attempts to incorporate what older adults say about old age, and what research suggests about both the pleasures and pains that come with it. Middle-age is a good time to think about older age, as we can develop habits then that will lead to successful aging.

By interacting with many older adults, I have learned that the best may be yet to come, but it also comes with challenges. My own memory isn't what it used to be, and I need to work harder to remember what is important. I am also reminded about aging when I see my children enjoying their birthdays, and how they seem to devour new information. Thinking about aging often only happens when it intersects with our personal lives. We have seen how our parents have aged, and we wonder what to expect for ourselves. At any stage in life, we are always presented with challenges, and there are many paradoxes and surprises about what old age is all about.

Psychological research, and many older-age role models, shows how we can enjoy old age.

There is no shortcut to successful aging, just as there is no way to avoid aging. There are many different ways to achieve successful aging. One plan may be to think about old age early in life, to identify the positives and anticipate the challenges, and to have your own role models of successful aging. Whatever your age, now is the time to think about successful aging.

Acknowledgments

I WANT TO THANK THE MANY OLDER ADULTS WHO WERE happy and willing to share their life stories and valuable insights. Interacting with older adults is my favorite part of studying the psychology of aging, and I hope that message is clear in the book. I would like to especially thank those people I interviewed that provided inspiration and insights for this book, specifically John Wooden, Frank Gehry, Maya Angelou, Bob Newhart, John Glenn, Annie Glenn, Phyllis Diller, Dave Brubeck, Jack LaLanne, Elaine LaLanne, Stan Berman, Albert Bandura, Jared Diamond, and Dr. Ruth Westheimer.

Many people provided me with supportive guidance and advice about this book, including Bob Bjork, Elizabeth Bjork, Keith Holyoak, Barbara Knowlton, Fergus Craik, Lynn Hasher, David Balota, Jan Duchek, Roddy Roediger, Larry Jacoby, Don MacKay, Nicole Anderson, Aimee Drolet, David Rosenbaum, Moshe Naveh-Benjamin, Ken Rosenfeld, Larry Rosenblum, Noah Goldstein, Jenessa Shapiro, Danny Oppenheimer, Matt Lieberman, Gary Small, Sonja Lyubomirsky, Aaron Benjamin, Chris Hertzog, Daniel Schacter, Mark McDaniel, Mara Mather, Laura Carstensen, Tyler Burge, Dave Kornhaber, Matt Rhodes, Lisa Geraci, Nate Kornell, Tom Bradbury, Ben Karney, Aaron Blaisdell, Gerardo Ramirez, Steve Lee, Annie Cerf, Alan Hartley, André Didierjean, Patrick Lemaire, Brian Siegel, Seth

Siegel, Patricia Greenfield, Joshua Kaufman, Vered Halamish, Dayna Touron, Greg Samanez-Larkin, Alison Chasteen, Tara Scanlan, Hal Hershfield, Shlomo Benartzi, Sian Beilock, Mario Mendez, Sheida Rabipour, Monica Moore, Ethan Goldstine, Sarah Barber, Mitchum Huehls, Jim Stigler, Scott Johnson, Dean Buonomano, Sherre Hirsch, Bruce Baker, Catherine Sarkisian, Carol Tavris, Jessica Logan, Iris Firstenberg, Moshe Rubinstein, Art Bornstein, David Brenman, Nan Wooden, Carole Burnett, Ed Geiselman, Chris Ardern, Sarah Hadomi, Nick Soderstrom, Howard Friedman, Ted Robles, Shelley Taylor, Story Musgrave, Charlie Heartsill, Jesse Rissman, David Walker, Phil Kellman, Roger Long, Michelle Craske, Greg Miller, Victoria Sork, Jared Diamond, Karl Pillemer, Igor Grossmann, Peter Rendell, Nate Rose, Daniel Glenn, Paul Williams, Martin Monti, and David McCabe. In addition, there are many who have worked with me in my laboratory at UCLA that have provided an exciting environment in which to do research, and contributed in key ways to many of the research studies and ideas that are presented in this book. This includes Shannon McGillivray, Michael Friedman, Teal Eich, Michael Cohen, Kou Murayama, Kenji Ikeda, Mary Hargis, Joe Hennessee, Adam Blake, Tyson Kerr, Catherine Middlebrooks, and Alex Siegel. There are likely many other names that I have forgotten. I have learned that tends to happen with age and when it takes you several years to write a book.

I appreciate the support from the UCLA Department of Psychology, an enriching place with many talented people. In addition, my research program has benefitted greatly from funding from the National Institute on Aging.

I am in debt to Joan Bossert at Oxford University Press, who took an early interest in this book proposal and provided critical advice and guidance during the entire process. Lynnee Argabright, Emily Perry, Phil Velinov, Jerri Hurlbutt, and many other talented people at Oxford University Press worked hard to improve the final product. I would like to thank Sara-Louise Brown for designing the creative cover art for the front cover of the book. Jamie Coyne helped transcribe the interviews and with editing. I appreciate the comments and reviews from all of the students in the UCLA Developmental Psychology and Human Memory graduate class. Jessica Castel provided useful edits and comments regarding the overall organization. I would like to in particular thank Doris Jean Long, as she provided timely and extremely thorough edits, many thoughtful comments in very clearly handwritten notes in the margins and ensuing discussions, useful personal practical and scientific insights, as well as some genuine encouragement.

My family has played so many roles in my life, this book, and my interest in successful aging. My parents showed me many of the pleasures and challenges of aging, and gave me the gift of growing up in a large family—something that was, and still is, enriched by my brother Evan and sisters Valerie, Jessica, and Deborah and their families. My wife Jami, ever since I told her I was going to write this book (almost 10 years ago), urged me to do it (for the next 10 years). She helped guide me throughout this journey, listened and commented on every aspect of the book, and provided direction, support, and constant encouragement. My wife is an incredible person. My grandparents and extended family provided many memorable examples of aging. My children, Eden, Claire, and Theo, show me all about the pleasures of aging at the other end of the spectrum.

I acknowledge the converted garage/home office where I would retreat to write, during early mornings, some late evenings, and in-between. There are many challenges and frustrations when writing a book, but there is great pleasure in working at home, with my children playing outside and visiting me when either they or I need a break. Hearing their excited voices as I write reminds me to enjoy the here-and-now, and not just what is ahead. They are also some of my favorite case studies of development and give me by far the most important reasons to age well.

If you've read this far, then thank you, too. Of course, I wrote a book so that people would read it, but I'm always amazed and surprised when people come up to me and say, "You know that study you described in Chapter 6, I found it really interesting because . . . ", or more simply say they learned something or agree or disagree with something in this book. I have learned that writing a book about aging is a very challenging task, as is trying to study the aging process, which in and of itself is always changing. I have relied on many interviews, personal observations, and fields of research to present some of the paradoxes and benefits of older age, but I am also aware of just how complex the aging process can be. I apologize for any oversimplifications, generalizations, or inaccuracies presented in the book. If you have any comments or insights to share about aging, I look forward hearing from you.

Notes

Chapter 1

1. Demos, V., & Jache, A. (1981). When you care enough: An analysis of attitudes toward aging in humorous birthday cards. *The Gerontologist, 21*, 209–215.
2. Alter, A. L., & Hershfield, H. E. (2014). People search for meaning when they approach a new decade in chronological age. *Proceedings of the National Academy of Sciences of the United States of America, 111*, 17066–17070.
3. Fell, J. (2012, May). 5 Questions: Elaine LaLanne. *Los Angeles Times*. Retrieved from http://articles.latimes.com/2012/may/26/health/la-he-five-questions-lalanne-20120526
4. Pew Research Center (2009). Growing old in America: Expectation vs. reality. Retrieved from http://www.pewsocialtrends.org/2009/06/29/growing-old-in-america-expectations-vs-reality/
5. Survey shows what boomers and seniors like to be called: By their name! CNN iReport. Posted December 5, 2013. Retrieved from http://ireport.cnn.com/docs/DOC-1066224
6. Graham, J. (2012, April 19). The new old age caring and coping: "Elderly" no more. *New York Times*. Retrieved from

https://newoldage.blogs.nytimes.com/2012/04/19/elderly-no-more/?_r=0

7. Rowe, J. W., & Kahn, R. L. (1998). *Successful aging: The MacArthur Foundation Study*. New York: Pantheon.

8. Cosco, T. D., Prina, A. M., Perales, J., Stephan, B. C., & Brayne, C. (2014). Operational definitions of successful aging: A systematic review. *International Psychogeriatrics, 26,* 373–381.

9. Merle, A. (2016, April 14). The reading habits of ultra-successful people. *Huffington Post*. Retrieved from http://www.huffingtonpost.com/andrew-merle/the-reading-habits-of-ult_b_9688130.html

10. Jeune, B., Robine, J. M., Young, R., Desjardins, B., Skytthe, A., & Vaupel, J. W. (2010). Jeanne Calment and her successors. Biographical notes on the longest living humans. In H. Maier, J. Gampe, B. Jeune, J. W. Vaupel, & J.-M. Robine (Eds.), *Supercentenarians* (pp. 285–323). Berlin, Heidelberg: Springer-Verlag.

11. Olshansky, S. J. (2011). Aging of US presidents. *Journal of the American Medical Association, 306,* 2328–2329.

12. Retrieved from http://www.musicvaultz.com/tag/pete-townshend/

13. Stephan, Y., Caudroit, J., & Chalabaev, A. (2011). Subjective health and memory self-efficacy as mediators in the relation between subjective age and life satisfaction among older adults. *Aging & Mental Health, 15,* 428–436; Stephan, Y., Chalabaev, A., Kotter-Grühn, D., & Jaconelli, A. (2013). "Feeling younger, being stronger": An experimental study of subjective age and physical functioning among older adults. *Journals of Gerontology. Series B, Psychological Sciences and Social Sciences, 68,* 1–7; Kotter-Grühn, D., Kleinspehn-Ammerlahn, A., Gerstorf, D., & Smith, J. (2009). Self-perceptions of aging predict mortality and change with approaching death: 16-year longitudinal results from the Berlin Aging Study. *Psychology and Aging, 24,* 654–667.

14. Rubin, D. C., & Berntsen, D. (2006). People over forty feel 20% younger than their age: Subjective age across the lifespan. *Psychonomic Bulletin & Review, 13,* 776–780.

15. Things might be wholly different for those under age 40. My son, who is turning 3, regularly tells people he is turning

8. I have also heard that teenagers may lie about their age, such as attempting to pose as 21.

16. Elejalde-Ruiz, A. (October 12, 2011). How old do you feel inside? *Chicago Tribune.* Retrieved from http://www.chicagotribune. com/lifestyles/health/sc-health-1012-senior-health-emotional-age-20111012-story.html

17. Dance, sing, just 'keep moving,' Dick Van Dyke tells seniors. An interview with Dick Van Dyke. Weekend Edition Sunday, NPR, October 11, 2015. Retrieved from http:// www.npr.org/2015/10/11/447591736/dance-sing-just-keep-moving-dick-van-dyke-tells-seniors

18. Hsu, L. M., Chung, J., & Langer, E. J. (2010). The influence of age-related cues on health and longevity. *Perspectives on Psychological Science, 5,* 632–648.

19. Hsu, L. M., Chung, J., & Langer, E. J. (2010). The influence of age-related cues on health and longevity. *Perspectives on Psychological Science, 5,* 632–648.

20. Gerstorf, D., Hülür, G., Drewelies, J., Eibich, P., Duezel, S., Demuth, I., . . . Lindenberger, U. (2015). Secular changes in late-life cognition and well-being: Towards a long bright future with a short brisk ending? *Psychology and Aging, 30,* 301–310.

21. While this books deals mostly with the psychology of aging, an excellent textbook that covers the more complex interactions of social, psychological, and biological factors that influence aging is Whitbourne, S. K., & Whitbourne, S. B. (2010). *Adult development and aging: Biopsychosocial perspectives.* Hoboken, NJ: John Wiley & Sons.

22. A common saying is that "the plural of anecdote is data," suggesting that anecdotes are insightful but it is more convincing if there are many observations that can be quantified in a research study.

23. I thank Dr. Jay Brenman for providing background regarding the life cycle and longevity of the fruit fly.

24. For an impressive example of this extension of life in the fruit fly, see Ulgherait, M., Rana, A., Rera, M., Graniel, J., & Walker, D. W. (2014). AMPK modulates tissue and organismal aging in a non-cell-autonomous manner. *Cell Reports, 8,* 1767–1780.

25. Schaie, K. W. (2005). What can we learn from longitudinal studies of adult development? *Research in Human Development, 2*, 133–158.

26. Rönnlund, M., Nyberg, L., Bäckman, L., & Nilsson, L. G. (2005). Stability, growth, and decline in adult life span development of declarative memory: Cross-sectional and longitudinal data from a population-based study. *Psychology and Aging, 20*, 3–18.

27. The Terman study is outlined in Howard S. Friedman and Leslie R. Martin's (two of the researchers who carried out follow-up analyses on Terman's original work) book entitled *The Longevity Project* and provides many surprising and myth-busting insights regarding what factors influence how well we age, and what types of people live well into old age. George Valliant's *Aging Well* describes a similar study done over a 50-year period.

28. Siegel, M., Bradley, E. H., & Kasl, S. V. (2003). Self-rated life expectancy as a predictor of mortality: Evidence from the HRS and AHEAD surveys. *Gerontology, 49*, 265–271.

29. Cacchione, P. Z., Powlishta, K. K., Grant, E. A., Buckles, V. D., & Morris, J. C. (2003). Accuracy of collateral source reports in very mild to mild dementia of the Alzheimer type. *Journal of the American Geriatrics Society, 51*, 819–823.

30. Baltes, P. B. (1997). On the incomplete architecture of human ontogeny: Selection, optimization, and compensation as foundation of developmental theory. *American Psychologist, 52*, 366.

31. Baltes, P. B., & Baltes, M. M. (1990). Psychological perspectives on successful aging: The model of selective optimization with compensation. *Successful Aging: Perspectives from the Behavioral Sciences, 1*, 1–34.

32. Carstensen, L. L. (2009). *A long bright future: An action plan for a lifetime of happiness, health, and financial security.* New York: Broadway Books.

33. Hummert, M. L., Garstka, T. A., Shaner, J. L., & Strahm, S. (1995). Judgments about stereotypes of the elderly attitudes, age associations, and typicality ratings of young, middle-aged, and elderly adults. *Research on Aging, 17*, 168–189.

34. Donlon M., Ashman, O., Levy, B. R. (2005). Revision of older television characters: A stereotype-awareness intervention. *Journal of Social Issues, 61*, 307–319.

35. Levy, B. (2009). Stereotype embodiment a psychosocial approach to aging. *Current Directions in Psychological Science, 18,* 332–336.
36. Levy, B. R., Ferrucci, L., Zonderman, A. B., Slade, M. D., Troncoso, J., & Resnick, S. M. (2016). A culture–brain link: Negative age stereotypes predict Alzheimer's disease biomarkers. *Psychology and Aging, 31,* 82–88.
37. Levy, B. R., Zonderman, A. B., Slade, M. D., & Ferrucci, L. (2009). Age stereotypes held earlier in life predict cardiovascular events in later life. *Psychological Science, 20,* 296–298.
38. Langer, E. J. (2009). *Counterclockwise.* New York: Random House Digital.
39. Iacono, D., Markesbery, W. R., Gross, M., Pletnikova, O., Rudow, G., Zandi, P., & Troncoso, J. C. (2009). The Nun Study. Clinically silent AD, neuronal hypertrophy, and linguistic skills in early life. *Neurology, 73,* 665–673.
40. Snowdon, D. A., Greiner, L. H., Mortimer, J. A., Riley, K. P., Greiner, P. A., & Markesbery, W. R. (1997). Brain infarction and the clinical expression of Alzheimer disease: The Nun Study. *Journal of the American Medical Association, 277,* 813–817.
41. Iacono, D., Markesbery, W. R., Gross, M., Pletnikova, O., Rudow, G., Zandi, P., & Troncoso, J. C. (2009). The Nun Study. Clinically silent AD, neuronal hypertrophy, and linguistic skills in early life. *Neurology, 73,* 665–673.
42. Cabeza, R., Anderson, N. D., Locantore, J. K., & McIntosh, A. R. (2002). Aging gracefully: Compensatory brain activity in high-performing older adults. *Neuroimage, 17,* 1394–1402.
43. Tucker, A. M., & Stern, Y. (2011). Cognitive reserve in aging. *Current Alzheimer Research, 8,* 354–360.
44. Reuter-Lorenz, P. A., & Park, D. C. (2014). How does it STAC up? Revisiting the scaffolding theory of aging and cognition. *Neuropsychology Review, 24,* 355–370.
45. Bennett, D. A., Schneider, J. A., Tang, Y., Arnold, S. E., & Wilson, R. S. (2006). The effect of social networks on the relation between Alzheimer's disease pathology and level of cognitive function in old people: A longitudinal cohort study. *Lancet Neurology, 5,* 406–412.
46. Erickson, K. I., Voss, M. W., Prakash, R. S., Basak, C., Szabo, A., Chaddock, L., . . . Wojcicki, T. R. (2011). Exercise training increases

size of hippocampus and improves memory. *Proceedings of the National Academy of Sciences of the United States of America, 108,* 3017–3022.

47. For this type of approach, see the insightful book by Karl Pillemer, aptly titled *30 Lessons for Living.* Pillemer interviewed more than 1,000 Americans over the age of 65 to get practical advice on all of life's issues, from family and children to money and careers.

48. Leigh, J. P., Tancredi, D. J., & Kravitz, R. L. (2009). Physician career satisfaction within specialties. *BMC Health Services Research, 9,* 166.

Chapter 2

1. Donlon, M., Ashman, O., & Levy, B. R. (2005) Revision of older television characters: A stereotype-awareness intervention. *Journal of Social Issues, 61,* 307–319.

2. Levy, B. R. (2009). Stereotype embodiment: A psychosocial approach to aging. *Current Directions in Psychological Science, 18,* 332–336.

3. Sarkisian, C. A., Prohaska, T. R., Wong, M. D., Hirsch, S., & Mangione, C. M. (2005). The relationship between expectations for aging and physical activity among older adults. *Journal of General Internal Medicine, 20,* 911–915.

4. Carstensen, L. L., Pasupathi, M., Mayr, U., & Nesselroade, J. R. (2000). Emotional experience in everyday life across the adult life span. *Journal of Personality and Social Psychology, 79,* 644–655.

5. Tergesen, A. (2014, November 30). Why everything you think about aging may be wrong. *Wall Street Journal.* Retrieved from https://www.wsj.com/articles/why-everything-you-think-about-aging-may-be-wrong-1417408057

6. Stone, A. A., Schwartz, J. E., Broderick, J. E., & Deaton, A. (2010). A snapshot of the age distribution of psychological well-being in the United States. *Proceedings of the National Academy of Sciences of the United States of America, 107,* 9985–9990.

7. Stone, A. A., Schwartz, J. E., Broderick, J. E., & Deaton, A. (2010). A snapshot of the age distribution of psychological well-being in the United States. *Proceedings of the National Academy of Sciences of the United States of America, 107,* 9985–9990.

8. Lacey, H. P., Smith, D. M., & Ubel, P. A. (2006). Hope I die before I get old: Mispredicting happiness across the adult lifespan. *Journal of Happiness Studies, 7,* 167–182.

9. Mather, M., & Carstensen, L. L. (2005). Aging and motivated cognition: The positivity effect in attention and memory. *Trends in Cognitive Sciences, 9,* 496–502.

10. Fingerman, K. L., Hay, E. L., & Birditt, K. S. (2004). The best of ties, the worst of ties: Close, problematic, and ambivalent social relationships. *Journal of Marriage and Family, 66,* 792–808.

11. Tergesen, A. (2014, November 30). Why everything you think about aging may be wrong. *Wall Street Journal.* Retrieved from https://www.wsj.com/articles/why-everything-you-think-about-aging-may-be-wrong-1417408057

12. Fingerman, K. L., Hay, E. L., & Birditt, K. S. (2004). The best of ties, the worst of ties: Close, problematic, and ambivalent social relationships. *Journal of Marriage and Family, 66,* 792–808.

13. English, T., & Carstensen, L. L. (2014). Selective narrowing of social networks across adulthood is associated with improved emotional experience in daily life. *International Journal of Behavioral Development, 38,* 195–202.

14. Tergesen, A. (2014, November 30). Why everything you think about aging may be wrong. *Wall Street Journal.* Retrieved from https://www.wsj.com/articles/why-everything-you-think-about-aging-may-be-wrong-1417408057

15. Bhattacharjee, A., & Mogilner, C. (2014). Happiness from ordinary and extraordinary experiences. *Journal of Consumer Research, 41,* 1–17.

16. Baltes, P. B., & Smith, J. (2003). New frontiers in the future of aging: From successful aging of the young old to the dilemmas of the fourth age. *Gerontology, 49,* 123–135.

17. Hawkley, L. C., & Cacioppo, J. T. (2010). Loneliness matters: A theoretical and empirical review of consequences and mechanisms. *Annals of Behavioral Medicine, 40,* 218–227.

18. Mather, M., & Ponzio, A. (2017). Emotion and aging. In L. Feldman Barrett, M. Lewis, & J. Haviland-Jones (Eds.), *Handbook of emotions* (pp. 319–335). New York: Guilford Press.

19. Mather, M., & Ponzio, A. (2017). Emotion and aging. In L. Feldman Barrett, M. Lewis, & J. Haviland-Jones (Eds.), *Handbook of emotions* (pp. 319–335). New York: Guilford Press.

20. Birditt, K. S., & Fingerman, K. L. (2003). Age and gender differences in adults' descriptions of emotional reactions to interpersonal problems. *Journals of Gerontology: Series B, 58,* P237–P245.
21. Seider, B. H., Shiota, M. N., Whalen, P., & Levenson, R. W. (2011). Greater sadness reactivity in late life. *Social Cognitive and Affective Neuroscience, 6,* 186–194.
22. Timmer, E., Westerhof, G. J., & Dittmann-Kohli, F. (2005). "When looking back on my past life I regret . . . ": Retrospective regret in the second half of life. *Death Studies, 29,* 625–644.
23. Bjälkebring, P., Västfjäll, D., & Johansson, B. (2013). Regulation of experienced and anticipated regret for daily decisions in younger and older adults in a Swedish one-week diary study. *Geropsych: The Journal of Gerontopsychology and Geriatric Psychiatry, 26,* 233–241.
24. Mather, M., Mazar, N., Gorlick, M. A., Lighthall, N. R., Burgeno, J., Schoeke, A., & Ariely, D. (2012). Risk preferences and aging: The "certainty effect" in older adults' decision making. *Psychology and Aging, 27,* 801–816.
25. Castel, A. D., Friedman, M. C., McGillivray, S., Flores, C. C., Murayama, K., Kerr, T., & Drolet, A. (2016). I owe you: Age-related similarities and differences in associative memory for gains and losses. *Aging, Neuropsychology, and Cognition, 23,* 549–565.
26. Broadbent, J., de Quadros-Wander, S., & McGillivray, J. (2014). Perceived control's influence on well-being in residential care vs. community dwelling older adults. *Journal of Happiness Studies, 15,* 845–855.
27. Suinn, R. M. (2001). The terrible twos—anger and anxiety: Hazardous to your health. *American Psychologist, 56,* 27–36.
28. Stone, A. A., Schwartz, J. E., Broderick, J. E., & Deaton, A. (2010). A snapshot of the age distribution of psychological well-being in the United States. *Proceedings of the National Academy of Sciences of the United States of America, 107,* 9985–9990.
29. Blanchard-Fields, F., & Coats, A. H. (2008). The experience of anger and sadness in everyday problems impacts age differences in emotion regulation. *Developmental Psychology, 44,* 1547–1556.

30. Fung, H. H., & Carstensen, L. L. (2006). Goals change when life's fragility is primed: Lessons learned from older adults, the September 11 attacks and SARS. *Social Cognition, 24,* 248–278.

31. Hsu, L. M., Chung, J., & Langer, E. J. (2010). The influence of age-related cues on health and longevity. *Perspectives on Psychological Science, 5,* 632–648.

32. Abel, E. L., & Kruger, M. L. (2010). Smile intensity in photographs predicts longevity. *Psychological Science, 21*(4), 542–544.

33. Danner, D., Snowdon, D., & Friesen, W. (2001). Positive emotions in early life and longevity: Findings from the nun study. *Journal of Personality and Social Psychology, 80,* 804–813.

34. Diener, E., & Chan, M. Y. (2011). Happy people live longer: Subjective well-being contributes to health and longevity. *Applied Psychology: Health and Well-Being, 3,* 1–43.

35. Dutton, J. (2012, March-April). In the lab with the world's leading laugh scientist. *Mental Floss Magazine.*

36. Provine, R. R. (2001). *Laughter: A scientific investigation.* New York: Penguin.

37. Cousins, N. (1976). Anatomy of an illness (as perceived by the patient). *New England Journal of Medicine, 295,* 1458–1463.

38. Severo, R., & Keepnews, P. (2012, August 22). Phyllis Diller, sassy comedian, dies at 95. *New York Times.* Retrieved from http://www.nytimes.com/2012/08/21/arts/television/phyllis-diller-sassy-comedian-dies-at-95.html

39. My grandmother Miriam Novitch dedicated her life to this cause, as outlined in her book, Novitch, M. (1981). *Spiritual Resistance: Art from Concentration Camps, 1940-1945.* Philadelphia: Jewish Publication Society of America. For a biography of her life and mission see Geva, S. (2015). "To collect the tears of the Jewish people": The story of Miriam Novitch. *Holocaust Studies, 21,* 73–92.

40. Biss, R. K., & Hasher, L. (2012). Happy as a lark: Morning-type younger and older adults are higher in positive affect. *Emotion, 12,* 437–441.

41. Lyubomirsky, S., King, L., & Diener, E. (2005). The benefits of frequent positive affect: Does happiness lead to success? *Psychological Bulletin, 131,* 803–855.

42. Cohn, M. A., Fredrickson, B. L., Brown, S. L., Mikels, J. A., & Conway, A. M. (2009). Happiness unpacked: Positive emotions

increase life satisfaction by building resilience. *Emotion, 9,* 361–368.

Chapter 3

1. Park, D. C., Lautenschlager, G., Hedden, T., Davidson, N. S., Smith, A. D., & Smith, P. K. (2002). Models of visuospatial and verbal memory across the adult life span. *Psychology and Aging, 17,* 299.
2. Hargis, M. B., Yue, C. L., Kerr, T., Ikeda, K., Murayama, K., & Castel, A. D. (2017). Metacognition and proofreading: The roles of aging, motivation, and interest. *Aging, Neuropsychology, and Cognition, 24,* 216–226.
3. Craik, F. I. M., & Salthouse, T. A. (Eds.). (2011). *The handbook of aging and cognition.* Hove, UK: Psychology Press.
4. Helmuth, L. (2003). The wisdom of the wizened. *Science, 299*(5611), 1300–1302.
5. Chasteen, A. L., Bhattacharyya, S., Horhota, M., Tam, R., & Hasher, L. (2005). How feelings of stereotype threat influence older adults' memory performance. *Experimental Aging Research, 3,* 235–260.
6. Rahhal, T. A., Hasher, L., & Colcombe, S. J. (2001). Instructional manipulations and age differences in memory: Now you see them, now you don't. *Psychology and Aging, 16,* 697–706.
7. Mazerolle, M., Régner, I., Barber, S. J., Paccalin, M., Miazola, A. C., Huguet, P., & Rigalleau, F. (2017). Negative aging stereotypes impair performance on brief cognitive tests used to screen for predementia. *Journals of Gerontology. Series B, Psychological Sciences and Social Science, 72*(6), 932–936.
8. Hess, T. M., & Hinson, J. T. (2006). Age-related variation in the influences of aging stereotypes on memory in adulthood. *Psychology and Aging, 21,* 621–625.
9. Adams, C., Smith, M. C., Pasupathi, M., & Vitolo, L. (2002). Social context effects on story recall in older and younger women: Does the listener make a difference? *Journals of Gerontology, 57,* P28–P40.
10. Rendell, P. G., Castel, A. D., & Craik, F. I. (2005). Memory for proper names in old age: A disproportionate impairment? *Quarterly Journal of Experimental Psychology Section A, 58,* 54–71.

11. Castel, A. D. (2005). Memory for grocery prices in younger and older adults: The role of schematic support. *Psychology and Aging, 20,* 718.

12. Mather, M., & Carstensen, L. L. (2005). Aging and motivated cognition: The positivity effect in attention and memory. *Trends in Cognitive Sciences, 9,* 496–502.

13. Castel, A. D. (2009). Memory and successful aging: A conversation with Coach John Wooden. *Association for Psychological Science Observer, 22,* 13–15.

14. Hertzog, C., & Dunlosky, J. (2011). Metacognition in later adulthood: Spared monitoring can benefit older adults' self-regulation. *Current Directions in Psychological Science, 20,* 167–173.

15. Some research suggests that taking pictures of things at museums actually reduces your memory for these things (Henkel, L. A. [2014]. Point-and-shoot memories: The influence of taking photos on memory for a museum tour. *Psychological Science, 25,* 396–402). However, other related research has shown that if you know the information is saved somewhere, it frees up your own memory to remember other things (Storm, B. C., & Stone, S. M. [2015]. Saving-enhanced memory: The benefits of saving on the learning and remembering of new information. *Psychological Science, 26,* 182–188). So, clearly, there are both some costs and benefits to relying on technology to help us remember.

16. McGillivray, S., & Castel, A. D. (2017). Older and younger adults' strategic control of metacognitive monitoring: The role of consequences, task experience and prior knowledge. *Experimental Aging Research, 43,* 233–256.

17. Cohen, M. S., Rissman, J., Suthana, N. A., Castel, A. D., & Knowlton, B. J. (2016). Effects of aging on value-directed modulation of semantic network activity during verbal learning. *NeuroImage, 125,* 1046–1062.

18. Burke, D. M., MacKay, D. G., Worthley, J. S., & Wade, E. (1991). On the tip of the tongue: What causes word finding failures in young and older adults? *Journal of Memory and Language, 30,* 542–579.

19. Ramscar, M., Hendrix, P., Shaoul, C., Milin, P., & Baayen, H. (2014). The myth of cognitive decline: Non-linear dynamics of lifelong learning. *Topics in Cognitive Science, 6,* 5–42.

20. Castel, A. D., Vendetti, M., & Holyoak, K. J. (2012). Fire drill: Inattentional blindness and amnesia for the location of fire extinguishers. *Attention, Perception, & Psychophysics, 74,* 1391–1396.
21. McBride, D. M., Coane, J. H., Drwal, J., & LaRose, S. A. M. (2013). Differential effects of delay on time-based prospective memory in younger and older adults. *Aging, Neuropsychology, and Cognition, 20,* 700–721.
22. Craik, F. I., & Bialystok, E. (2006). Planning and task management in older adults: Cooking breakfast. *Memory & Cognition, 34,* 1236–1249.
23. Fantz, A. (2015, January 6). After leaving a child in a car, 'that pain . . . never goes away'. CNN. Retrieved from http://www.cnn.com/2014/07/03/us/hot-car-deaths/
24. Schmidt, H. G., & Boshuizen, H. P. A. (1993). On the origins of intermediate effects in clinical case recall. *Memory & Cognition, 21,* 338–351.
25. Roediger, H. L., & McDermott, K. B. (1995). Creating false memories: Remembering words not presented in lists. *Journal of Experimental Psychology: Learning, Memory and Cognition, 24,* 803–814.
26. McCabe, D. P., & Smith, A. D. (2002). The effect of warnings on false memories in young and older adults. *Memory & Cognition, 30,* 1065–1077.
27. Radvansky, G. A., Pettijohn, K. A., & Kim, J. (2015). Walking through doorways causes forgetting: Younger and older adults. *Psychology and Aging, 30,* 259–265.
28. Betty White doesn't understand why people say she's had a 'comeback'. *Huffington Post,* March 31, 2015. Retrieved from http://www.huffingtonpost.com/2015/03/31/betty-white-age-comeback_n_6972348.html
29. Roediger III, H. L., & Karpicke, J. D. (2006). Test-enhanced learning: Taking memory tests improves long-term retention. *Psychological Science, 17,* 249–255.
30. Meyer, A. N., & Logan, J. M. (2013). Taking the testing effect beyond the college freshman: Benefits for lifelong learning. *Psychology and Aging, 28,* 142–147.
31. Blumen, H. M., Rajaram, S., & Henkel, L. (2013). The applied value of collaborative memory research in aging: Behavioral and

neural considerations. *Journal of Applied Research in Memory and Cognition, 2,* 107–117.

32. Seamon, J. G., Punjabi, P. V., & Busch, E. A. (2010). Memorising Milton's *Paradise Lost*: A study of a septuagenarian exceptional memoriser. *Memory, 18,* 498–503.

33. Bio, Hegdahl, Douglas Brent. Retrieved from http://www.pownetwork.org/bios/h/h135.htm

34. Brainy Quote. John Wooden. Retrieved from http://www.brainyquote.com/quotes/authors/j/john_wooden_4.html

35. Routledge, C., Arndt, J., Wildschut, T., Sedikides, C., Hart, C. M., Juhl, J., . . . Schlotz, W. (2011). The past makes the present meaningful: Nostalgia as an existential resource. *Journal of Personality and Social Psychology, 101,* 638–652.

36. Bohanek, J. G., Marin, K. A., Fivush, R., & Duke, M. P. (2006). Family narrative interaction and children's sense of self. *Family Process, 45,* 39–54.

37. The answers are: giraffe; Wrigley's chewing gum; and New Zealand, in 1893.

38. McGillivray, S., Murayama, K., & Castel, A. D. (2015). Thirst for knowledge: The effects of curiosity and interest on memory in younger and older adults. *Psychology and Aging, 30,* 835–841.

39. Couch H. N. (1959). *Cicero on the art of growing old. A translation and subjective evaluation of the essay entitled Cato the Elder on Old Age.* Providence, RI: Brown University Press.

Chapter 4

1. Baltes, P. B., & Smith, J. (1990). Toward a psychology of wisdom and its ontogenesis. In R. J. Sternberg (Ed.), *Wisdom: Its nature, origins, and development* (pp. 87–120). New York: Cambridge University Press.

2. Jeste, D. V., & Oswald, A. J. (2014). Individual and societal wisdom: Explaining the paradox of human aging and high well-being. *Psychiatry, 77,* 317–330.

3. Isaacson, W. (2007). *Einstein: His life and universe.* New York: Simon & Schuster.

4. Personal interview with Maya Angelou, February 2, 2011.

5. Baltes, P. B., Staudinger, U. M., Maercker, A., & Smith, J. (1995). People nominated as wise: A comparative study of wisdom-related knowledge. *Psychology and Aging, 10*, 155–166.

6. Grossmann, I., Na, J., Varnum, M. E., Park, D. C., Kitayama, S., & Nisbett, R. E. (2010). Reasoning about social conflicts improves into old age. *Proceedings of the National Academy of Sciences of the United States of America, 107*, 7246–7250.

7. Goldberg, E. (2006). *The wisdom paradox: How your mind can grow stronger as your brain grows older.* New York: Penguin.

8. Salthouse, T. A. (2012). Consequences of age-related cognitive declines. *Annual Review of Psychology, 63*, 201–226.

9. Blanchard-Fields, F. (2007). Everyday problem solving and emotion: An adult developmental perspective. *Current Directions in Psychological Science, 16*, 26–31.

10. Birditt, K. S., & Fingerman, K. L. (2005). Do we get better at picking our battles? Age group differences in descriptions of behavioral reactions to interpersonal tensions. *Journals of Gerontology, 60*, P121–P128.

11. Hess, T. M., & Auman, C. (2001). Aging and social expertise: The impact of trait-diagnostic information on impressions of others. *Psychology and Aging, 16*, 497–510.

12. Bailey, P. E., Szczap, P., McLennan, S. N., Slessor, G., Ruffman, T., & Rendell, P. G. (2016). Age-related similarities and differences in first impressions of trustworthiness. *Cognition and Emotion, 30*, 1017–1026.

13. Ross, M., Grossmann, I., & Schryer, E. (2014). Contrary to psychological and popular opinion, there is no compelling evidence that older adults are disproportionately victimized by consumer fraud. *Perspectives on Psychological Science, 9*, 427–442.

14. Guilford, J. P. (1967). *The nature of human intelligence.* New York: McGraw Hill.

15. Madore, K. P., Jing, H. G., & Schacter, D. L. (2016). Divergent creative thinking in young and older adults: Extending the effects of an episodic specificity induction. *Memory & Cognition, 44*, 974–988.

16. Simonton, D. K. (1997). Creative productivity: A predictive and explanatory model of career trajectories and landmarks. *Psychological Review, 104*, 66–89.

17. Galenson, D. W. (2003). *The life cycles of modern artists: Theory, measurement, and implications* (No. w9539). Cambridge, MA: National Bureau of Economic Research.

18. Kaufman, J. C., & Beghetto, R. A. (2009). Beyond big and little: The four C model of creativity. *Review of General Psychology, 13*,1–12.

19. McFadden, S. H., & Basting, A. D. (2010). Healthy aging persons and their brains: Promoting resilience through creative engagement. *Clinics in Geriatric Medicine, 26*, 149–161.

20. Dillon, N. (2009, April 20). Jeff Skiles, Sully's heroic co-pilot from flight 1549, has smooth return to cockpit after furlough. *Daily News*. Retrieved from http://www.nydailynews.com/news/jeff-skiles-sully-heroic-co-pilot-flight-1549-smooth-return-cockpit-furlough-article-1.363958

21. Flight 1549: A routine takeoff turns ugly. CBS News, *60 Minutes*, February 8, 2009. Retrieved from http://www.cbsnews.com/news/flight-1549-a-routine-takeoff-turns-ugly/

22. Salthouse, T. A. (2000). Aging and measures of processing speed. *Biological Psychology, 54*, 35–54.

23. Diamond, J. (2013, January 29). The daily shower can be a killer. *New York Times*. Retrieved from http://www.nytimes.com/2013/01/29/science/jared-diamonds-guide-to-reducing-lifes-risks.html

24. Bishai, D., Trevitt, J. L., Zhang, Y., McKenzie, L. B., Leventhal, T., Gielen, A. C., & Guyer, B. (2008). Risk factors for unintentional injuries in children: Are grandparents protective? *Pediatrics, 122*, e980–e987.

25. Kornell, N. (2011). How grandparents unlock kids learning potential. *Psychology Today*. Retrieved from https://www.psychologytoday.com/blog/everybody-is-stupid-except-you/201108/how-grandparents-unlock-kids-learning-potential

26. Bohanek, J. G., Marin, K. A., Fivush, R., & Duke, M. P. (2006). Family narrative interaction and children's sense of self. *Family Process, 45*, 39–54.

27. Crystal, B. (2013). *Still foolin' 'em: Where I've been, where I'm going, and where the hell are my keys?* New York: Henry Holt and Co.

Chapter 5

1. Verghese, J., Lipton, R. B., Katz, M. J., Hall, C. B., Derby, C. A., Kuslansky, G., . . . Buschke, H. (2003). Leisure activities and the risk of dementia in the elderly. *New England Journal of Medicine, 348,* 2508–2516.

2. Cheng, S. T., Chan, A. C., & Yu, E. C. (2006). An exploratory study of the effect of mahjong on the cognitive functioning of persons with dementia. *International Journal of Geriatric Psychiatry, 21,* 611–617.

3. Bengtsson, S. L., Nagy, Z., Skare, S., Forsman, L., Forssberg, H., & Ullén, F. (2005). Extensive piano practicing has regionally specific effects on white matter development. *Nature Neuroscience, 8,* 1148–1150.

4. Amer, T., Kalender, B., Hasher, L., Trehub, S. E., & Wong, Y. (2013). Do older professional musicians have cognitive advantages? *PloS One, 8,* e71630.

5. Bialystok, E., Craik, F. I., & Freedman, M. (2007). Bilingualism as a protection against the onset of symptoms of dementia. *Neuropsychologia, 45,* 459–464.

6. Spreng, R. N., Drzezga, A., Diehl-Schmid, J., Kurz, A., Levine, B., & Perneczky, R. (2011). Relationship between occupation attributes and brain metabolism in frontotemporal dementia. *Neuropsychologia, 49,* 3699–3703.

7. Shimamura, A. P., Berry, J. M., Mangels, J. A., Rusting, C. L., & Jurica, P. J. (1995). Memory and cognitive abilities in university professors: Evidence for successful aging. *Psychological Science,* 271–277.

8. Castel, A. D. (2007). Aging and memory for numerical information: The role of specificity and expertise in associative memory. *Journals of Gerontology, 62,* 194–196.

9. Carlson, M. C., Parisi, J. M., Xia, J., Xue, Q. L., Rebok, G. W., Bandeen-Roche, K., & Fried, L. P. (2011). Lifestyle activities and memory: Variety may be the spice of life. *Journal of the International Neuropsychological Society, 18,* 286–294.

10. Horhota, M., Lineweaver, T., Ositelu, M., Summers, K., & Hertzog, C. (2012). Young and older adults' beliefs about effective ways to mitigate age-related memory decline. *Psychology and Aging, 27,* 293–304.

11. Boots, E. A., Schultz, S. A., Almeida, R. P., Oh, J. M., Koscik, R. L., Dowling, M. N., . . . Asthana, S. (2015). Occupational complexity and cognitive reserve in a middle-aged cohort at risk for Alzheimer's disease. *Archives of Clinical Neuropsychology, 7,* 634–642.

12. Personal interview with Maya Angelou, February 2, 2011.

13. Hultsch, D. F., Hertzog, C., Small, B. J., & Dixon, R. A. (1999). Use it or lose it: Engaged lifestyle as a buffer of cognitive decline in aging? *Psychology and Aging, 14,* 245–263.

14. Salthouse, T. A. (2006). Mental exercise and mental aging evaluating the validity of the "use it or lose it" hypothesis. *Perspectives on Psychological Science, 1,* 68–87.

15. Hertzog, C., McGuire, C. L., Horhota, M., & Jopp, D. (2010). Does believing in "use it or lose it" relate to self-rated memory control, strategy use, and recall? *Journal of Aging and Human Development, 70,* 61–87.

16. Ball, K., Berch, D. B., Helmers, K. F., Jobe, J. B., Leveck, M. D., Marsiske, M., . . . Unverzagt, F. W. (2002). Effects of cognitive training interventions with older adults: A randomized controlled trial. *Journal of the American Medical Association, 288,* 2271–2281.

17. Park, D. C., Lodi-Smith, J., Drew, L., Haber, S., Hebrank, A., Bischof, G. N., & Aamodt, W. (2014). The impact of sustained engagement on cognitive function in older adults: The Synapse Project. *Psychological Science, 25,* 103–112.

18. Stine-Morrow, E. A., Parisi, J. M., Morrow, D. G., & Park, D. C. (2008). The effects of an engaged lifestyle on cognitive vitality: A field experiment. *Psychology and Aging, 23,* 778.

19. Jackson, J. J., Hill, P. L., Payne, B. R., Roberts, B. W., & Stine-Morrow, E. A. L. (2012). Can an old dog learn (and want to experience) new tricks? Cognitive training increases openness in older adults. *Psychology and Aging, 27,* 286–292.

20. Sun, F. W., Stepanovic, M. R., Andreano, J., Barrett, L. F., Touroutoglou, A., & Dickerson, B. C. (2016). Youthful brains in older adults: Preserved neuroanatomy in the default mode and salience networks contributes to youthful memory in superaging. *Journal of Neuroscience, 36,* 9659–9668.

21. Feldman Barrett, L. (2016, December 31). Grey matter: How to become a "superager." *New York Times.* Retrieved from

https://www.nytimes.com/2016/12/31/opinion/sunday/how-to-become-a-superager.html?_r=0

22. Marzorati, G. (2016). *Late to the Ball*. New York: Scribner.

23. Marzorati, G. (2016, April 29). Better aging though practice, practice, practice. *New York Times*. Retrieved from http://www.nytimes.com/2016/05/01/opinion/better-aging-through-practice-practice-practice.html?_r=0

24. Erickson, K. I., Voss, M. W., Prakash, R. S., Basak, C., Szabo, A., Chaddock, L., . . . Wojcicki, T. R. (2011). Exercise training increases size of hippocampus and improves memory. *Proceedings of the National Academy of Sciences of the United States of America, 108*, 3017–3022.

25. Hayes, S. M., Alosco, M. L., Hayes, J. P., Cadden, M., Peterson, K. M., Allsup, K., . . . Verfaellie, M. (2015). Physical activity is positively associated with episodic memory in aging. *Journal of the International Neuropsychological Society, 21*, 780–790.

26. Tracy, K. (2005). *Ellen: The real story of Ellen DeGeneres*. New York: Pinnacle Books.

27. Personal interview with John Glenn, December 13, 2012.

28. O'Donovan, G., Hamer, M., & Stamatakis, E. (2017). Relationships between exercise, smoking habit and mortality in more than 100,000 adults. *International Journal of Cancer, 140*, 1819–1827.

29. Bialystok, E., Craik, F. I., & Freedman, M. (2007). Bilingualism as a protection against the onset of symptoms of dementia. *Neuropsychologia, 45*, 459–464.

30. Lawton, D. M., Gasquoine, P. G., & Weimer, A. A. (2015). Age of dementia diagnosis in community dwelling bilingual and monolingual Hispanic Americans. *Cortex, 66*, 141–145.

31. Alexander, W. (2015). *Flirting with French*. New York: Workman Publishing.

32. Pillai, J. A., Hall, C. B., Dickson, D. W., Buschke, H., Lipton, R. B., & Verghese, J. (2011). Association of crossword puzzle participation with memory decline in persons who develop dementia. *Journal of the International Neuropsychological Society, 17*, 1006–1013.

33. Verghese, J., Lipton, R. B., Katz, M. J., Hall, C. B., Derby, C. A., Kuslansky, G., . . . Buschke, H. (2003). Leisure activities and the risk of dementia in the elderly. *New England Journal of Medicine, 348*, 2508–2516.

34. Hambrick, D. Z., Salthouse, T. A., & Meinz, E. J. (1999). Predictors of crossword puzzle proficiency and moderators of age–cognition relations. *Journal of Experimental Psychology: General, 128,* 131–164.

35. I have created a computer program that can make reading more like a crossword puzzle. This program, called "Adaptext" (still in its research phrases) allows people to fill in the blanks of key words while they read texts, books, or articles on a computer screen, making the reading process more like an engaging and challenging puzzle, and one that can improve memory for these key words.

36. Wöllner, C., & Halpern, A. R. (2015). Attentional flexibility and memory capacity in conductors and pianists. *Attention, Perception, and Psychophysics, 78,* 198–208.

37. Habib, M., & Besson, M. (2009). What do music training and musical experience teach us about brain plasticity? *Music Perception, 26,* 279–285.

38. Mammarella, N., Fairfield, B., & Cornoldi, C. (2007). Does music enhance cognitive performance in healthy older adults? The Vivaldi effect. *Aging Clinical and Experimental Research, 19,* 394–399.

39. Lindsay, J., Laurin, D., Verreault, R., Hébert, R., Helliwell, B., Hill, G. B., & McDowell, I. (2002). Risk factors for Alzheimer's disease: A prospective analysis from the Canadian Study of Health and Aging. *American Journal of Epidemiology, 156,* 445–453.

40. Langa, K. M., Larson, E. B., Crimmins, E. M., Faul, J. D., Levine, D. A., Kabeto, M. U., & Weir, D. R. (2017). A Comparison of the prevalence of dementia in the United States in 2000 and 2012. *JAMA Internal Medicine, 177,* 51–58.

41. Lachman, M. E., Agrigoroaei, S., Murphy, C., & Tun, P. A. (2010). Frequent cognitive activity compensates for education differences in episodic memory. *American Journal of Geriatric Psychiatry, 18,* 4–10.

42. 95-Year-old woman graduates from college. ABC News, May 12, 2007. Retrieved from http://abcnews.go.com/GMA/LifeStages/story?id=3167970

43. Flora, C. (2016, July 5). The golden age of teaching yourself anything. *Psychology Today.* Retrieved from

https://www.psychologytoday.com/articles/201607/
the-golden-age-teaching-yourself-anything

44. Eck, A. (2014, October 27). Dark chocolate could improve memory by 25%, but you'd have to eat seven bars a day. NOVA, PBS. Retrieved from http://www.pbs.org/wgbh/nova/next/body/seven-bars-dark-chocolate-improve-memory-25/

45. Goody, M. (2015, May 28). Why a journalist scammed the media into spreading bad chocolate science. NPR News. Retrieved from http://www.npr.org/sections/thesalt/2015/05/28/410313446/why-a-journalist-scammed-the-media-into-spreading-bad-chocolate-science

46. Berkman, L. F., & Syme, S. L. (1979). Social networks, host resistance, and mortality: A nine-year follow-up study of Alameda County residents. *American Journal of Epidemiology, 109,* 186–204.

47. Teo, A. R., Choi, H., Andrea, S. B., Valenstein, M., Newsom, J. T., Dobscha, S. K., & Zivin, K. (2015). Does mode of contact with different types of social relationships predict depression in older adults? *Journal of the American Geriatrics Society, 63,* 2014–2022.

48. U.S. Bureau of Labor Statistics, 2015.

49. Anderson, N. D., Damianakis, T., Kröger, E., Wagner, L. M., Dawson, D. R., Binns, M. A., . . . Cook, S. L. (2014). The benefits associated with volunteering among seniors: A critical review and recommendations for future research. *Psychological Bulletin, 140,* 1505–1533.

50. Carlson, M. C., Saczynski, J. S., Rebok, G. W., Seeman, T., Glass, T. A., McGill, S., . . . Fried, L. P. (2008). Exploring the effects of an "everyday" activity program on executive function and memory in older adults. *The Gerontologist, 48,* 793–801.

Chapter 6

1. Agnvall, E. (2016, August). Keep your brain young by staying fit. *AARP Bulletin.*

2. Clarke, D. D., & Sokoloff, L. (1998). *Regulation of cerebral metabolic rate. Basic neurochemistry: Molecular, cellular and*

medical aspects (6th ed.). Philadelphia: Lippincott Williams & Wilkins.

3. Max Planck Institute for Human Development and Stanford Center on Longevity. (2014, October 20). A consensus on the brain training industry from the scientific community. Retrieved from http://longevity3.stanford.edu/blog/2014/10/15/the-consensus-on-the-brain-training-industry-from-the-scientific-community-2/

4. Federal Trade Commission. (2016, January 5). Lumosity to pay $2 million to settle FTC deceptive advertising charges for its "brain training" program. Retrieved from https://www.ftc.gov/news-events/press-releases/2016/01/lumosity-pay-2-million-settle-ftc-deceptive-advertising-charges

5. Owen, A. M., Hampshire, A., Grahn, J. A., Stenton, R., Dajani, S., Burns, A. S., . . . Ballard, C. G. (2010). Putting brain training to the test. *Nature, 465*(7299), 775–778.

6. Toril, P., Reales, J. M., & Ballesteros, S. (2014). Video game training enhances cognition of older adults: A meta-analytic study. *Psychology and Aging, 29,* 706–716.

7. Anguera, J. A., Boccanfuso, J., Rintoul, J. L., Al-Hashimi, O., Faraji, F., Janowich, J., . . . Gazzaley, A. (2013). Video game training enhances cognitive control in older adults. *Nature, 501*(7465), 97–101.

8. Hambrick, S. (2014, December 14). Brain training doesn't make you smarter. *Scientific American.* Retrieved from http://www.salon.com/2014/12/04/brain_training_doesnt_make_you_smarter_partner/

9. Roenker, D. L., Cissell, G. M., Ball, K. K., Wadley, V. G., & Edwards, J. D. (2003). Speed-of-processing and driving simulator training result in improved driving performance. *Human Factors, 45,* 218–233.

10. Ross, L. A., Freed, S. A., Edwards, J. D., Phillips, C. B., & Ball, K. (2017). The impact of three cognitive training programs on driving cessation across 10 years: A randomized controlled trial. *The Gerontologist, 57,* 838–846.

11. Simons, D. J., Boot, W. R., Charness, N., Gathercole, S. E., Chabris, C. F., Hambrick, D. Z., & Stine-Morrow, E. A. (2016). Do "brain-training" programs work? *Psychological Science in the Public Interest, 17,* 103–186.

12. Rabipour, S., & Davidson, P. S. (2015). Do you believe in brain training? A questionnaire about expectations of computerised cognitive training. *Behavioural Brain Research, 295,* 64–70.

13. Clark, B. B., Robert, C., & Hampton, S. A. (2016). The technology effect: How perceptions of technology drive excessive optimism. *Journal of Business and Psychology, 31,* 87–102.

14. Foroughi, C. K., Monfort, S. S., Paczynski, M., McKnight, P. E. & Greenwood, P. M. (2016). Placebo effects in cognitive training. *Proceedings of the National Academy of Sciences of the United States of America, 113,* 7470–7474.

15. Jaeggi, S. M., Buschkuehl, M., Jonides, J., & Perrig, W. J. (2008). Improving fluid intelligence with training on working memory. *Proceedings of the National Academy of Sciences of the United States of America, 105,* 6829–6833.

16. Uhls, Y. T., Michikyan, M., Morris, J., Garcia, D., Small, G. W., Zgourou, E., & Greenfield, P. M. (2014). Five days at outdoor education camp without screens improves preteen skills with nonverbal emotion cues. *Computers in Human Behavior, 39,* 387–392.

17. This is a useful review of some of the recent relevant work on how exercise helps neurogenesis in mice: Clark, P. J., Kohman, R. A., Miller, D. S., Bhattacharya, T. K., Brzezinska, W. J., & Rhodes, J. S. (2011). Genetic influences on exercise-induced adult hippocampal neurogenesis across 12 divergent mouse strains. *Genes, Brain and Behavior, 10,* 345–353.

18. Van Praag, H., Shubert, T., Zhao, C., & Gage, F. H. (2005). Exercise enhances learning and hippocampal neurogenesis in aged mice. *Journal of Neuroscience, 25,* 8680–8685.

19. I credit Moshe Rubenstein for sharing this with me, as when he was describing this finding to a friend, his friend then asked him jokingly, "Where can I get such a wheel?!"

20. Kaplan, S. (2016, July). Does reading fiction make you a better person? *Washington Post.* Retrieved from https://www.washingtonpost.com/news/speaking-of-science/wp/2016/07/22/does-reading-fiction-make-you-a-better-person/?utm_term=.1f7a1f585596

21. Mar, R. A., Oatley, K., Hirsh, J., de la Paz, J., & Peterson, J. B. (2006). Bookworms versus nerds: Exposure to fiction versus non-fiction, divergent associations with social ability, and the

simulation of fictional social worlds. *Journal of Research in Personality, 40,* 694–712.

22. Ward, M. (2016, November 16). Warren Buffett's reading routine could make you smarter, science suggests. CNBC. Retrieved from http://www.cnbc.com/2016/11/16/warren-buffetts-reading-routine-could-make-you-smarter-suggests-science.html

23. Wilson, R. S., Boyle, P. A., Yu, L., Barnes, L. L., Schneider, J. A., & Bennett, D. A. (2013). Life-span cognitive activity, neuropathologic burden, and cognitive aging. *Neurology, 81,* 314–321.

24. Evans, M. D., Kelley, J., Sikora, J., & Treiman, D. J. (2010). Family scholarly culture and educational success: Books and schooling in 27 nations. *Research in Social Stratification and Mobility, 28,* 171–197.

25. Almeida, O. P., Yeap, B. B., Alfonso, H., Hankey, G. J., Flicker, L., & Norman, P. E. (2012). Older men who use computers have lower risk of dementia. *PloS One, 7,* e44239.

26. Small, G. W., Moody, T. D., Siddarth, P., & Bookheimer, S. Y. (2009). Your brain on Google: Patterns of cerebral activation during Internet searching. *American Journal of Geriatric Psychiatry, 17,* 116–126.

27. Smith, A. (2014, April). Older adults and technology use. Pew Research Center. Retrieved from http://www.pewinternet.org/2014/04/03/older-adults-and-technology-use/

28. Doward, J. (2015, May 16). Schools that ban mobile phones see better academic results. *The Guardian.* Retrieved from http://www.theguardian.com/education/2015/may/16/schools-mobile-phones-academic-results

29. I sometimes enjoy the struggle and challenge of installing a new water filter or fixing a leaking sink, but also realize that sometimes bigger plumbing jobs are best left to an expert.

30. Hampton, D. (2014, September 10). Rethinking the brain benefits of wine. Retrieved from http://www.thebestbrainpossible.com/rethinking-red-wine/

31. Brickman, A. M., Khan, U. A., Provenzano, F. A., Yeung, L. K., Suzuki, W., Schroeter, H., . . . Small, S. A. (2014). Enhancing dentate gyrus function with dietary flavanols improves cognition in older adults. *Nature Neuroscience, 17,* 1798–1803.

32. Belluck, P. (2014, October). To improve a memory, consider chocolate. *New York Times*. Retrieved from https://www.nytimes.com/2014/10/27/us/a-bite-to-remember-chocolate-is-shown-to-aid-memory.html?_r=0

33. Bjork, E. L., & Bjork, R. A. (2014). Making things hard on yourself, but in a good way: Creating desirable difficulties to enhance learning. In M. A. Gernsbacher & J. Pomerantz (Eds.), *Psychology and the real world: Essays illustrating fundamental contributions to society* (2nd ed., pp. 59–68). New York: Worth.

34. Li, F., Fisher, K. J., & Harmer, P. (2005). Improving physical function and blood pressure in older adults through cobblestone mat walking: A randomized trial. *Journal of the American Geriatrics Society, 53,* 1305–1312.

35. Maillot, P., Perrot, A., & Hartley, A. (2012). Effects of interactive physical-activity video-game training on physical and cognitive function in older adults. *Psychology and Aging, 27,* 589–600.

36. Bredesen, D. E. (2014). Reversal of cognitive decline: A novel therapeutic program. *Aging, 6,* 707–717.

37. Greenberg, S. (2009, Jan 5). John Wooden: I'm not afraid of death. *Sporting News Magazine.* Retrieved from https://2thinkgood.com/2012/05/28/john-wooden-rip/

38. National Institute on Aging, Go4Life. (n.d.). Improve your balance. Retrieved from https://go4life.nia.nih.gov/exercises/balance

39. Cooper, R., Strand, B. H., Hardy, R., Patel, K. V., & Kuh, D. (2014). Physical capability in mid-life and survival over 13 years of follow-up: British Birth Cohort Study. *British Medical Journal, 348,* g2219.

Chapter 7

1. Bergua, V., Fabrigoule, C., Barberger-Gateau, P., Dartigues, J. F., Swendsen, J., & Bouisson, J. (2006). Preferences for routines in older people: associations with cognitive and psychological vulnerability. *International Journal of Geriatric Psychiatry, 21,* 990–998.

2. Leisure in retirement. Beyond the bucket list. A Merrill-Lynch survey by Age Wave (2016). Retrieved from http://agewave. com/wp-content/uploads/2016/05/2016-Leisure-in-Retirement_ Beyond-the-Bucket-List.pdf

3. Cole, C., Laurent, G., Drolet, A., Ebert, J., Gutchess, A., ... Peters, E. (2008). Decision making and brand choice by older consumers. *Marketing Letters, 19*, 355–365.

4. LaLanne, J. (2009). *Live young forever: 12 steps to optimum health, fitness & longevity.* Brampton, Ontario: Robert Kennedy.

5. Gill, T. M., Guralnik, J. M., Pahor, M., Church, T., Fielding, R. A., King, A. C., ... Allore, H. G. (2016). Effect of structured physical activity on overall burden and transitions between states of major mobility disability in older persons: Secondary analysis of a randomized, controlled trial. *Annals of Internal Medicine, 165*, 883–840.

6. Go4Life. https://go4life.nia.nih.gov/

7. Notthoff, N., & Carstensen, L. L. (2014). Positive messaging promotes walking in older adults. *Psychology and Aging, 29*, 329–341.

8. Austin, S., Qu, H., & Shewchuk, R. M. (2013). Age bias in physicians' recommendations for physical activity: A behavioral model of healthcare utilization for adults with arthritis. *Journal of Physical Activity and Health, 10*, 222–231.

9. Koch, S., Holland, R. W., Hengstler, M., & van Knippenberg, A. (2009). Body locomotion as regulatory process: Stepping backward enhances cognitive control. *Psychological Science, 20*, 549–550.

10. Marcell, T. J., Hawkins, S. A., & Wiswell, R. A. (2014). Leg strength declines with advancing age despite habitual endurance exercise in active older adults. *Journal of Strength & Conditioning Research, 28*, 504–513.

11. O'Keefe, J. H., & Lavie, C. J. (2013). Run for your life . . . at a comfortable speed and not too far. *Heart, 99*, 516–519.

12. Hughes, L. (2017, May 22). Can you hold a plank as long as 71-year-old Cher? *Women's Health.* Retrieved from http://www. womenshealthmag.com/fitness/cher-workout-plank

13. Retrieved from http://bragg.com/about/lalanne_gospel.html

14. Conason, J. (2013, Aug/Sept). Bill Clinton explains why he became a vegan. *AARP Magazine*. Retrieved from http://www.aarp.org/health/healthy-living/info-08-2013/bill-clinton-vegan.html

15. Seller, P. (2015, February 25). Warren Buffets secret to staying young: "I eat like a six year old." *Fortune Magazine*. http://fortune.com/2015/02/25/warren-buffett-diet-coke/

16. As described by a younger reporter (Arash Markazi, ESPN Senior Writer) who would also be there: Markazi, A. (2010, October). Where everybody knew his name. Retrieved from http://www.espn.com/blog/los-angeles/ucla/post/_/id/3105/where-everyone-knew-his-name

17. I can vouch for how delicious this donut is, and it is my favorite, so I think Wooden had good taste.

18. Teicholz, N. (2014). *The big fat surprise: Why butter, meat and cheese belong in a healthy diet.* New York: Simon and Schuster.

19. Cattel, J. (2016, February). The key to living longer could be eating like your grandparents. Retrieved from http://greatist.com/eat/eat-like-great-grandparents

20. U.S. National Library of Medicine. Sleep disorders in older adults. Medline Plus. Retrieved from https://medlineplus.gov/ency/article/000064.htm

21. Mander, B. A., Rao, V., Lu, B., Saletin, J. M., Lindquist, J. R., Ancoli-Israel, S., . . . Walker, M. P. (2013). Prefrontal atrophy, disrupted NREM slow waves and impaired hippocampal-dependent memory in aging. *Nature Neuroscience, 16,* 357–364.

22. Grigsby-Toussaint, D. S., Turi, K. N., Krupa, M., Williams, N. J., Pandi-Perumal, S. R., & Jean-Louis, G. (2015). Sleep insufficiency and the natural environment: Results from the US behavioral risk factor surveillance system survey. *Preventive Medicine, 78,* 78–84.

23. Moss, T. G., Carney, C. E., Haynes, P., & Harris, A. L. (2015). Is daily routine important for sleep? An investigation of social rhythms in a clinical insomnia population. *Chronobiology International, 32,* 92–102.

24. Zisberg, A., Gur-Yaish, N., & Shochat, T. (2010). Contribution of routine to sleep quality in community elderly. *Sleep, 33,* 509–514.

25. Mednick, S. C., & Ehrman, M. (2006). *Take a nap!: Change your life.* New York: Workman Publishing.

26. Foley, D., Ancoli-Israel, S., Britz, P., & Walsh, J. (2004). Sleep disturbances and chronic disease in older adults. *Journal of Psychosomatic Research, 56,* 497–502.

27. Trompeter, S. E., Bettencourt, R., & Barrett-Connor, E. (2012). Sexual activity and satisfaction in healthy community-dwelling older women. *American Journal of Medicine, 125,* 37–43.

28. Erber, J. T., & Szuchman, L. T. (2015). *Great myths of aging.* Hoboken, NJ: Wiley Blackwell.

29. Westheimer, R. K. (2005). *Sex after 50: Revving up the romance, passion and excitement!* Fresno, CA: Linden Publishing.

30. Krug, N. (2015, June 3). Dr. Ruth, 87, still shocking us with her sex talk. *Washington Post.* Retrieved from https://www.washingtonpost.com/news/arts-and-entertainment/wp/2015/06/03/dr-ruth-87-still-shocking-us-with-her-sex-talk/?utm_term=.6037e9e7918d

31. Joanisse, M., Gagnon, S., & Voloaca, M. (2012). Overly cautious and dangerous: An empirical evidence of the older driver stereotypes. *Accident Analysis & Prevention, 45,* 802–810.

32. Erber, J. T., & Szuchman, L. T. (2015). *Great myths of aging.* Hoboken, NJ: Wiley Blackwell.

33. Karlawish, J. (2014, September 20). Too young to die, too old to worry. *New York Times Sunday Review.* Retrieved from http://www.nytimes.com/2014/09/21/opinion/sunday/too-young-to-die-too-old-to-worry.html?_r=0

34. Nepal, A. (2010, November 29). Winning Langley gave up smoking at 102 and died within a year. Retrieved from http://xnepali.net/winnie-langley-gave-up-smoking-at-102-and-died-within-a-year/

35. UC Irvine Institute for Memory Impairments and Neurological Disorders (UCI MIND). The 90+ Study. Retrieved from https://www.mind.uci.edu/research/90plus-study/

36. Penninx, B. W., Van Tilburg, T., Kriegsman, D. M., Deeg, D. J., Boeke, A. J. P., & van Eijk, J. T. M. (1997). Effects of social support and personal coping resources on mortality in older age. *American Journal of Epidemiology, 146,* 510–519.

37. Fratiglioni, L., Paillard-Borg, S., & Winblad, B. (2004). An active and socially integrated lifestyle in late life might protect against dementia. *Lancet Neurology, 3,* 343–353.

38. Zauberman, G., Ratner, R. K., & Kyu Kim, B. (2008). Memories as assets: Strategic memory protection in choice over time. *Journal of Consumer Research, 35,* 715–728.

39. Meske, C., Sanders, G. F., Meredith, W. H., & Abbott, D. A. (1994). Perceptions of rituals and traditions among elderly persons. *Activities, Adaptation & Aging, 18,* 13–26.

40. Fiese, B. H. (2006). *Family routines and rituals.* New Haven, CT: Yale University Press.

41. Rosenthal, C. J., & Marshall, V. W. (1988). Generational transmission of family ritual. *American Behavioral Scientist, 31,* 669–684.

42. Wahlheim, C. N., Dunlosky, J., & Jacoby, L. L. (2011). Spacing enhances the learning of natural concepts: An investigation of mechanisms, metacognition, and aging. *Memory & Cognition, 39,* 750–763.

Chapter 8

1. Pew Research Center. (2009). Growing old in America: Expectations vs reality. Retrieved from http://www.pewsocialtrends.org/2009/06/29/growing-old-in-america-expectations-vs-reality/

2. Ibid.

3. Wu, C., Odden, M. C., Fisher, G. G., & Stawski, R. S. (2016). Association of retirement age with mortality: A population-based longitudinal study among older adults in the USA. *Journal of Epidemiology and Community Health, 70,* 917–923.

4. Merrill Lynch & Age Wave. (2016). Leisure in retirement: Beyond the bucket list. A Merrill Lynch Retirement Study conducted in partnership with Age Wave. Retrieved from https://agewave.com/wp-content/uploads/2016/05/2016-Leisure-in-Retirement_Beyond-the-Bucket-List.pdf .

5. Castel, A. D. (2007). Aging and memory for numerical information: The role of specificity and expertise in associative memory. *Journals of Gerontology, 62,* 194–196.

6. Spreng, R. N., Rosen, H. J., Strother, S., Chow, T. W., Diehl-Schmid, J., Freedman, M., . . . Morelli, S. A. (2010). Occupation

attributes relate to location of atrophy in frontotemporal lobar degeneration. *Neuropsychologia, 48,* 3634–3641.

7. Sterns, H. L., & Gray, J. H. (1999). Work, leisure, and retirement. *Gerontology,* 355–389.

8. This book doesn't address how people think about death, but there are excellent books that review this important topic, as younger and older people certainly have different viewpoints and levels of acceptance about death.

9. Dave, D., Rashad, I., & Spasojevic, J. (2006). *The effects of retirement on physical and mental health outcomes* (No. w12123). National Bureau of Economic Research.

10. Perreira, K. M., & Sloan, F. A. (2001). Life events and alcohol consumption among mature adults: A longitudinal analysis. *Journal of Studies on Alcohol, 62,* 501–508.

11. Merrill Lynch & Age Wave. (2016). Leisure in retirement: Beyond the bucket list. A Merrill Lynch Retirement Study conducted in partnership with Age Wave. Retrieved from https://agewave. com/wp-content/uploads/2016/05/2016-Leisure-in-Retirement_ Beyond-the-Bucket-List.pdf

12. Reitzes, D. C., Mutran, E. J., & Fernandez, M. E. (1998). The decision to retire: A career perspective. *Social Science Quarterly,* 79(3), 607–619.

13. Vaillant, G. E., DiRago, A. C., & Mukamal, K. (2006). Natural history of male psychological health: Retirement satisfaction. *American Journal of Psychiatry, 163,* 682–688.

14. Dion, J. (2014, November). The healing nature of friendship. Retrieved from https://www.stitch.net/blog/2014/11/ healing-nature-friendship/

15. Moen, P., Kim, J. E., & Hofmeister, H. (2001). Couples' work/ retirement transitions, gender, and marital quality. *Social Psychology Quarterly,* 64(1), 55–71.

16. Stock, R. (2011, January). Lunch date with ROMEO gives guys a chance to connect. AARP. Retrieved from http://www.aarp.org/ relationships/friends/info-01-2011/romeo_retired_men_club. html

17. Heid, M. (2015, March). You asked: How many friends do I need? *Time Magazine.* Retrieved from http://time.com/3748090/ friends-social-health/

18. Doyle, A. C. (1930). *The Complete Sherlock Holmes* (Vol. 2). New York: Doubleday Books.

19. Ekerdt, D. J. (1986). The busy ethic: Moral continuity between work and retirement. *The Gerontologist, 26*, 239–244.

20. Festini, S. B., McDonough, I. M., & Park, D. C. (2016). The busier the better: Greater busyness is associated with better cognition. *Frontiers in Aging Neuroscience, 8.*

21. Ironside, V. (2007). *No! I don't want to join a book club: Diary of a 60th year.* London: Penguin UK. When I looked for her book at my local library, all five large-print copies were checked out (probably by older adults), but the single regular print copy was available. Older adults who don't want to join a book club seem to want to read a book about why they don't want to join a book club!

22. Captain Sully retiring from US Airlines. CBS News, March 3, 2010. Retrieved from http://www.cbsnews.com/news/captain-sully-retiring-from-us-airways/

23. Quote from the Brubeck Institute, University of the Pacific Support Message. Retrieved from http://www.pacific.edu/Brubeck-Home/Support.html

24. Personal interview with Bob Newhart, March 3, 2011.

25. Berrin, D. (2017, May). An interview with Sherry Lansing. *The Jewish Journal.*

26. Dance, sing, just "keep moving," Dick Van Dyke tells seniors. An interview with Dyke Van Dyke. Weekend Edition Sunday, NPR. Retrieved from http://www.npr.org/2015/10/11/447591736/dance-sing-just-keep-moving-dick-van-dyke-tells-seniors

27. Diamond, J. (2012). *The world until yesterday: What can we learn from traditional societies?* New York: Penguin.

28. Freudenheim, M. (2005, March). More help wanted: Older works please apply. *New York Times.* Retrieved from http://www.nytimes.com/2005/03/23/business/more-help-wanted-older-workers-please-apply.html?_r=0#story-continues-1

29. Volz, J. (2000). Successful aging: The second 50. *American Psychology Association Monitor,* Volume 31.

30. Plaschke, B. (2017, April 4). Behind the scenes with Vin Scully on opening day of his retirement. *Los Angeles Times.* Retrieved from http://www.latimes.com/sports/dodgers/la-sp-vin-scully-plaschke-20170404-story.html

31. Schott, B. (2015, December 16). Getting to the heart of David Letterman. *Whitefish Review.* Retrieved from http://www.whitefishreview.org/archives/2015/12/david-letterman-interview/

32. Battaglio, S. (2017, August 8). David Letterman will do a six episode talk show for Netflix. *Los Angeles Times.* Retrieved from http://www.latimes.com/business/hollywood/la-fi-ct-letterman-netflix-20170808-story.html

33. Gillett, E. (2015, July). Meet the 93-year-old woman who still works 5 days a week and never wants to retire. Retrieved from http://www.businessinsider.com/betty-reid-soskin-interview-2015-7

34. Abdul-Jabbar, K. (2014, February). Kareem Abdul-Jabbar's three rules of retirement. *The Rotarian.* Retrieved from http://therotarianmagazine.com/three-rules-of-retirement

35. Williams, C. (2016, April). Why it pays to work less. *The Economist 1843 Magazine.* Retrieved from https://www.1843magazine.com/ideas/the-daily/why-it-pays-to-work-less

36. Smith, A., & McCulloch, J. R. (1838). *An Inquiry into the Nature and Causes of the Wealth of Nations.* Edinburgh: A. and C. Black and W. Tait.

37. Gruenewald, T. L., Tanner, E. K., Fried, L. P., Carlson, M. C., Xue, Q. L., Parisi, J. M., . . . Seeman, T. E. (2016). The Baltimore Experience Corps Trial: Enhancing generativity via intergenerational activity engagement in later life. *Journals of Gerontology, 71,* 661–670.

38. Patrick, D. (2016, November 7). Just my type. *Sports Illustrated.*

39. Tergesen, A. (2014, March 30). The long (long) wait to be a grandparent. *Wall Street Journal.* Retrieved from https://www.wsj.com/articles/SB10001424052702303775504579395501172676002

40. Kaufman, G., & Elder, G. H. (2003). Grandparenting and age identity. *Journal of Aging Studies, 17,* 269–282.

41. Baker, L. A., Silverstein, M., & Putney, N. M. (2008). Grandparents raising grandchildren in the United States: Changing family forms, stagnant social policies. *Journal of Societal & Social Policy, 7,* 53–69.

42. Merrill Lynch & Age Wave. (2016). Leisure in retirement: Beyond the bucket list. A Merrill Lynch Retirement Study conducted in partnership with Age Wave. Retrieved from https://agewave.

com/wp-content/uploads/2016/05/2016-Leisure-in-Retirement_
Beyond-the-Bucket-List.pdf

43. Burn, K. F., Henderson, V. W., Ames, D., Dennerstein, L., & Szoeke, C. (2014). Role of grandparenting in postmenopausal women's cognitive health. *Menopause, 21,* 1069–1074.

44. Bates, J. S., & Taylor, A. C. (2012). Grandfather involvement and aging men's mental health. *American Journal of Men's Health, 6,* 229–239.

Chapter 9

1. Personal interview with John Glenn, December 13, 2012.

2. Abdul-Jabbar, K. (2014, February). Kareem Abdul-Jabbar's three rules of retirement. *The Rotarian.* Retrieved from http://therotarianmagazine.com/three-rules-of-retirement

3. Abdul-Jabbar, K. (2017). *Coach Wooden and me: Our 50-year friendship on and off the court.* New York: Grand Central Publishing.

4. Mroczek, D. K., & Kolarz, C. M. (1998). The effect of age on positive and negative affect: A developmental perspective on happiness. *Journal of Personality and Social Psychology, 75,* 1333–1349.

5. Pew Research Center (2009). Growing old in America: Expectations vs reality. Retrieved from http://www.pewsocialtrends.org/2009/06/29/growing-old-in-america-expectations-vs-reality/

6. Sarkisian, C. A., Steers, W. N., Hays, R. D., & Mangione, C. M. (2005). Development of the 12-item expectations regarding aging survey. *The Gerontologist, 45,* 240–248.

7. Davis, M. M., Bond, L. A., Howard, A., & Sarkisian, C. A. (2011). Primary care clinician expectations regarding aging. *The Gerontologist, 51,* 856–866.

8. Bowen, C. E., & Skirbekk, V. (2017). Old age expectations are related to how long people want to live. *Ageing and Society, 37*(9), 1898–1923.

9. Haslam, C., Morton, T. A., Haslam, S. A., Varnes, L., Graham, R., & Gamaz, L. (2012). When the age is in, the wit is out: Age-related self-categorization and deficit expectations reduce performance on clinical tests used in dementia assessment. *Psychology and Aging, 27,* 778–784.

10. Levy, B. R., Pilver, C., Chung, P. H., & Slade, M. D. (2014). Subliminal strengthening improving older individuals' physical function over time with an implicit-age-stereotype intervention. *Psychological Science, 25,* 2127–2135.

11. Levy, B. R., Slade, M. D., Murphy, T. E., & Gill, T. M. (2012). Association between positive age stereotypes and recovery from disability in older persons. *Journal of the American Medical Association, 308,* 1972–1973.

12. Locke, E. A., & Latham, G. P. (2006). New directions in goal-setting theory. *Current Directions in Psychological Science, 15,* 265–268.

13. Depp, C. A., & Jeste, D. V. (2006). Definitions and predictors of successful aging: A comprehensive review of larger quantitative studies. *American Journal of Geriatric Psychiatry, 14,* 6–20.

14. Thornton, J. E., Collins, J. B., Birren, J. E., & Svensson, C. (2011). Guided autobiography's developmental exchange: What's in it for me? *International Journal of Aging and Human Development, 73,* 227–251.

15. Kenyon, G., Bohlmeijer, E., & Randall, W. L. (Eds.). (2010). *Storying later life: Issues, investigations, and interventions in narrative gerontology.* New York: Oxford University Press.

16. Perkins, L. (2014, August). Why grandma might not be the best babysitter. *Huffington Post.* Retrieved from http://www.huffingtonpost.com/lynn-perkins/why-grandma-might-not-be-_b_5682844.html

17. Greenstein, M., & Holland, J. (2014). *Lighter as we go: Virtues, character strengths, and aging.* New York: Oxford University Press.

18. Smith-Sloman, C. (2016, November 20). NYU plans to house local senior citizens with students. *New York Post.* Retrieved from http://nypost.com/2016/11/20/nyu-plans-to-house-local-senior-citizens-with-students/

19. Painter, J. A., Elliott, S. J., & Hudson, S. (2009). Falls in community-dwelling adults aged 50 years and older prevalence and contributing factors. *Journal of Allied Health, 38,* 201–207.

20. An excellent book about advice from older adults about life-long love is Pillemer, K. A. (2012). *30 lessons for loving: Advice from the wisest Americans on love, relationships, and marriage.* New York: Penguin.

21. Berrin, D. (2017, May). An interview with Sherry Lansing. *The Jewish Journal.*

22. Pillemer, K. (2011). *30 lessons for living: Tried and true advice from the wisest Americans.* New York: Penguin.

23. Pillemer, K. A. (2016, September). Stop. Worrying. Now. *Psychology Today.* Retrieved from https://www.psychologytoday.com/articles/201609/16-life-lessons?collection=1093092

24. DeLiema, M., Yon, Y., & Wilber, K. H. (2016). Tricks of the trade: Motivating sales agents to con older adults. *The Gerontologist, 56,* 335–344.

25. Ross, M., Grossmann, I., & Schryer, E. (2014). Contrary to psychological and popular opinion, there is no compelling evidence that older adults are disproportionately victimized by consumer fraud. *Perspectives on Psychological Science, 9,* 427–442.

26. Federal Bureau of Investigation. (n.d.) Scams and safety: Fraud against seniors. Retrieved from https://www.fbi.gov/scams-and-safety/common-fraud-schemes/seniors

27. Castle, E., Eisenberger, N. I., Seeman, T. E., Moons, W. G., Boggero, I. A., Grinblatt, M. S., & Taylor, S. E. (2012). Neural and behavioral bases of age differences in perceptions of trust. *Proceedings of the National Academy of Sciences of the United States of America, 109,* 20848–20852.

28. Bailey, P. E., Slessor, G., Rieger, M., Rendell, P. G., Moustafa, A. A., & Ruffman, T. (2015). Trust and trustworthiness in young and older adults. *Psychology and Aging, 30,* 977–986.

29. Criss, D. (2016, August 24). 91-year-old flips the script on a man who tried to rob him. CNN. Retrieved from http://www.cnn.com/2016/08/24/health/old-man-shoots-would-be-robber-trnd/?iid=ob_article_footer_expansion

30. Dweck, C. S. (2008). *Mindset: The new psychology of success.* New York: Random House Digital, Inc.

31. Plaks, J. E., & Chasteen, A. L. (2013). Entity versus incremental theories predict older adults' memory performance. *Psychology and Aging, 28,* 948–957.

32. Stephan, Y., Chalabaev, A., Kotter-Grühn, D., & Jaconelli, A. (2013). "Feeling younger, being stronger": An experimental study of subjective age and physical functioning among older adults. *Journals of Gerontology, 68,* 1–7.

33. Fung, H. H., & Carstensen, L. L. (2006). Goals change when life's fragility is primed: Lessons learned from older adults, the September 11 attacks and SARS. *Social Cognition, 24,* 248–278.
34. Brokaw, T. (2000). *The greatest generation.* New York: Random House.

Index